S0-BRN-056

MODERN CONSTITUTIONS

A Collection of the Fundamental Laws of Twenty-
two of the Most Important Countries of
the World, with Historical and
Bibliographical Notes

By
WALTER FAIRLEIGH DODD

VOLUME II

CHICAGO
THE UNIVERSITY OF CHICAGO PRESS
LONDON
T. FISHER UNWIN, 1 ADELPHI TERRACE
1909

This scarce antiquarian book is included in our special *Legacy Reprint Series*. In the interest of creating a more extensive selection of rare historical book reprints, we have chosen to reproduce this title even though it may possibly have occasional imperfections such as missing and blurred pages, missing text, poor pictures, markings, dark backgrounds and other reproduction issues beyond our control. Because this work is culturally important, we have made it available as a part of our commitment to protecting, preserving and promoting the world's literature.

TABLE OF CONTENTS
VOLUME I

TABLE OF CONTENTS
VOLUME II

ITALY

Under the control of the first Napoleon Italy for the first time assumed a compact political organization. Piedmont, Genoa, Parma, Tuscany, and part of the Papal States were annexed to France; Lombardy, Venetia, Modena, Romagna, and the Marches formed the kingdom of Italy with Eugène Beauharnais as viceroy; Naples was a dependent kingdom under Murat; the island territories of Sicily and Sardinia alone remained free from French influence. With the fall of Napoleon the first kingdom of Italy came to an end; Murat by his support of Napoleon in 1815 forfeited the kingdom of Naples; the French boundaries were limited so as to exclude the Italian conquests.

The principle of legitimacy was the basis upon which Italy was reorganized by the Congress of Vienna; the Bourbons returned to Naples, the House of Savoy to Piedmont; Parma, Modena, and Lucca were restored to royal rulers; the Papal States were returned to the pope; the two republics of Genoa and Venetia were suppressed; Genoa went to Piedmont to strengthen that state against French aggression; Lombardy was restored to Austria, which also gained Venetia. Piedmont alone among the purely Italian states was strengthened by the work of the Congress of Vienna. Through the possession of a large part of Italy, with Austrian houses ruling in Tuscany, Modena, and Parma, and through a secret treaty with Naples, Austria became practically the master of Italy and remained so until expelled by the combined forces of France and Sardinia in 1859.

With the restoration of the monarchs almost all traces of French reforms in Italy disappeared and as far as possible the prerevolutionary principles of government were re-established. All political activity was now forbidden; but liberal sentiments and aspirations for national unity had taken hold of the people and were fostered in the universities, by scientific gatherings, and in the secret organization of the Carbonari. Italian literature of the period 1815–48 took on a patriotic character, though most of the political writing was done by Italian exiles in foreign countries.

The first fruits of the liberal agitation were the revolutions of 1820 and 1821 in Naples and Piedmont; in Naples the Spanish constitution of 1812 was proclaimed; in Piedmont the same constitution was granted but withdrawn; both movements were suppressed with the aid of Austrian troops. A similar fate befell the revolutions which broke out in 1831 in the Estates of the Church, Parma, and Modena. From 1831 to 1848 several unsuccessful uprisings occurred; but the revolutionary propaganda was actively carried on and the ground was being prepared for a larger movement.

The liberal movement gained force through the election of a liberal pope in 1846; the pope committed himself to a reform of the government of the Papal States. Charles Albert of Sardinia showed himself in sympathy with the national feeling against Austria; the revolution broke out first in Naples and Sicily. Within the early months of 1848 four constitutions were granted: that of the Two Sicilies, on February 10; the Tuscan constitution on February 15; the constitution of Sardinia, on March 4; the constitution of the Temporal Power, on March 14. The Sicilian constitution of July 10, 1848, and that of the Roman Republic, of February 9, 1849, marked the more advanced stages of the revolutions in Rome and Sicily.

All Italy for a time united in the national movement; the pope and the king of Naples were forced to send troops to aid in the liberation of Italy from Austrian despotism; Charles Albert of Sardinia at last put himself at the head of the national movement; but the Italian forces were unorganized; the pope and Naples withdrew from the movement at the first opportunity; the defeats of Custozza and Novara showed the hopelessness of further struggle. Sardinia itself lost nothing by the defeat, and its new king, Victor Emmanuel, by remaining faithful to the constitution of 1848 provided the one constitutional state about which might center later efforts toward Italian unity. Throughout the rest of Italy the reaction carried away everything of liberal reforms, and brought with it the proscription of all who had taken part in the liberal movements.

The wars of 1848–49 failed because of deficient organization. The kingdom of Sardinia as the only possible leader in future movements immediately began to organize for the coming conflict, and soon there came to the head of affairs Cavour, who was destined to take the leading part in uniting Italy. When Sardinia again faced Austria it was not alone and unprepared, but with a well-drilled army and with the alliance of France.

The war of 1859 gave only Lombardy to Sardinia, to compensate for the loss of Nice and Savoy which were the price paid for French support, but it set in motion a movement which went far toward creating a united Italy. Tuscany, Parma, Modena, and the Romagna rose, expelled their rulers, and by plebiscites declared for union with Sardinia; their union with this state was effected by decrees of March 18 and 22, 1860. Assisted by Garibaldi Sicily and Naples drove out their Bourbon ruler, and were united with Sardinia on December 17, 1860. Umbria and the Marches, conquered from the pope by Sardinian arms, were united with the Italian state on December 17, 1860. Venetia was added in 1866 as a result of Italy's alliance with Prussia against Austria; Rome was occupied when the French soldiers were called home in 1870.

The Sardinian constitution of 1848 had step by step been extended over the whole of Italy; the kingdom of Italy was formally constituted in 1861. The Sardinian constitution contains no provision for amendment, and its text remains unchanged. The principle has gained acceptance that it may be altered by the regular legislative processes; so it is that the constitution, though the most important instrument of government, does not fully represent the present constitutional organization of Italy.[1] Aside from the constitution perhaps the most important law is that regulating the relations of the Italian government to the Holy See; the pope has, however, consistently refused to recognize this law or to receive the subsidy provided by it.

SELECT BIBLIOGRAPHY

ITALY. *Codice politico amministrativo.* (6th ed., Firenze, 1907. Manuali Barbèra.) A collection of all laws, ordinances, and regulations concerning the Italian government and public administration.

[1] See Ruiz, *Annals of the American Academy of Political and Social Science,* VI, 227.

KING, BOLTON. *A History of Italian Unity.* (London, 1899. 2 vols.) The best history of the Italian national movement. There are also briefer accounts in English by Countess Martinengo Cesaresco and by Stillman.

ARANGIO RUIZ, GAETANO. *Storia costituzionale del regno di Italia, 1848–1898.* (Firenze, 1898.) The best work for the period covered.

KING, BOLTON AND OKEY, THOMAS. *Italy To-day.* (London, 1901.) An excellent account of the present political and social condition of Italy.

BRUSA, E. *Das Staatsrecht des Königreichs Italien.* (Freiburg, 1892. Handbuch des oeffentlichen Rechts.) An excellent study of Italian constitutional law.

DEL GUERRA, ENRICO. *L'Amministrazione pubblica in Italia.* (Firenze, 1893.) A convenient guide to the administrative organization of Italy.

GRECO, GENNARO. *Il nuovo diritto amministrativo Italiano.* Parte speciale. Vol. I. (Napoli, 1896.) A brief outline of the central and local administrative organization.

MEUCCI, LORENZO. *Istituzioni di diritto amministrativo.* (4th ed., Torino, 1898.) A discussion of legal principles rather than of the actual administrative organization.

CARNAZZA, GABRIELLO. *Il diritto costituzionale Italiano.* (Catania, 1886.)

ORLANDO, V. E. *Principes de droit public et constitutionnel.* (Paris, 1902.) French translation of an Italian work, which, though general in character, devotes much of its attention to Italy.

BRUNIALTI, ATTILIO. *Il diritto costituzionale e la politica nelle scienza e nelle istituzioni.* (Torino, 1896-1900. 2 vols.) A general work which devotes much attention to Italy.

BRUNIALTI, ATTILIO. *Lo Stato e la chiesa in Italia.* (Torino, 1892.) A rather extensive treatise issued as the preface to Vol. VIII of the *Biblioteca di Scienze Politiche.* Scaduto is regarded as the leading authority upon the relations of church and state in modern Italy, but the editor has not been able to examine his works.

MOSCA, GAETANO. *Appunti di diritto costituzionale.* (Milan, 1908.) A brief summary of Italian constitutional law.

CONSTITUTION OF ITALY[1]

(March 4, 1848)

ARTICLE 1. The apostolic Roman Catholic religion is the only religion of the state. Other cults now existing are tolerated, in conformity with the law.

ART. 2. The state is governed by a representative monarchical government. The throne is hereditary according to the Salic law.

ART. 3. The legislative power shall be exercised collectively by the King and two houses, the Senate and the House of Deputies.

ART. 4. The person of the King is sacred and inviolable.

ART. 5. To the King alone belongs the executive power. He is the supreme head of the state; commands all land and naval forces; declares war; makes treaties of peace, alliance, commerce, and other treaties, communicating them to the houses as soon as the interest and security of the state permit, accompanying such notice with opportune explanations; treaties involving financial obligations or alterations of the territory of the state shall not take effect until after they have received the approval of the houses.

ART. 6. The King appoints to all of the offices of the state, and makes the necessary decrees and regulations for the execution of the laws, without suspending their execution or granting exemptions from the law.

ART. 7. The King alone approves and promulgates the laws.

ART. 8. The King may grant pardons and commute sentences.

ART. 9. The King shall convene the two houses each year. He may prorogue their sessions and dissolve the House

[1] In the preparation of this text assistance has been received from the translation made by Drs. S. M. Lindsay and L. S. Rowe, and issued as a supplement to the *Annals of the American Academy of Political and Social Science* of November, 1894.

of Deputies, in which case he shall convene a new House within a period of four months.

ART. 10.   The initiative in legislation shall belong both to the King and the two houses. All bills, however, imposing taxes or relating to the budget shall first be presented to the House of Deputies.

ART. 11.   The King shall attain his majority upon the completion of his eighteenth year.

ART. 12.   During the King's minority, the prince who is his nearest relative in the order of succession to the throne, shall be regent of the kingdom, provided he be twenty-one years of age.

ART. 13.   Should the prince upon whom the regency devolves be still in his minority and this duty pass to a more distant relative, the regent who actually takes office shall continue in the regency until the King becomes of age.

ART. 14.   In the absence of male relatives the regency shall devolve upon the queen-mother.

ART. 15.   In default also of a queen-mother, the regent shall be elected by the legislative houses, convened within ten days by the ministers.

ART. 16.   The preceding provisions with reference to the regency are applicable in case the King who has attained his majority is physically incapable of reigning. Under such circumstances, if the heir presumptive to the throne be eighteen years of age, he shall be regent of full right.

ART. 17.   The queen-mother shall be guardian of the King until he has completed his seventh year; from this time his guardianship shall pass into the hands of the regent.

ART. 18.   All rights pertaining to the civil power in matters of ecclesiastical benefices and in the execution of all regulations whatsoever coming from foreign countries shall be exercised by the King.[2]

[2] The clause, "regulations from foreign countries," refers to papal decrees, ecclesiastical ordinances, and orders; at the time of the adoption of this constitution Rome was foreign territory.

ART. 19. The civil list of the crown shall remain, during the present reign, at an amount equal to the average for the past ten years.

The King shall continue to have the use of the royal palaces, villas, gardens, and their appurtenances, and also of all chattels intended for the use of the crown, of which a speedy inventory shall be made by a responsible ministry.

In future the above-mentioned civil list of the crown shall be fixed for the duration of each reign by the first legislature subsequent to the King's accession to the throne.

ART. 20. The property which the King now possesses in his own right, together with that to which he may hereafter acquire title, either for a consideration or gratuitously in the course of his reign, shall form his private patrimony.

The King may dispose of his private patrimony either during his life or by will, exempt from the provisions of the civil law as to the amount thus disposable. In all other cases, the King's patrimony shall be subject to the laws that govern other property.

ART. 21. The law shall provide an annual civil list for the heir apparent to the throne when he has attained his majority, and even earlier in case of his marriage; for the allowances to the princes of the royal family and of royal blood, under the above-mentioned conditions; for the dowries of the princesses and for the dowries of the queens.

ART. 22. Upon ascending the throne, the King shall take an oath in the presence of the two houses to observe faithfully the present constitution.

ART. 23. The regent, before entering on the duties of that office, shall swear fidelity to the King and faithful observance of this constitution and of the laws of the state.

THE RIGHTS AND DUTIES OF CITIZENS

ART. 24. All inhabitants of the kingdom, whatever their rank or title, are equal before the law.

All shall equally enjoy civil and political rights and shall be eligible to civil and military office, except as otherwise provided by law.

Art. 25. All shall contribute without distinction to the burdens of the state, in proportion to their possessions.

Art. 26. Individual liberty is guaranteed.

No one shall be arrested or brought to trial except in the cases provided for and according to the forms prescribed by law.

Art. 27. The domicile is inviolable. No search of a house shall take place except by virtue of law and in the manner prescribed by law.

Art. 28. The press shall be free, but the law may suppress abuses of this freedom.

Nevertheless, Bibles, catechisms, liturgical and prayer books shall not be printed without the previous consent of the bishop.[8]

Art. 29. Property of all kinds whatsoever is inviolable.

In all cases, however, where the public welfare, legally ascertained, requires it, property may be taken and transferred in whole or in part, upon payment of a just indemnity in accordance with law.

Art. 30. No tax shall be levied or collected without the consent of the houses and the approval of the King.

Art. 31. The public debt is guaranteed.

All obligations of the state to its creditors are inviolable.

Art. 32. The right to assemble peaceably and without arms, is recognized, subject, however, to the laws that may regulate the exercise of this privilege in the interest of the public welfare.

This privilege is not applicable to meetings in public places or places open to the public, which shall remain entirely subject to police control.

---

[8] The second section of this article has been practically abrogated. The law actually places no restrictions upon the publication of religious books.

THE SENATE

ART. 33. The Senate shall be composed of members who have attained the age of forty years, appointed for life by the King without limit of numbers, and from the following categories of citizens:

1) Archbishops and bishops of the state.

2) The president of the House of Deputies.

3) Deputies after having served in three legislatures, or after six years of service.

4) Ministers of state.

5) Ministers secretaries of state.

6) Ambassadors.

7) Envoys extraordinary after three years of such service.

8) The first presidents of the Courts of Cassation and the Court of Accounts.

9) The first presidents of the Courts of Appeal.

10) The attorney-general of the Court of Cassation and the prosecutor-general, after five years of service.

11) The presidents of the chambers of the Courts of Appeal after three years of service.

12) The councilors of the Courts of Cassation and of the Court of Accounts, after five years of service.

13) The advocates-general and fiscals-general of the Courts of Appeal, after five years of service.

14) General officers of the land and naval forces; major-generals and rear-admirals after five years of active service in this capacity.

15) The councilors of state after five years of service.

16) The members of the Councils of Division [4] after three elections to their presidency.

17) The intendants-general, after seven years of service.

[4] At the time of the adoption of this constitution the "Division" in Piedmont corresponded to the "Province" in modern Italy. The Councils of Division are therefore the elective representative bodies of the Provinces, now known as the Provincial Councils.

18) Members of the Royal Academy of Science of seven years' standing.

19) Regular members of the Superior Council of Public Instruction, after seven years of service.

20) Those who by their services or eminent merit have done honor to their country.

21) Persons who, for at least three years, have paid direct property or business taxes to the amount of 3,000 lire.

ART. 34. By virtue of their position the princes of the royal family shall be members of the Senate. They shall take rank immediately after the president. They shall enter the Senate at the age of twenty-one and have a vote at twenty-five.

ART. 35. The president and vice-presidents of the Senate shall be appointed by the King. The Senate shall choose its secretaries from among its own members.

ART. 36. The Senate may be constituted a High Court of Justice by decree of the King to try crimes of high treason and attempts upon the safety of the state, and to try ministers impeached by the House of Deputies.

When acting in this capacity, the Senate is not a political body. It shall not then occupy itself with any other judicial matters than those for which it was convened; any other action shall be null and void.

ART. 37. No senator shall be arrested except by virtue of an order of the Senate, unless he be taken in the commission of an offense. The Senate shall be the sole judge of the imputed misdemeanors of its members.

ART. 38. Legal documents as to births, marriages, and deaths of members of the royal family shall be presented to the Senate and deposited by that body among its archives.

THE HOUSE OF DEPUTIES

ART. 39. The elective house shall be composed of deputies chosen by the electoral districts as provided by law.[5]

[5] The election of deputies is now controlled by the royal decree of March 28, 1895, which is a consolidation of all laws in force passed before

Art. 40.   No person shall be a member of the House who is not a subject of the King, thirty years of age, in the enjoyment of all civil and political rights, and of the other qualifications required by law.

Art. 41.   Deputies shall represent the nation as a whole, and not the several provinces from which they are chosen.

No binding instructions may therefore be given by the electors.

Art. 42.   Deputies shall be elected for five years; their power shall cease *ipso facto* at the expiration of this period.

Art. 43.   The president, vice-presidents, and secretaries of the House of Deputies shall be chosen by the House from among its own members at the beginning of each session, for the entire session.

Art. 44.   If a deputy ceases for any reason to perform his duties, the electoral district that chose him shall be called upon at once to proceed with a new election.

Art. 45.   Deputies shall be privileged from arrest during the sessions, except when taken in the commission of an offense, and no deputy may be proceeded against in criminal matters without the previous consent of the House.

Art. 46.   No warrant of arrest for debts[6] may be executed against a deputy during the sessions of the House, nor within a period of three weeks preceding or following the same.

that date. Italy is divided into 508 districts, each of which elects one deputy. Voters must possess the following qualifications: (1) be Italian citizens; (2) have attained the age of twenty-one years; (3) be able to read and write; (4) have successfully passed the examinations in the subjects comprised in the course of compulsory elementary education. The fourth qualification is not required of officials, graduates of colleges, professional men, of those who pay an annual direct tax of not less than 19.80 lire, of those who pay an agricultural rental of 500 lire, of those who pay house rent of from 150 to 400 lire according to the population of the commune in which they live, of those who have served two years in the army, and of certain other less important classes.

[6] The Mancini law of December 6, 1877, has done away with personal arrest for debts.

Art. 47.   The House of Deputies shall have power to impeach ministers of the crown and to bring them to trial before the High Court of Justice.

PROVISIONS COMMON TO BOTH HOUSES

Art. 48.   The sessions of the Senate and House of Deputies shall begin and end at the same time.

Every meeting of one house, at a time when the other is not in session, is illegal and its acts are entirely void.

Art. 49.   Senators and deputies before entering upon the duties of their office shall take an oath to be loyal to the King, to observe faithfully the constitution and laws of the state, and to perform their duties with the inseparable welfare of King and country as the sole end in view.

Art. 50.   The office of senator or deputy shall not carry with it any compensation or remuneration.

Art. 51.   Senators and deputies shall not be called to account for opinions expressed or votes given in the houses.

Art. 52.   The sessions of the houses shall be public.

Upon the written request of ten members secret sessions may be held.

Art. 53.   No session or vote of either house shall be legal or valid unless an absolute majority of its members is present.

Art. 54.   Action on any question shall be taken only by a majority of the votes cast.

Art. 55.   All bills shall first be submitted for preliminary examination to committees elected by each house.   Any proposition discussed and approved by one house shall be transmitted to the other for its consideration and approval; after passing both houses it shall be presented to the King for his approval.

Bills shall be discussed article by article.

Art. 56.   Any bill rejected by one of the three legislative powers shall not again be introduced during the same session.

Art. 57.   Every person who has attained his majority shall have the right to send petitions to the houses, which shall order them to be examined by a committee; on report of the committee each house shall decide whether such petitions are to be taken into consideration, and in case of an affirmative decision, they shall be referred to the competent minister or to one of the sections of the house for action.[7]

ART. 58. No petition may be presented in person to either house.

Legally organized bodies alone shall have the right to petition under a collective name.

ART. 59. The houses shall not receive any deputation, nor give hearing to others than their own members, ministers, and commissioners of the government.

ART. 60. Each house shall be the sole judge of the qualifications and elections of its own members.

ART. 61. The Senate and the House of Deputies shall make their own rules and regulations respecting their methods of procedure in the performance of their respective duties.

ART. 62. Italian shall be the official language of the houses.

The use of French shall, however, be permitted to the members coming from districts where French is used, and in replying to them.[8]

ART. 63. Votes shall be taken by rising and sitting, by division, or by secret ballot. The latter method, however, shall always be employed for the final vote on a law and in all cases of a personal character.

ART. 64. No one shall at the same time hold the office of senator and of deputy.

THE MINISTERS

ART. 65. The King appoints and dismisses his ministers.

ART. 66. The ministers shall have no vote in either house unless they are members thereof.

[7] The House of Deputies is divided into nine sections or "uffici," among which legislative business is divided by the president of the House.

[8] This clause applied principally to Savoy which became a part of France, by the terms of the treaty of March 24, 1860.

They shall have entrance to both houses and shall be heard upon request.

ART. 67. The ministers are responsible.

Laws and governmental acts shall not take effect until they shall have received the signature of a minister.

THE JUDICIARY

ART. 68. Justice emanates from the King and shall be administered in his name by the judges whom he appoints.

ART. 69. Judges appointed by the King, except cantonal judges, shall be irremovable, after three years of service.[9]

ART. 70. Courts, tribunals, and judges shall be retained as at present existing. No modification shall be introduced except by law.[10]

ART. 71. No one shall be withdrawn from his ordinary legal jurisdiction.

It shall, therefore, not be lawful to create extraordinary tribunals or commissions.[11]

ART. 72. The proceedings of courts in civil cases and the

[9] A law of 1859 re-enacted December 6, 1865, permits transfers of judges, provided they preserve the same grade and salary. By a decree of January 4, 1880, a legal commission of five members must be consulted with regard to such transfers.

[10] There are in Italy five independent Courts of Cassation, or courts of last resort, those of Turin, Florence, Naples, Palermo, and Rome. However, the Court of Cassation of Rome has gradually received exclusive jurisdiction over several important matters; a law of December 12, 1875, granted this court exclusive jurisdiction over conflicts between other courts as to their respective powers, in cases involving the revenues of the state, in cases involving the suppression of religious corporations, and in certain other matters; a law of March 31, 1877, extends its competence over conflicts between administrative officers and the courts; the law of December 6, 1888, made the Court of Cassation of Rome the only court of final jurisdiction in criminal matters. In civil matters, however, the courts of Turin, Florence, Naples, and Palermo still retain jurisdiction coextensive with that of the court at Rome.

[11] The code of penal procedure, however, in Article 766 provides that in case of reasonable suspicion, or on the grounds of public safety, a person may be removed for trial from the regularly constituted jurisdiction.

hearings in criminal cases shall be public, as provided by law.

ART. 73. The interpretation of the laws, in the form obligatory upon all citizens, belongs to the legislative power.

GENERAL PROVISIONS

ART. 74. Communal and provincial institutions and the boundaries of the communes and provinces shall be regulated by law.[12]

ART. 75. Military conscriptions shall be regulated by law.

ART. 76. A communal militia shall be established upon a basis fixed by law.

ART. 77. The state retains its flag, and the blue cockade is the only national one.[13]

ART. 78. The knightly orders now in existence shall be maintained with their endowments, which shall not be used for other purposes than those specified in the acts by which they were established.

The King may create other orders and prescribe their constitutions.

ART. 79. Titles of nobility shall be borne by those who have a right to them. The King may confer new titles.

ART. 80. No one may receive orders, titles, or pensions from a foreign power without the consent of the King.

ART. 81. All laws contrary to the provisions of the present constitution are abrogated.

TRANSITORY PROVISIONS

ART. 82. This statute shall go into effect on the day of the first meeting of the houses, which shall take place immediately after the elections. Until that time urgent public

[12] A royal decree of May 4, 1898, combined into one text all of the laws relating to provincial and communal organization. The kingdom is divided into provinces, circondari, mandamenti, and communes, and the system of provincial and communal government is to a large extent copied from France.

[13] The Italian tricolor of green, white, and red was adopted by royal proclamation of March 23, 1848.

service shall be provided for by royal ordinances according to the mode and form now in vogue, excepting, however, the authentications and registrations in the courts which are from now on abolished.

ART. 83.   In the execution of this statute the King reserves to himself the right to make the laws for the press, elections, communal militia, and the reorganization of the Council of State.

Until the publication of the laws for the press, the regulations now in force on this subject shall remain valid.

ART. 84.   The ministers are intrusted with and are responsible for the execution and full observance of these transitory provisions.

LAW OF THE PAPAL GUARANTIES
(May 13, 1871)

TITLE I.   PREROGATIVES OF THE SUPREME PONTIFF
AND OF THE HOLY SEE

ARTICLE 1.   The person of the Supreme Pontiff is sacred and inviolable.

ART. 2.   Any attempt against the person of the Supreme Pontiff and the provocation to commit such an attempt shall be punished with the same penalty as similar offenses against the person of the King.

Public offenses and insults committed directly against the person of the Supreme Pontiff, by speech, by act, or by the means indicated in Art. 1 of the law of the press, shall be punished with the penalty fixed by Art. 19 of the said law.

The crimes above mentioned shall be proceeded against by the public prosecutor and tried by the Court of Assize.

The discussion of religious matters shall be entirely free.

ART. 3.   The Italian government grants to the Supreme Pontiff, within the kingdom, sovereign honors, and guarantees to him the pre-eminence customarily accorded to him by Catholic sovereigns.

He may maintain the usual number of guards for his person and for the custody of the palaces, without prejudice to the duties of such guards, according to the laws in force in the kingdom.

ART. 4. An annual income of 3,225,000 lire is reserved for the Holy See.

With this sum, equal to that of the Roman budget for "Holy Apostolic Palaces, Sacred College, Ecclesiastical Congregations, Secretary of State, and Diplomatic Corps abroad," it is intended to provide for the Supreme Pontiff and for the various ecclesiastical needs of the Holy See, for the ordinary and extraordinary maintenance and custody of the apostolic palaces and their annexes, for the compensation and pensions of the guards mentioned in the preceding article and of the attachés of the pontifical court, and for casual expenses; as well as for the regular maintenance and custody of the museums and library attached to the apostolic palaces, and for the compensation and pensions of their employees.

This dotation shall be entered in the great book of the public debt as a perpetual and inalienable income in the name of the Holy See, and during the vacancy of the See, it shall continue to be paid to supply all the needs of the Roman church during such interval.

It shall remain free from every form of state, provincial, or communal taxation or other burden, and shall not be diminished even in case the Italian government should later decide to assume the expenses of the museums and of the library.

ART. 5. Besides the dotation mentioned in the preceding article the Supreme Pontiff shall have the use of the apostolic Vatican and Lateran palaces with all buildings, gardens, and lands appertaining thereto, and also the villa of Castel Gandolfo with all its appurtenances.

These palaces, the villa and its annexes, as well as the museums, the library, and the collections of art and of archaeology connected therewith, are inalienable and are exempt from all taxation or charges and from seizure for a public purpose.

ART. 6. During the vacancy of the pontifical chair no judicial or political authority shall for any reason hinder or limit the personal liberty of cardinals.

The government shall see to it that assemblies of conclave and ecumenical councils are not disturbed by external violence.

ART. 7. No public official or agent of the public force in the performance of the duties of his office, shall enter the places or palaces which are the permanent or temporary residence of the Supreme Pontiff, or during the sessions of the ecumenical council or conclave, without the authorization of the Pope, conclave, or council.

ART. 8. Papers, documents, books, or registers deposited in pontifical offices or congregations, invested with a purely spiritual character, shall be free from the legal processes of visit, search, or sequestration.

ART. 9. The Supreme Pontiff shall be entirely free to fulfil all the functions of his spiritual ministry, and to this end may affix to the doors of basilicas and churches of Rome notices relating to such ministry.

ART. 10. Ecclesiastics at Rome who officially take part in the promulgation of acts pertaining to the spiritual ministry of the Holy See shall not on this account be subjected to any examination, investigation, or control by the civil authorities.

Every foreigner invested with ecclesiastical office at Rome shall enjoy all the privileges and immunities of Italian citizens, in accordance with the laws of the kingdom.

ART. 11. Envoys of foreign governments to the Holy See shall be entitled within the kingdom to all the prerogatives and immunities accorded to other diplomatic agents, according to the usages of international law.

All offenses against them shall be subject to the same penalties as are provided for offenses against envoys of foreign powers to the Italian government.

Envoys of the Holy See to foreign governments shall, within the territory of the kingdom, be entitled to privileges and immunities of the same character while going to or returning from their mission.

ART. 12. The Supreme Pontiff corresponds freely with the episcopacy and with the whole Catholic world, without any interference from the Italian government.

To this end he shall have the right to establish his own postal and telegraph offices at the Vatican or at any of his other residences, served by employees chosen by himself.

The pontifical post-office may transmit sealed packages of correspondence directly to foreign offices, or may send them through the Italian offices. In either case transmission of dispatches or correspondence bearing the papal stamp shall be made free of charge within Italian territory.

Couriers sent out in the name of the Supreme Pontiff are, within the kingdom, placed on an equal footing with couriers of foreign governments.

Telegraphic connections between the pontifical telegraph system and that of the state shall be made at the expense of the state.

Telegrams sent to the state offices with pontifical authentication shall be received and transmitted within the kingdom in the same manner as telegrams of state, and without charge.

Telegrams of the Supreme Pontiff or sent by his order, which bear the papal stamp, shall enjoy the same privileges if presented to any telegraph office of the kingdom.

Telegrams addressed to the Supreme Pontiff shall be exempt from the tax imposed upon those who receive telegrams.

ART. 13. Within the city of Rome and within the six subsidiary sees, the seminaries, academies, colleges, and other catholic institutions founded for the education and training of ecclesiastics shall continue under the sole control of the Holy See, without any interference from the educational authorities of the state.

TITLE II. RELATION OF THE STATE TO THE CHURCH

ART. 14. Every special restriction upon the exercise of the right of members of the Catholic clergy to assemble is abolished.

ART. 15. The government renounces the right to an apostolic legation in Sicily, and to the appointment or nomination to the major benefices throughout the kingdom.

Bishops shall not be required to swear fidelity to the King.

Major and minor benefices may be conferred only upon Italian citizens, except in the city of Rome and in the subsidiary sees.

Nothing is changed with respect to the collation to benefices of royal patronage.

ART. 16. The *exequatur* and *placet regio* and all other forms of government authorization for the publication or execution of ecclesiastical acts are abolished.

But, until otherwise provided by a special law mentioned in Art. 18, such *exequator* and *placet regio* shall be required for acts disposing of ecclesiastical property and for appointments to major and minor benefices, except those in the city of Rome and in the subsidiary sees.

The provisions of the civil law relating to the creation and management of ecclesiastical institutions, and to the sale of their property, remain unchanged.

ART. 17. In matters of spiritual discipline there shall be no appeal from decisions of ecclesiastical authorities, nor shall such decisions be recognized or executed by the civil authorities.

The determination of the legal effects of such decisions and of other acts of the ecclesiastical authority shall belong to the civil authorities.

If, however, such acts are contrary to the laws of the state or opposed to public order, or encroach upon the rights of individuals they shall be of no effect and shall be subject to the criminal laws, if they constitute offenses.

ART. 18. A future law shall provide for the reorganization, preservation, and administration of the ecclesiastical property within the state.

ART. 19. All regulations now in force contrary to this law are repealed.

JAPAN

In 1867 the Shogun, until then the real ruler of Japan, surrendered his powers to the Emperor. The disappearance of the Shogunate weakened the feudal system, which was, however, made the basis of the first representative organization. In February, 1868, a superior council and seven ministerial departments were organized; a deliberative assembly was convened, its members to be composed of delegates appointed by the feudal chiefs. In the same year the Emperor took an oath that "the system of a deliberative assembly should be adopted and that all measures should be taken in conformity with public opinion." The organization of government upon a feudal basis proved unsatisfactory; the deliberative assembly was abolished in 1870, and the feudal régime itself was suppressed in 1871.

An agitation in favor of national representative institutions began in 1874, but those in charge of the government considered such a step premature; in 1878 representative provincial councils were created. Beginning in 1880 a vigorous political propaganda was conducted in favor of the establishment of a representative assembly; an imperial edict of October 12, 1881, announced that the first Imperial Diet would be convened in 1890.

Between 1881 and 1889 important reforms were made in the organization of the government. The constitution was promulgated on February 11, 1889, and at the same time were issued the Imperial House Law, the ordinance concerning the House of Peers, the Law of the Houses, the election law for members of the House of Representatives, and the law of finance. The first Diet was formally opened on November 29, 1890.

SELECT BIBLIOGRAPHY

Ito, Hirobumi. *Commentaries on the Constitution of the Empire of Japan.* Translated by Miyoji Ito. (Tokyo, 1889.) A brief commentary by the author of the constitution.

GOLLIER, THÉOPHILE. *Essai sur les institutions politiques du Japon.* (Brussels, 1903.) An excellent account of the structure of the Japanese government.

NOSAWA TAKEMATSU. *Étude sur la constitution du Japon.* (Paris, 1896.)

FURUYA, HISATSUNA. *Système représentatif au Japon.* (Brussels, 1899.) A study of the history and organization of the Japanese Diet.

KAWAKAMI, KARL KIYOSHI. *The Political Ideas of Modern Japan.* (Iowa City, Iowa, 1903.)

CONSTITUTION OF JAPAN [1]
(February 11, 1889)

CHAPTER I.   THE EMPEROR

ARTICLE 1.   The Empire of Japan shall be reigned over and governed by a line of emperors unbroken for ages eternal.

ART. 2.   The imperial throne shall be succeeded to by imperial male descendants, according to the provisions of the Imperial House Law.[2]

ART. 3.   The Emperor is sacred and inviolable.

ART. 4.   The Emperor is the head of the Empire, combining in himself the rights of sovereignty, and exercises them, according to the provisions of the present constitution.

ART. 5.   The Emperor exercises the legislative power with the consent of the Imperial Diet.

ART. 6.   The Emperor gives sanction to laws, and orders them to be promulgated and executed.

ART. 7.   The Emperor convokes the Imperial Diet, opens, closes, and prorogues it, and dissolves the House of Representatives.

[1] This text has been adopted almost without change from the official English translation issued from Tokyo in 1889; the difficulty of obtaining revision makes it necessary to give this constitution in the untechnical language in which it here appears.

[2] By the Imperial House Law the succession is in the male descendants of the Emperor, in accordance with the law of primogeniture; when the Emperor has no descendants the crown goes to the male relative of the nearest collateral male line.

ART. 8.   The Emperor, in consequence of an urgent necessity to maintain public safety or to avert public calamities, issues, when the Imperial Diet is not sitting, imperial ordinances in the place of laws.

Such imperial ordinances are to be laid before the Imperial Diet at its next session, and when the Diet does not approve the said ordinances, the government shall declare them to be invalid for the future.

ART. 9.   The Emperor issues, or causes to be issued, the ordinances necessary for the carrying out of the laws, or for the maintenance of the public peace and order, and for the promotion of the welfare of the subjects.   But no ordinance shall in any way alter any of the existing laws.

ART. 10.   The Emperor determines the organization of the different branches of the administration, and the salaries of all civil and military officers, and appoints and dismisses the same.   Exceptions especially provided for in the present constitution or in other laws shall be in accordance with the respective provisions (bearing thereon).

ART. 11.   The Emperor has the supreme command of the army and navy.

ART. 12.   The Emperor determines the organization and peace standing of the army and navy.

ART. 13.   The Emperor declares war, makes peace, and concludes treaties.

ART. 14.   The Emperor proclaims a state of siege.

The conditions and effects of a state of siege shall be determined by law.

ART. 15.   The Emperor confers titles of nobility, rank, orders, and other marks of honor.

ART. 16.   The Emperor orders amnesty, pardon, commutation of punishment, and rehabilitation.

ART. 17.   A regency shall be instituted in conformity with the provisions of the Imperial House Law.

The regent shall exercise the powers appertaining to the Emperor, in his name.

CHAPTER II. RIGHTS AND DUTIES OF SUBJECTS

ART. 18. The conditions necessary for being a Japanese subject shall be determined by law.

ART. 19. Japanese subjects may, according to qualifications determined in laws or ordinances, be appointed to civil or military offices equally, and may fill any other public offices.

ART. 20. Japanese subjects are amenable to service in the army or navy, according to the provisions of law.

ART. 21. Japanese subjects are amenable to the duty of paying taxes, according to the provisions of law.

ART. 22. Japanese subjects shall have the liberty of abode and of changing the same within the limits of law.

ART. 23. No Japanese subject shall be arrested, detained, tried, or punished, unless according to law.

ART. 24. No Japanese subject shall be deprived of his right of being tried by the judges determined by law.

ART. 25. Except in the cases provided for in the law, the house of no Japanese subject shall be entered or searched without his consent.

ART. 26. Except in the cases mentioned in the law, the secrecy of the letters of every Japanese subject shall remain inviolable.

ART. 27. The right of property of every Japanese subject shall remain inviolable.

Measures necessary to be taken for the public benefit shall be provided for by law.

ART. 28. Japanese subjects shall, within limits not prejudicial to peace and order, and not antagonistic to their duties as subjects, enjoy freedom of religious belief.

ART. 29. Japanese subjects shall, within the limits of law, enjoy the liberty of speech, writing, publication, public meeting, and association.

ART. 30. Japanese subjects may present petitions, by observing the proper forms of respect, and by complying with the rules specially provided for the same.

ART. 31. The provisions in the present chapter shall not affect the exercise of the powers appertaining to the Emperor, in times of war or in cases of national emergency.

ART. 32. Each and every one of the provisions contained in the preceding articles of the present chapter, that are not in conflict with the laws or the rules and discipline of the army and navy, shall apply to the officers and men of the army and navy.

CHAPTER III. THE IMPERIAL DIET

ART. 33. The Imperial Diet shall consist of two houses, a House of Peers and a House of Representatives.[3]

ART. 34. The House of Peers shall, in accordance with the ordinance concerning the House of Peers, be composed of the members of the imperial family, of the orders of nobility, and of those persons who have been nominated thereto by the Emperor.[4]

ART. 35. The House of Representatives shall be composed of members elected by the people, according to the provisions of the election law.[5]

ART. 36. No one shall at one and the same time be a member of both houses.

[3] The internal organization of the two houses is regulated by the Law of the Houses, of February 11, 1889. By Art. 3 of this law it is provided that "the president and vice-president of the House of Representatives shall both of them be nominated by the Emperor from among three candidates respectively elected by the House for each of those offices."

[4] See imperial ordinance concerning House of Peers, p. 33.

[5] The election law of 1889 was amended in 1900. At present the right to vote is enjoyed by male subjects twenty-five years of age, who have resided in the election district for one year, and pay a tax of ten yen (about five dollars). Before 1900 the tax qualification was fifteen yen. On account of the relative poverty of the people the present tax qualification limits the suffrage to a small proportion of the adult male population. In general all male subjects thirty years of age are eligible as representatives; the representatives are chosen in single election districts.

ART. 37.   Every law requires the consent of the Imperial Diet.

ART. 38.   Both houses shall vote upon projects of law submitted to them by the government, and may respectively initiate projects of law.

ART. 39.   A bill, which has been rejected by either the one or the other of the two houses, shall not be again brought in during the same session.

ART. 40.   Both houses may make representations to the government as to laws or upon any other subject.   When, however, such representations are not accepted, they cannot be made a second time during the same session.

ART. 41.   The Imperial Diet shall be convoked every year.

ART. 42.   A session of the Imperial Diet shall last during three months.   In case of necessity, the duration of a session may be prolonged by imperial order.

ART. 43.   When urgent necessity arises, an extraordinary session may be convoked, in addition to the ordinary one.

The duration of an extraordinary session shall be determined by imperial order.

ART. 44.   The opening, closing, prolongation of session, or prorogation of the Imperial Diet shall be effected simultaneously for both houses.

In case the House of Representatives has been ordered to dissolve, the House of Peers shall at the same time be prorogued.

ART. 45.   When the House of Representatives has been ordered to dissolve, members shall be caused by imperial order to be newly elected, and the new House shall be convoked within five months from the day of dissolution.

ART. 46.   No debate shall be opened and no vote shall be taken in either house of the Imperial Diet, unless not less than one-third of the whole number of the members thereof is present.

ART. 47.   Votes shall be taken in both houses by absolute

majority. In the case of a tie, the president shall have the casting vote.

ART. 48. The deliberations of both houses shall be held in public. The deliberations may, however, upon demand of the government or by resolution of the house, be held in secret sitting.

ART. 49. Both houses of the Imperial Diet may respectively present addresses to the Emperor.

ART. 50. Both houses may receive petitions presented by subjects.

ART. 51. Both houses may enact, besides what is provided for in the present constitution and in the Law of the Houses, rules necessary for the management of their internal affairs.

ART. 52. No member of either house shall be held responsible outside the respective houses, for any opinion uttered or for any vote given in the house. When, however, a member himself has given publicity to his opinions by public speech, by documents in print or in writing, or by any other similar means, he shall, in the matter, be amenable to the general law.

ART. 53. The members of both houses shall, during the session, be free from arrest, unless with the consent of the house, except in cases where taken *in flagrante delicto,* or of offenses connected with a state of internal commotion or with a foreign trouble.

ART. 54. The ministers of state and the delegates of the government may, at any time, take seats and speak in either house.

CHAPTER IV. THE MINISTERS OF STATE AND THE PRIVY COUNCIL

ART. 55. The respective ministers of state shall give their advice to the Emperor, and be responsible for it.

All laws, imperial ordinances and imperial rescripts of

whatever kind, that relate to the affairs of state, require the countersignature of a minister of state.

ART. 56. The Privy Council shall, in accordance with the provisions for the organization of the Privy Council, deliberate upon important matters of state, when they have been consulted by the Emperor.

CHAPTER V.   THE JUDICIAL POWER

ART. 57. The judicial power shall be exercised by the courts of law according to law, in the name of the Emperor.

The organization of the courts of law shall be determined by law.

ART. 58. The judges shall be appointed from among those who possess proper qualifications according to law.

No judge shall be deprived of his position, unless by way of criminal sentence or disciplinary punishment.

Rules for disciplinary punishment shall be determined by law.

ART. 59. Trials and judgments of a court shall be conducted publicly. When, however, there exists any fear that such publicity may be prejudicial to peace and order, or to the maintenance of public morality, the public trial may be suspended by provision of law or by the decision of the court.

ART. 60. All matters that fall within the competency of special tribunals shall be specially provided for by law.

ART. 61. No suit which relates to rights alleged to have been infringed by the illegal measures of the executive authorities, and which should come within the competency of the Court of Administrative Litigation specially established by law, shall be taken cognizance of by a court of law.

CHAPTER VI.   FINANCE

ART. 62. The imposition of a new tax or the modification of the rates (of an existing one) shall be determined by law.

However, all such administrative fees or other revenue having the nature of compensation shall not fall within the category of the above clause.

The raising of national loans and the contracting of other liabilities to the charge of the national treasury, except those that are provided in the budget, shall require the consent of the Imperial Diet.

ART. 63. The taxes levied at present shall, in so far as they are not remodeled by a new law, be collected according to the old system.

ART. 64. The expenditure and revenue of the state require the consent of the Imperial Diet by means of an annual budget.

Any and all expenditures exceeding the appropriations set forth in the titles and paragraphs of the budget, or that are not provided for in the budget, shall subsequently require the approbation of the Imperial Diet.

ART. 65. The budget shall be first laid before the House of Representatives.

ART. 66. The expenditures of the Imperial House shall be defrayed every year out of the national treasury, according to the present fixed amount for the same, and shall not require the consent thereto of the Imperial Diet, except in case an increase thereof is found necessary.

ART. 67. Those expenditures already fixed and based upon the powers belonging to the Emperor by the constitution, and such expenditures as may have arisen by the effect of law, or that relate to the legal obligations of the government, shall neither be rejected nor reduced by the Imperial Diet, without the concurrence of the government.

ART. 68. In order to meet special requirements, the government may ask the consent of the Imperial Diet to a certain amount as a continuing expenditure fund, for a previously fixed number of years.

ART. 69. In order to supply deficiencies, which are unavoidable, in the budget, and to meet requirements unprovided for in the same, a reserve fund shall be provided in the budget.

ART. 70. When the Imperial Diet cannot be convoked, owing to the external or internal condition of the country, in case of urgent need for the maintenance of public safety the government may enact all necessary financial measures, by means of an imperial ordinance.

In the case mentioned in the preceding clause, the matter shall be submitted to the Imperial Diet at its next session, and its approbation shall be obtained thereto.

ART. 71. When the Imperial Diet has not voted on the budget, or when the budget has not been brought into actual existence, the government shall carry out the budget of the preceding year.

ART. 72. The final account of the expenditures and revenue of the state shall be verified and confirmed by the Board of Audit, and it shall be submitted by the government to the Imperial Diet, together with the report of verification of the said board.

The organization and competency of the Board of Audit shall be determined by a special law.

CHAPTER VII.   SUPPLEMENTARY RULES

ART. 73. When it may become necessary in future to amend the provisions of the present constitution, a project to that effect shall be submitted to the Imperial Diet by imperial order.

In the above case, neither house shall open the debate, unless not less than two-thirds of the whole number of members are present, and no amendment shall be passed, unless a majority of not less than two-thirds of the members present is obtained.

ART. 74. No modification of the Imperial House Law shall be required to be submitted to the deliberation of the Imperial Diet.

No provision of the present constitution can be modified by the Imperial House Law.

ART. 75. No modification shall be introduced into the constitution, or into the Imperial House Law, during the time of a regency.

ART. 76. Existing legal enactments, such as laws, regulations, ordinances, or by whatever names they may be called, shall, so far as they do not conflict with the present constitution, continue in force.

All existing contracts or orders, that entail obligations upon the government, and that are connected with expenditure, shall come within the scope of Art. 67.

IMPERIAL ORDINANCE CONCERNING THE HOUSE OF PEERS

ARTICLE 1. The House of Peers shall be composed of the following members:

1) The members of the imperial family.

2) Princes and marquises.

3) Counts, viscounts, and barons who have been elected thereto by the members of their respective orders.

4) Persons who have been specially nominated by the Emperor, on account of meritorious services to the state or of erudition.

5) Persons who have been elected, one member for each Fu (city) and Ken (prefecture), by and from among the tax payers of the highest amount of direct national taxes on land, industry, or trade therein, and who have afterward been appointed thereto by the Emperor.

ART. 2. The male members of the imperial family shall take seats in the House on reaching their majority.

ART. 3. The members of the orders of princes and of marquises shall become members on reaching the full age of twenty-five years.

ART. 4. The members of the orders of counts, viscounts, and barons, who after reaching the full age of twenty-five years, have been elected by the members of their respective orders, shall become members for a term of seven years. Rules for their election shall be specially determined by imperial ordinance.

The number of members mentioned in the preceding clause shall not exceed one-fifth of the entire number of the respective orders of counts, viscounts, and barons.

ART. 5. Any man of above the age of thirty years, who has been appointed a member by the Emperor for meritorious services to the state or for erudition, shall be a life member.

ART. 6. One member shall be elected in each Fu and Ken from among and by the fifteen male inhabitants thereof of above the full age of thirty years, paying therein the highest amount of direct national taxes on land, industry, or trade. When the person thus elected receives his appointment from the Emperor, he shall become a member for the term of seven years. Rules for such elections shall be specially determined by imperial ordinance.

ART. 7. The number of members appointed by the Emperor for meritorious services to the state, or for erudition, or from among men paying the highest amount of direct national taxes on land, industry, or trade in each Fu or Ken, shall not exceed the number of the members having the title of nobility.

ART. 8. The House of Peers shall, when consulted by the Emperor, pass upon rules concerning the privileges of the nobility.

ART. 9. The House of Peers decides upon the qualification of its members and upon disputes concerning elections thereto. The rules for these decisions shall be resolved upon by the House of Peers and submitted to the Emperor for his sanction.

ART. 10. When a member has been sentenced to confinement, or to any severer punishment, or has been declared bankrupt, he shall be expelled by imperial order.

With respect to the expulsion of a member, as a disciplinary punishment in the House of Peers, the president shall report the facts to the Emperor for his decision.

Any member who has been expelled shall be incapable of again becoming a member, unless permission so to do has been granted by the Emperor.

ART. 11.   The president and vice-president shall be nominated by the Emperor, from among the members, for a term of seven years.

If an elected member is nominated president or vice-president, he shall serve in that capacity for the term of his membership.

ART. 12.   Every matter, other than those for which provision has been made in the present imperial ordinance, shall be dealt with according to the provisions of the Law of the Houses.

ART. 13.   When in the future any amendment or addition is to be made to the provisions of the present imperial ordinance, the matter shall be submitted to the vote of the House of Peers.

MEXICO

The first important movement for Mexican independence from Spain was that of 1810, headed by the priest, Miguel Hidalgo i Costilla; this insurrection was suppressed without difficulty, and Hidalgo was executed. The revolutionary forces, however, were not entirely crushed, and soon a more formidable revolution occurred under the leadership of Morelos; a popular assembly was convened in 1813 which declared Mexico independent and adopted the republican constitution of October 22, 1814.

This movement was also suppressed, and Mexico remained quiet until after the Spanish revolution of 1820. Augustin de Iturbide, one of the Spanish military commanders, now joined the revolutionary forces, and the plan of Iguala, drawn up by the insurgents on February 24, 1821, was generally supported by the people; by this plan Mexico was erected into an independent limited monarchy and the throne was offered to Ferdinand VII of Spain. The new Spanish viceroy, O'Donojú, who had been appointed by the then liberal government of Spain, agreed to the general principles of this plan; if neither Ferdinand VII nor any male member of his family would accept the crown, an emperor was to be chosen by the Mexican legislature. Both Ferdinand and the Spanish Cortes disapproved the terms made by O'Donojú, and on March 18, 1822, Iturbide was chosen emperor of Mexico, with the title of Augustin I. Both Monarchists and Republicans combined against the new emperor who was forced to abdicate and leave the country after a reign of little more than a year.

Upon the disappearance of Iturbide the republic was immediately proclaimed. A constitutional convention was convened, which on January 31, 1824, adopted a constitutional act as the basis for a new constitution; by this act it was declared that "the nation adopts the republican, representative, popular, federal form of government." The republican constitution of October 4, 1824, which erected the provinces into states, was in many respects a copy of the constitution of the United States. This constitution was nominally in force for eleven years, but its operation was frequently interrupted by revolutions.

In Mexico as in the Argentine Republic the most important political question was that of centralization or federalism. General Santa Anna, who became president of the republic for the second time in 1834, allied himself with the supporters of centralization. The Congress which met in 1835 undertook the alteration of the constitution of 1824, and the seven constitutional laws of December 29, 1836, entirely changed the organization of the government. The states were abolished and replaced by departments with limited powers; each department was governed by an elected council of seven members, and by a governor, appointed by the president of the republic from a list of three candidates presented by the departmental council. Slight changes were introduced by the constitution of June 12, 1843, which consolidated the constitutional laws of 1836 into one instrument. The federalists regaining control, the constitution of 1824 was restored on August 22, 1846.

Between 1836 and 1855 there were few years when Mexico was not in a state of civil war. Santa Anna, who had regained power in 1846 and had fled from the country in the succeeding year, again became president in 1853, and by his arbitrary conduct aroused strong opposition. The garrison of Ayutla took the lead in the movement by demanding on March 1, 1854, that Santa Anna should cease to exercise power and that a temporary president be chosen for the purpose of convening a constitutional convention; the so-called Plan of Ayutla was adopted with some changes by the garrison of Acapulco on March 11, 1854, and was generally accepted throughout the country. Santa Anna abandoned the presidency and a constitutional convention met on February 18, 1856; in May of the same year the new president issued a "provisional organic statute of the Mexican Republic," which was replaced by the constitution of February 5, 1857.

The constitution of 1857 has been frequently amended; all changes are noted in the text given below. This constitution has been continuously in force since 1857, except for the period of the short-lived empire of Maximilian, during a portion of which the autocratic provisional statute of April 10, 1865, was operative throughout the greater part of Mexican territory.

SELECT BIBLIOGRAPHY

Mexico. *Constitución de los Estados Unidos Mexicanos . . . . con sus adiciones y reformas, leyes orgánicas y reglamentarios.* Texto vigente de la constitución. (México, 1905.) The latest official edition of the Mexican constitution and important complementary laws.

Montiel y Duarte, Isidro Antonio. *Derecho público Mexicano.* (México, 1871–82. 4 vols. and appendix.) A documentary history of Mexican constitutions.

Gamboa, José M. *Leyes constitucionales de México durante el siglo XIX.* (México, 1901.) A convenient collection of Mexican constitutional documents.

Mexico. *Constituciones políticas de los estados de la república Mexicana.* (México, 1902. 2 vols.)

Torre, Juan de la. *La constitución federal de 1857 y leyes organicas.* (2d ed., Mexico, 1896.) A convenient private collection of laws bearing on the organization of government; a new edition was probably issued in 1905.

Coronado, Mariano. *Elementos de derecho constitucional Mexicano.* (2d ed., Guadalajara, 1899.) This work and that of Ruiz have not been examined by the editor but they are referred to in high terms by Cruzada, *Bibliografía juridica Mexicana* (México, 1905).

Ruiz, Eduardo. *Curso de derecho constitucional y administrativo.* (México, 1888.)

Garcia Granados, Ricardo. *La constitución de 1857 y las leyes de reforma en México.* (México, 1906.) An excellent historical outline.

CONSTITUTION OF MEXICO [1]
(February 5, 1857)

In the name of God and by the authority of the Mexican people.

The representatives of the different states, of the district and of the territories which compose the Republic of Mexico, called by the plan proclaimed in Ayutla the first of March, eighteen hundred and fifty-four, amended in Acapulco the

[1] In the preparation of this text assistance has been received from the translation made by Professor Bernard Moses and issued in the *Annals of the American Academy of Political and Social Science* of July, 1891, and from that contained in Rodriguez, *American Constitutions.*

eleventh day of the same month and year, and by the summons issued the seventeenth of October, eighteen hundred and fifty-five, to constitute the nation under the form of a popular, representative, democratic republic, exercising the powers with which they are invested, do comply with the requirements of their high office, by decreeing the following political constitution of the Mexican Republic, on the indestructible basis of its legitimate independence, proclaimed the sixteenth of September, eighteen hundred and ten, and consummated the twenty-seventh of September, eighteen hundred and twenty-one.

TITLE I

SECTION I. THE RIGHTS OF MAN

ARTICLE 1. The Mexican people recognize that the rights of man are the basis and the object of social institutions. Consequently they declare that all the laws and all the authorities of the country should respect and maintain the guaranties which the present constitution establishes.

ART. 2. In the Republic all are born free. Slaves who set foot upon the national territory shall recover, by that act alone, their liberty, and shall have a right to the protection of the laws.

ART. 3. Instruction shall be free. The law shall determine what professions require a diploma for their exercise, and what requisites are necessary to obtain such diplomas.

ART. 4. Everyone shall be free to engage in any honorable and useful profession, industrial pursuit, or occupation suitable to him, and to avail himself of its products. The exercise of these liberties shall not be hindered except by judicial sentence when such exercise injures the rights of a third party, or by executive order issued in the manner specified by law, when it offends the rights of society.

ART. 5. No one shall be obliged to perform personal work without just compensation and without his full consent [unless the work be imposed as a penalty by the judicial authority].

[With respect to public services the following only shall be obligatory, under provisions which shall be established by law: military service, the electoral functions, municipal offices, and service upon the jury; all of these except military service shall be gratuitous as well as obligatory.]

The state shall not permit the execution of any contract, covenant, or agreement which has for its object the [abridgement], loss, or irrevocable sacrifice of the liberty of man, whether by reason of labor, education, or religious vows.

[The law, therefore, does not recognize monastic orders, nor may it permit their establishment, whatever may be the denomination or the object for which it may be sought to create them.]   Nor shall any agreement be permitted by which a man agrees to his own proscription or exile.[2]

ART. 6.   The expression of ideas shall not be the object of any judicial or administrative investigation, except in case it attacks morality, the rights of a third party, provokes some crime or misdemeanor, or disturbs public order.

ART. 7.   The liberty to write and to publish writings on any subject whatsoever is inviolable.   No law or authority shall establish previous censorship, or require authors or printers to give bond, or restrict the liberty of the press, which shall have no other limits than respect for private life, morality, and the public peace.   Crimes which are committed by means of the press shall be judged by the competent tribunals of the Federation or by those of the states or of the Federal District and the Territory of Lower California, in accordance with the penal laws.[3]

ART. 8.   The right of petition, exercised in writing in a

[2] As amended September 25, 1873, and June 10, 1898. The change in the first clause and the addition of the second clause were made in 1898. The other changes were made in 1873. For the relation of church and state, see additions to the constitution, of September 25, 1873.

[3] As amended May 15, 1883. The last sentence originally read: "Crimes of the press shall be judged by one jury which determines the facts, and by another which applies the law and designates the punishment."

peaceful and respectful manner, is inviolable; but in political matters only citizens of the Republic may exercise it. To every petition a written answer shall be returned by the authority to whom it may have been addressed, and the latter is obliged to make the result known to the petitioner.

ART. 9.   No one shall be deprived of the right peacefully to associate or unite with others for any lawful purpose; but only citizens of the Republic may assemble in order to take part in the political affairs of the country. No armed assembly shall have the right to deliberate.

ART. 10.   Everyone shall have the right to possess and carry arms for his security and legitimate defense. The law shall designate what arms are prohibited, and the punishment to be incurred by those who carry them.

ART. 11.   Everyone shall have the right to enter and leave the Republic, to travel through its territory, and to change his residence, without the necessity of a letter of security, passport, safe conduct, or other similar requisite. The exercise of this right shall not affect the legitimate power of the judicial or executive authorities in cases of criminal or civil responsibility.

ART. 12.   There are not nor shall there be recognized in the Republic, titles of nobility, or prerogatives or hereditary honors. Only the people, legally represented, may decree recompenses in honor of those who have rendered or may render eminent services to the country or to humanity.

ART. 13.   In the Mexican Republic no one shall be judged by special laws or by special tribunals. No person or corporation shall have privileges or enjoy emoluments which are not in compensation for a public service and are not established by law. Martial law may exist only for crimes and offenses which have a definite connection with military discipline. The law shall determine with absolute clearness the cases included in this exception.

ART. 14.   No retroactive law shall be enacted. No one

shall be judged or sentenced but by virtue of laws made prior to the act, and exactly applicable to it, and by a tribunal which shall have been previously established by law.

ART. 15. Treaties shall never be made for the extradition of political offenders, or for the extradition of petty offenders who may have been slaves in the country where the offense was committed; nor agreements or treaties by virtue of which are altered the guaranties and rights which this constitution grants to the man and to the citizen.

ART. 16. No one shall be molested in his person, family, domicile, papers, or possessions, except by virtue of a written order from a competent authority, which shall establish and set forth the legal grounds for the proceeding. In cases where one is detected in the commission of an offense, any person may apprehend the offender and his accomplices, placing them without delay at the disposal of the nearest authorities.

ART. 17. No one shall be arrested for debts of a purely civil character. No one shall exercise violence in order to enforce his rights. The tribunals shall always be prompt to administer justice, which shall be gratuitous, judicial costs being consequently abolished.

ART. 18. Imprisonment shall take place only for crimes which deserve corporal punishment. In any stage of the proceedings in which it shall appear that such a punishment cannot be imposed upon the accused, he shall be set at liberty under bail. In no case shall the imprisonment or detention be prolonged for failure to pay fees or any other pecuniary charge.

ART. 19. No detention shall exceed the term of three days, unless justified by a warrant, showing the cause of imprisonment and having the other requisites established by law. The mere lapse of this term shall render liable the authority that orders or consents to such detention and the agents, ministers, wardens, or jailers who execute it. Any maltreatment in the apprehension or in the confinement of the prisoners, any hardship which may be inflicted without legal ground, or any tax or contribution in the prisons, is an abuse which the laws should correct and the authorities severely punish.

ART. 20.   In every trial the accused shall have the following guaranties:

I. That the grounds of the proceedings and the name of the accuser, if there shall be one, be made known to him.

II. That his preliminary examination be made within forty-eight hours, counted from the time he may be placed at the disposal of the judge.

III. That he be confronted with the witnesses who testify against him.

IV. That he be furnished with all the information on record, which he may need for his defense.

V. That he be heard in his defense, either personally or by counsel, or by both, as he may desire. In case he should have no one to defend him, a list of official counselors shall be shown to him, in order that he may choose one or more to act as his counsel.

ART. 21.   The imposition of penalties properly so called shall belong exclusively to the judicial authority. The political and administrative authorities shall only have power to impose, as corrective measures, fines to the extent of five hundred dollars, or imprisonment to the extent of one month, in the cases and in the manner which the law shall expressly determine.

ART. 22.   Punishments by multilation and infamy, by branding, flogging, the bastinado, torture of every kind, excessive fines, confiscation of property, or any other unusual or extraordinary penalties, shall be forever prohibited.

ART. 23.   The penalty of death for political offenses is abolished. With reference to other offenses, the penalty of death shall only be imposed in case of treason during a foreign war, parricide, homicide with treachery, premeditation, or advantage, arson, selling or forcing another into involuntary servitude, highway robbery, piracy, and grave offenses of a military character.[4]

ART. 24. No criminal case shall have more than three trials.[5] No one shall be tried twice for the same offense, whether by the judgment he be acquitted or condemned. The practice of suspending trial is abolished.[6]

ART. 25. Sealed correspondence sent through the mails shall be free from any examination. The violation of this guaranty is an offense which the law shall punish severely.

ART. 26. In time of peace no soldier may require quarters, supplies, or other real or personal services, without the consent of the owner. In time of war he may do so, but only in the manner prescribed by law.

ART. 27. Private property shall not be taken without the consent of the owner, except for a public purpose, and upon previous indemnification. The law shall determine the authority which may make the condemnation and the conditions upon which it may be carried out.

Religious corporations and institutions, whatever may be their character, denomination, duration, or object, and civil corporations when they are under the patronage, direction, or administration of religious organizations or of ministers of any religious denomination, shall have no legal capacity to acquire or administer any real property other than the buildings destined immediately and directly to the service and object of such corporations and institutions; nor shall they acquire or administer funds secured upon real estate.

Corporations and civil institutions which are not included within the above restrictions, may acquire and administer, besides the buildings referred to, immovable property and

---

[4] As amended, May 14, 1901.

[5] I. e., trial before the court of first instance, and two trials on appeal.

[6] "Absolver de la instancia," to suspend proceedings, usually because of insufficient evidence, it being possible to have a new trial upon the same charge; practically the same as the *nolle prosequi* of English law.

funds secured upon immovable property, which they may require for their support and purposes, under subjection to the requirements and limitations of a federal law which shall be passed by the Congress of the Union.[7]

ART. 28.   There shall be no monopolies, nor exclusive privileges of any kind nor prohibitions under the guise of protection to industry. The only exceptions to this shall be those relative to the coining of money, to the mails, and to the privileges which, for a limited time, the law may grant to inventors or to the perfecters of some improvement.

ART. 29.   In cases of invasion, grave disturbance of the public peace, or in any other cases which may place society in great danger or distress, only the President of the Republic, with the concurrence of the Council of Ministers and with the approbation of the Congress of the Union, and in the recess thereof, of the Permanent Committee, may suspend the guaranties established by this constitution, with the exception of those which protect the life of man; but such suspension shall be made for a limited time, by means of general orders, and shall not be limited to a particular individual.

If the suspension should take place during the session of Congress, that body shall grant the authorizations which it deems necessary in order that the executive may properly meet the situation. If the suspension should take place during the recess, the Permanent Committee shall convene the Congress without delay, in order that it may grant such authorizations.

SECTION II.   MEXICANS

ART. 30.   Mexicans are:

I. All those born, within or without the territory of the Republic, of Mexican parents.

[7] As altered by amendment of May 14, 1901. This amendment restricted the powers of religious corporations, and extended the powers of civil corporations; it repeals, by implication, Art. 3 of the additions to the constitution, of September 25, 1873. See additions to the constitution, of September 25, 1873, for relations of church and state.

II. Foreigners who are naturalized in conformity with the laws of the Federation.

III. Foreigners who acquire real estate in the Republic, or have Mexican children, if they do not declare their intention to retain their nationality.

ART. 31. It shall be the duty of every Mexican:

I. To defend the independence, the territory, the honor, the rights, and interests of his country.

[II. To perform his services in the army or national guard, in conformity with the respective organic laws.[8]]

III. To contribute in the proportional and equitable manner provided by law, toward public expenses as well of the Federation, as of the state, and of the municipality in which he resides.

ART. 32. Mexicans shall be preferred to foreigners, under equal circumstances, for all employments, offices, or commissions within the appointment of the authorities, in which the condition of citizenship may not be indispensable. Laws shall be enacted to improve the condition of industrious Mexicans, by rewarding those who distinguish themselves in any science or art, by encouraging labor, and by founding industrial colleges and manual training schools.

SECTION III. FOREIGNERS

ART. 33. Foreigners are those who do not possess the qualifications specified in Art. 30. They shall have the right to the guaranties established by Title I, Sec. I, of the present constitution, except that in all cases the government shall have the power to expel pernicious foreigners. They shall be under obligation to contribute toward the public expenses in the manner which the laws may provide, and to obey and respect the institutions, laws, and authorities of the country, subjecting themselves to the decisions and sentences of the courts, without power to seek other protection than that which the laws grant to Mexicans.

* Amendment of June 1, 1898.

SECTION IV. MEXICAN CITIZENS

ART. 34. Citizens of the Republic are all those who, in addition to the quality of Mexicans, have the following qualifications:

I. Have completed the age of eighteen years if they are married, or of twenty-one if unmarried.

II. Have an honest means of livelihood.

ART. 35. The prerogatives of the citizen are:

I. To vote at popular elections.

II. To be eligible for any office filled by popular election, and to serve in any other office or employment, provided he have the qualifications fixed by law.

III. To associate with others to discuss the political affairs of the country.

IV. To enlist in the army or in the national guard for the defense of the Republic or its institutions [under the conditions which the laws shall prescribe].[a]

V. To exercise in all cases the right of petition.

ART. 36. It shall be the duty of every citizen of the Republic:

I. To enroll himself in the register of the inhabitants of the municipality in which he lives, stating the property which he owns, or the industry, profession, or labor by which he subsists.

II. To enlist in the national guard.

III. To vote at popular elections, in the district to which he belongs.

IV. To discharge the duties of the federal offices to which he may be elected, which in no case shall be gratuitous.

ART. 37. The character of citizen is lost:

I. By naturalization in a foreign country.

II. By serving officially the government of another country or by accepting its decorations, titles, or employments without previous permission from the federal Congress; excepting

[a] As amended June 10, 1898.

literary, scientific, and humanitarian titles, which may be freely accepted.

ART. 38. The law shall prescribe the cases and the manner in which the rights of citizenship shall be lost or suspended, and the manner in which they may be regained.

TITLE II

SECTION I. NATIONAL SOVEREIGNTY AND THE FORM OF GOVERNMENT

ART. 39. The national sovereignty is vested essentially and originally in the people. All public power emanates from the people, and is instituted for their benefit. The people have at all times the inalienable right to alter or modify the form of their government.

ART. 40. It is the will of the Mexican people to constitute themselves into a federal, democratic, representative republic, composed of states, free and sovereign in all that concerns their internal government, but united into a federation established according to the principles of this fundamental law.

ART. 41. The people exercise their sovereignty through the federal powers in the matters belonging to the Union, and through those of the states in the matters relating to the internal affairs of the latter, within the limits respectively established by this federal constitution, and by the separate constitutions of the states, which latter shall in no case contravene the stipulations of the federal compact.

SECTION II. INTEGRAL PARTS OF THE FEDERATION AND OF THE NATIONAL TERRITORY

ART. 42. The national territory comprises the integral parts of the Federation and the adjacent islands in both oceans.

ART. 43. The integral parts of the Federation are: the states of Aguascalientes, Campeche, Coahuila, Colima, Chiapas, Chihuahua, Durango, Guanajuato, Guerrero, Hidalgo, Jalisco,

México, Michoacán, Morelos, Nuevo León, Oaxaca, Puebla, Querétaro, San Luis Potosí, Sinaloa, Sonora, Tabasco, Tamaulipas, Tlaxcala, Valle de México, Vera Cruz, Yucatán, Zacatecas, the territory of Lower California, the territory of Tepic, formed from the seventh canton of the state of Jalisco, and the territory of Quintana Roo.

The territory of Quintana Roo shall be formed from the eastern portion of the peninsula of Yucatán, and shall be bounded by a dividing line beginning on the north coast of the Gulf of Mexico at the meridian eighty-seven degrees, thirty-two minutes longitude west of Greenwich, from there to its intersection with the twenty-first degree of parallel, and from thence continued to the parallel which passes near the lighthouse Sur de Chemax, twenty kilometers to the east of this point; thence to the vertex of the angle formed by the lines which divide the states of Yucatán and Campeche, near Put, thence descending southward to the boundaries of the republics of Mexico and of Guatemala.[10]

ART. 44. The states of Aguascalientes, Chiapas, Chihuahua, Durango, Guerrero, México, Puebla, Querétaro, Sinaloa, Sonora, Tamaulipas, and the territory of Lower California shall preserve the boundaries which they now have.

ART. 45. The states of Colima and Tlaxcala shall preserve in their new character of states the boundaries which they had as territories of the Federation.

ART. 46. The state of the Valle de México shall be formed from the territory now constituting the Federal District, but it shall not become a state until after the supreme federal powers are removed to some other place.

ART. 47. The state of Nuevo León and Coahuila shall comprise the territory formerly belonging to the two separate

[10] The present text is that introduced by amendment of November 24, 1902. Campeche became a state April 29, 1863; Coahuila, November 18, 1868; Hidalgo, January 15, 1869; Morelos, April 16, 1869. The territory of Tepic was created December 12, 1884, and that of Quintana Roo, November 24, 1902.

states of which it is now formed, except a part of the Bonanza Hacienda, which shall be reunited to Zacatecas, exactly as it was before its annexation to Coahuila.[11]

ART. 48. The states of Guanajuato, Jalisco, Michoacán, Oaxaca, San Luis Potosí, Tabasco, Vera Cruz, Yucatán, and Zacatecas shall recover the extent and boundaries which they had on the thirty-first of December, eighteen hundred and fifty-two, with the alterations established in the following article.

ART. 49. The town of Contepec, now belonging to Guanajuato, shall be annexed to Michoacán. The municipality of Ahualulco, belonging to Zacatecas, shall be annexed to San Luis Potosí. The municipalities of Ojo Caliente and San Francisco de los Adames, belonging to San Luis, as well as the towns of Nueva Tlaxcala and San Andrés del Teul, belonging to Jalisco, shall be annexed to Zacatecas. The department of Túxpam shall continue to form a part of Vera Cruz. The canton of Huimanguillo, belonging to Vera Cruz, shall be annexed to Tabasco.

TITLE III. DIVISION OF POWERS

ART. 50. The supreme power of the Federation shall be divided for its exercise into legislative, executive, and judicial. Two or more of these powers shall never be united in one person or corporation, nor shall the legislative power be vested in one individual.

SECTION I. LEGISLATIVE POWER

ART. 51. The legislative power of the nation is vested in a general Congress, which shall be divided into two houses, one of Deputies, and the other of Senators.[12]

[11] Altered by the admission of Coahuila to separate statehood.

[12] As amended November 13, 1874. This article originally read: "The exercise of the supreme legislative power is vested in one assembly, which shall be denominated the Congress of the Union." Amendments of November 13, 1874, recast the government on the basis of the bicameral system.

ART. 52.   The House of Deputies shall consist of representatives of the nation, chosen entirely anew every two years by the Mexican citizens.[13]

ART. 53.   One deputy shall be elected for each sixty thousand inhabitants, or for a fraction thereof which exceeds twenty thousand, having regard to the general census of the Federal District and of each state and territory.   The state or territory in which the population is less than that fixed in this article shall, nevertheless, elect one deputy.[14]

ART. 54.   For each deputy there shall be elected one substitute.

ART. 55.   The election of deputies shall be indirect in the first degree, and by secret ballot, in the manner which the electoral law shall provide.[15]

ART. 56.   The following qualifications are required of deputies: To be Mexican citizens in the enjoyment of their rights; to be twenty-five years of age on the day of the opening of the session; to be residents of the state or territory in which the election is held, and not to belong to the ecclesiastical state.

[13] As amended November 13, 1874.

[14] As amended December 18, 1901. The previous ratio was one deputy for every forty thousand inhabitants.

[15] The election of President, vice-president, members of the Supreme Court, senators, and deputies is regulated by laws of December 18, 1901, and May 24, 1904. Each state and territory is divided into electoral districts having 60,000 inhabitants; these electoral districts are in turn divided into election precincts, each precinct having 500 inhabitants. Each precinct chooses a delegate to an electoral college of the district. The electoral college of each district, met at its capital, chooses a deputy and an alternate to the Congress of the Union, and votes for senator or senators, President and vice-president of the Republic, if it should be the year for a presidential election, and members of the Supreme Court of Justice. If no candidate for the Senate receives a majority of the votes of the electoral bodies of a state, the state legislature elects from among those having the highest number of votes. When no candidate for the presidency, vice-presidency, senatorship from the Federal District, or membership in the Supreme Court of Justice has a majority of the electoral votes, the House of Deputies chooses one of the two candidates having the highest number of votes.

Residence is not lost by absence in the discharge of a public office of popular election.

ART. 57. The positions of deputy [and of senator] are incompatible with any salaried commission or office of the Union.[16]

ART. 58. Deputies [and senators], from the day of their election until the day on which their trust is concluded, shall not accept any [commission or] employment within the appointment of the federal executive, for which a salary is received, without the previous license of the respective house. The same provision is applicable to the substitutes of deputies [and of senators] when in the exercise of their functions.[17]

[A. The Senate shall consist of two senators for each state and of two for the Federal District. The election of senators shall be indirect in the first degree. The legislature of each state shall declare elected the person who shall have obtained a majority of the votes cast, or shall elect, in the manner provided by the electoral law, from among those who shall have obtained the highest number of votes. For each senator there shall be elected a substitute.[17]]

[B. The Senate shall be renewed by halves every two years. Senators named in the second place shall go out at the end of the first two years, and thereafter those who have held longest.[17]]

[C. The same qualifications are required for a senator as for a deputy, except that of age, which shall be at least thirty years on the day of the opening of the session.[17]]

ART. 59. Deputies [and senators] are inviolable for their opinions expressed in the performance of their duties and shall never be called to account for them.[18]

ART. 60. Each house shall be the judge of the elections

[16] As amended November 13, 1874.

[17] As amended November 13, 1874. Slight changes in language are not noted. Important additions are bracketed.

[18] As amended November 13, 1874.

of its members, and shall pass upon any question which may arise concerning them.[19]

ART. 61. The houses shall not open their sessions nor exercise their functions without the presence, in the Senate of two-thirds, and in the House of Deputies, of more than one-half of the whole number of their members, but the members present in either house shall meet on the day appointed by law and compel the attendance of absent members under penalties provided by law.[19]

ART. 62. Congress shall hold two regular sessions each year: the first, which may be extended for thirty working days, shall commence on the sixteenth day of September and end on the fifteenth day of December; and the second, which may be extended for fifteen working days, shall commence on the first day of April and end on the last day of May.[19]

ART. 63. At the opening of the sessions of Congress the President of the Union shall be present and shall deliver an address in which he shall give information of the state of the country. The president of the Congress shall reply in general terms.

ART. 64. Every action of Congress shall have the form of a law or decree. Laws and decrees shall be communicated to the executive, signed by the presidents of both houses, and by a secretary of each of them, and shall be promulgated in this form: "The Congress of the United Mexican States decrees:" (text of the law or decree).[19]

PARAGRAPH II.   INITIATION AND ENACTMENT OF LAWS

ART. 65. The right to initiate laws or decrees shall belong:

I. To the President of the Union.

II. To the deputies and senators of the general Congress.

III. To the legislatures of the states.[19]

[19] As amended November 13, 1874.

Art. 66. Bills introduced by the President of the Republic, by the legislatures of the states, or by deputations from the same, shall be at once referred to a committee. Those introduced by deputies or senators shall be subject to the procedure prescribed by the rules of debate.[20]

Art. 67. No bill which shall have been rejected in the house of its origin, before passing to the other house, shall be again presented in the sessions of that year.[20]

Art. 68. The second session shall be devoted, with preference over all other matters, to the examination and voting of the appropriations for the succeeding fiscal year, the levying of the taxes necessary to meet such expenses, and the examination of the accounts of the past year, which the executive shall submit.

Art. 69. On the last day but one of the first session, the executive shall present to the House of Deputies the estimates of appropriations for the following year, and the accounts of the preceding year. Both of these shall be referred to a committee of five representatives, appointed on the same day, whose duty it shall be to examine such documents, and to present a report concerning them at the second meeting of the second session.[20]

Art. 70. Bills and resolutions may be introduced indiscriminately in either house, except that those which relate to loans, taxes, and imposts, or to the recruiting of troops, shall first be discussed in the House of Deputies.[21]

Art. 71. Every bill, the consideration of which does not belong exclusively to one of the houses, shall be discussed successively in both, the rules of debate being observed with respect to the form, intervals, and mode of procedure in discussions and voting.

A. A bill approved in the house where it originated, shall be sent to the other house for its consideration. If the latter

[20] As amended November 13, 1874.

[21] As amended November 13, 1874. All of Art. 70 as it now stands is new.

body approves the bill, it shall be forwarded to the executive, who, if he has no objections to make, shall publish it immediately.

B. Every bill shall be considered approved by the executive if not returned with objections to the house where it originated, within ten working days, unless during this term Congress shall have closed or suspended its session, in which case the return should be made on the first working day of the next session.

C. A bill rejected wholly or in part by the executive shall be returned with his objections to the house where it originated. It shall be discussed again by this body and if it should be confirmed by an absolute majority of votes, shall be sent again to the other house. If passed by the same majority in that house the bill shall become law, and shall be returned to the executive for promulgation. The vote upon such a law or decree shall be by name.

D. A bill wholly rejected by the house of revision shall be returned with objections to the house in which it originated. If, having been examined anew, the bill should be approved by an absolute majority of the members present, it shall be returned to the house which rejected it, which shall again consider it, and, if approving it by the same majority, shall transmit it to the executive for the purposes of clause A; but if the bill be rejected, it shall not again be presented until the succeeding sessions.

E. If a bill should be rejected only in part, or amended by the revising house, the new consideration in the house of its origin shall relate only to the rejected parts or to the amendments, without power to alter in any way the articles agreed upon. If the amendments made in the revising house are approved by an absolute majority of the votes present in the house where it originated, the bill shall be transmitted to the executive for the purposes of clause A. But if the amendments made by the revising house shall be rejected by the majority of votes in the house where the bill originated, the bill shall be returned to the revising house in order that the arguments of the house where it originated may be taken into consideration; and if by an absolute majority of the votes present such amendments are rejected in this second revision, the bill, in so far as it has been approved by both houses, shall be transmitted to the executive for the purposes of clause A; but if the revising house should insist upon such amendments by an absolute majority of the votes present, the whole bill shall not again be considered until the following sessions, unless both houses agree, by the absolute majority of their members present, to the promulgation of the law or decree only with the articles agreed upon, and that the amendments shall be reserved to be examined and voted upon in the following sessions.

F. The same procedure required for the enactment of laws shall be observed in their interpretation, amendment, or repeal.

G. Both houses shall hold their meetings in the same place and shall not move to another without first having agreed upon the removal, and upon the time and manner of making it, designating the same place for the meeting of both. But if the two houses, agreeing to the removal, should differ as to the time, manner, or place, the executive shall terminate the difference, by choosing one of the extremes of the dispute. Neither house shall suspend its sessions for more than three days without the consent of the other.

H. When the general Congress meets in extraordinary session it shall occupy itself exclusively with the object or objects designated in the summons; and if the object of the special session shall not have been accomplished by the day upon which the regular session should begin, the extraordinary session shall, nevertheless, be closed, leaving the unfinished business to be taken up in the regular session.

The executive of the Union shall have no right to object to the resolutions of Congress when it adjourns its sessions, or exercises the functions of an electoral body or of a jury.[22]

[22] As amended November 13, 1874. All of Art. 71 as it now stands was introduced by amendment.

PARAGRAPH III. THE POWERS OF CONGRESS

ART. 72. The Congress shall have power:

I. To admit new states or territories into the Federal Union, incorporating them into the nation.

II. To erect territories into states when they shall have a population of eighty thousand inhabitants and the elements necessary to provide for their political existence.

III. To form new states within the territories of those existing, it being necessary to this end:

1) That the section or sections which ask to be erected into a state have a population of at least one hundred and twenty thousand inhabitants.

2) That proof be given to Congress that they have the elements sufficient to provide for their political existence.

3) That the legislatures of the states, whose territories are affected, shall have been heard concerning the expediency or inexpediency of erecting the new state; they shall be obliged to make their report within six months from the date of the communication addressed to them with reference to the matter.

4) That the executive of the Federation shall likewise be heard, his report to be made within seven days from the date upon which he shall have been asked for it.

5) That two-thirds of the deputies and senators present in their respective houses shall have voted for the erection of the new state.

6) That the resolution of Congress shall have been ratified by the majority of the legislatures of the states, after the examination of a copy of the proceedings; provided that the legislatures of the states whose territories are affected shall have given their consent.

7) If the legislatures of the states whose territories are affected shall not have given their consent the ratification mentioned in the preceding clause should be made by two-thirds of the legislatures of the other states.[23]

[23] As amended November 13, 1874.

IV. To settle finally the boundaries of the states, terminating the differences which may arise between them relative to the demarcation of their respective territories, except when the differences are of a judicial character.

V. To change the residence of the supreme powers of the Federation.

VI. To legislate in all matters concerning the Federal District and territories.[24]

VII. To approve the estimates of the federal expenses, which the executive shall annually submit to it, and to impose the taxes necessary to meet such expenses.[25]

VIII. To establish rules under which the executive may make loans on the credit of the nation; to approve such loans and to recognize and order the payment of the national debt.

IX. To establish tariffs on foreign commerce, and to prevent, by general provisions, onerous restrictions from being established upon the commerce between the states.

X. To promulgate mining and commercial codes, binding throughout the whole Republic; banking institutions shall be regulated by the commercial code.[26]

XI. To create or abolish federal public offices, and to fix, increase, or decrease their salaries.

XII. To confirm the nominations which the executive may make of ministers, diplomatic agents, and consuls, of superior officers of the treasury, of colonels and other superior officers of the national army and navy.[27]

XIII. To approve the treaties, agreements, or diplomatic conventions which the executive may make.[27]

[24] As amended October 31, 1901.

[25] Changed by amendment of November 13, 1874. See sec. A, clause 6, of this article.

[26] As amended December 14, 1883. This clause originally read: "To establish the general bases of mercantile legislation."

[27] By amendment of November 13, 1874, these matters were placed within the exclusive power of the Senate. See sec. B of this article.

XIV. To declare war, upon examination of the facts submitted to it by the executive.

XV. To regulate the manner in which letters of marque may be issued; to enact laws according to which the prizes on sea and land shall be adjudged good or bad; and to frame the maritime law of peace and war.

XVI. To permit or to forbid the entrance of foreign troops into the territory of the Federation, and to permit fleets of other powers to be stationed in the waters of the Republic for more than one month.[28]

XVII. To permit the departure of national troops beyond the borders of the Republic.[28]

XVIII. To raise and maintain the army and navy of the Union, and to regulate their organization and service.

XIX. To make regulations for the purpose of organizing, arming, and disciplining the national guard, reserving respectively to the citizens who compose it the appointment of the commanders and officers, and to the states the power of instructing it in conformity with the discipline prescribed by such regulations.

XX. To consent to the use by the executive of the national guard outside of its respective states and territories, determining the strength of the force required.[28]

XXI. To enact laws on naturalization, colonization, and citizenship.

XXII. To enact laws on the general means of communication and on post-roads and post-offices.

XXIII. To establish mints, regulate the conditions of coinage, determine the value of foreign coins, and to adopt a general system of weights and measures.

XXIV. To make rules for the occupation and alienation of public lands and concerning the prices thereof.

---

[28] By amendment of November 13, 1874, these matters were placed within the exclusive power of the Senate. See sec. B of this article.

XXV. To grant pardons for offenses cognizable by the tribunals of the Federation.

XXVI. To grant rewards or recompense for eminent services rendered to the country or to humanity.[29]

XXVII. To extend for thirty working days the first period of its regular sessions.

XXVIII. To make rules for its internal government and take the necessary measures to compel the attendance of absent members, and to punish the faults or omissions of those present.

XXIX. To appoint and remove freely the employees in the offices of its secretaryship, and those of the chief auditorship, which offices shall be organized as the law may provide.

XXX. To enact all laws which may be necessary and proper for the execution of the foregoing powers and of all other powers granted by this constitution to the authorities of the Union.[30]

[A.[31] The House of Deputies shall have exclusive power:

I. To constitute itself an electoral college for the exercise of the powers granted to it by law, with respect to the election of the President and vice-president of the Republic, members of the Supreme Court of Justice, and senators for the Federal District.[32]

II. To accept or to decide concerning the resignations and leaves of absence of the President and vice-president of the Republic, and concerning the resignations of the members of the Supreme Court of Justice.[33]

---

[29] As amended June 2, 1882.

[30] Two clauses were added by amendment of April 24, 1896, and were repealed May 6, 1904. They related to the election of President *ad interim* and to the granting of leave of absence to the President.

[31] Added by amendment of November 13, 1874.

[32] As amended May 6, 1904.

[33] As amended May 6, 1904. Clause II had also been amended April 24, 1896.

III. By means of an inspecting committee from its own body, to watch over the exact performance of the duties of the chief auditorship.

IV. To appoint the principal officers and other employees of the chief auditorship.

V. To constitute itself a jury of accusation, for the high functionaries mentioned in Art. 103.

VI. To examine the accounts which the President shall annually present, to approve the annual estimate of expenses, and to initiate the taxes which in its judgment should be levied to defray such expenses.]

[B.[34] The Senate shall have exclusive power:

I. To approve the treaties and diplomatic conventions concluded by the executive with foreign powers.

II. To confirm the nominations which the President of the Republic may make of ministers, diplomatic agents, consuls-general, superior officers of the treasury, colonels and other superior officers of the national army and navy, in the manner provided by law.

III. To authorize the executive to permit the departure of national troops beyond the borders of the Republic, the passage of foreign troops through the national territory, and the stationing of fleets of another power in the waters of the Republic for more than one month.

IV. To consent to the use by the executive of the national guard outside of its respective states and territories, determining the strength of the force required.

V. To declare, when the constitutional legislative and executive powers of a state shall have disappeared, that the time has arrived for the appointment of a provisional governor of such state, who shall call elections in conformity with the constitutional laws of the state. The appointment of a governor shall be made by the federal executive with the approval of the Senate, or in its recess of the Permanent Committee. Such ap-

[34] Added by amendment of November 13, 1874.

pointed governor shall not be elected constitutional governor in the elections which are held by virtue of his summons.

VI. To decide any political questions which may arise between the powers of a state, if any one of them applies to the Senate for this purpose, or when the constitutional order shall have been interrupted by armed conflict in consequence of such questions. In such a case, the Senate shall make its decision in conformity with the general constitution of the Republic and with the constitution of the state.

The exercise of the powers specified in this and in the preceding clause shall be regulated by law.

VII. To constitute itself a court of impeachment, in conformity with Art. 105 of the constitution.]

[C.[35] Each of the houses shall have power, without the intervention of the other:

I. To pass economic resolutions with reference to its internal organization.

II. To communicate with the other house and with the executive of the Union, by means of committees from its own body.

III. To appoint the employees of its secretariat, and to make the internal regulations for this office.

IV. To issue summons for extraordinary elections to fill vacancies in their respective memberships.]

ART. 73. During the recesses of Congress there shall be a Permanent Committee composed of twenty-nine members, fifteen of whom shall be deputies and fourteen senators, appointed by their respective houses on the evening before the day for the close of the session.[36]

ART. 74. The Permanent Committee shall have the fol-

---

[35] Added by amendment of November 13, 1874.
[36] As amended November 13, 1874.

lowing powers [without prejudice to others which this Constitution confers upon it].[87]

I. To give its consent to the use of the national guard in the cases mentioned in Art. 72, clause XX.

II. To determine, by itself or upon the proposal of the executive, after hearing him in the first case, upon the convocation of Congress or of one of its houses into extraordinary session, the vote of two-thirds of the members present being necessary in either case. The summons shall set forth the object or objects of the extraordinary session.[88]

III. To approve the appointments referred to in Art. 85, clause III.

IV. To administer the oath of office to the President of the Republic, and to the members of the Supreme Court of Justice, in the cases provided for by this constitution.[89]

V. To report upon all matters which have not been acted upon, in order that the next legislature may immediately take them up as unfinished business.

SECTION II.   THE EXECUTIVE POWER

ART. 75.   The exercise of the supreme executive power of the Union shall be vested in a single individual, who shall be called "President of the United Mexican States."

ART. 76.   The election of the President shall be indirect in the first degree, and by secret ballot, in such manner as may be prescribed by the election law.

ART. 77.   In order to become President it is necessary to be a Mexican citizen by birth, in the exercise of his rights, thirty-five years of age at the time of the election, not to belong to the ecclesiastical order, and to be a resident of the country at the time when the election is held.

ART. 78.   The President and vice-president of the Repub-

[87] Amended May 6, 1904.

[88] As amended November 13, 1874.

[89] See Art. 4 of additions to the constitution, of September 25, 1873.

lic shall enter upon the performance of their duties on the first day of December, and shall continue in office for six years.[40]

ART. 79. The electors who choose the President of the Republic shall also elect on the same day and in the same manner, a vice-president, who shall have the qualifications required for President by Art. 77.

The vice-president of the Republic shall be *ex officio* president of the Senate, with voice, but without vote, except in case of a tie. The vice-president may, without restriction, fill any office within the appointment of the President; in this case as in the case of other absences of the vice-president, the presidency of the Senate shall be filled in the manner provided by law.[41]

ART. 80. When the President of the Republic does not present himself on the day fixed by law for the assumption of his duties, or when his inability is permanent, or if he has been granted leave to resign his office, the vice-president of the Republic shall assume the exercise of the executive power, by force of law, without the necessity of a new oath.

If the inability of the President should be permanent, the vice-president shall take his place until the end of the period for which he was elected; in any other case the vice-president shall act until the President presents himself for the discharge of his duties.[42]

ART. 81. If at the beginning of a constitutional period neither the President-elect nor vice-president-elect presents him-

---

[40] As amended May 6, 1904. This amendment extended the presidential term from four to six years; the office of vice-president first appears by amendments of 1904. This article was also amended May 5, 1878, October 21, 1887, and December 20, 1890. The amendments of 1878 and 1887 imposed restrictions upon the President's succeeding himself in office.

[41] As amended May 6, 1904. This article had been previously amended October 3, 1882, and April 24, 1896; the latter amendment made elaborate provisions for the election of substitute President and President *ad interim*, who were to be chosen after a vacancy occurred.

[42] As amended May 6, 1904.

self, or if the election shall not have been held and its result declared by the first of December, the President whose term of office has expired, shall retire, nevertheless, and the secretary of state for foreign affairs shall immediately assume the executive power, in the capacity of President *ad interim;* and should there be no such secretary, or should he be prevented, one of the other secretaries, following the order of the law which establishes their rank, shall assume the executive power.

A similar procedure shall be followed when, in case of permanent or temporary absence of the President, the vice-president does not present himself, or if the vice-president, although in the discharge of his functions, should have been granted leave to resign; and if, in the course of the term, there should occur the permanent absence of both officials.

In case of the permanent absence of the President and vice-president, the Congress of the Union, or in its recess the Permanent Committee, shall immediately call an extraordinary election.

When the absence of both of these officials occurs in the last year of the constitutional term, no election shall be called, but the secretary who assumes the executive power shall continue to exercise it until the new President takes possession, or until he is superseded in conformity with the foregoing provisions.

The citizens chosen in the extraordinary elections shall enter upon their duties immediately upon making the proper declaration, and shall remain in office for the unexpired portion of the constitutional term.

When one of the secretaries of state assumes the executive power for a short period of time he shall discharge its functions without the necessity of an oath.[43]

ART. 82. The offices of President and vice-president of the Republic may not be resigned except for grave cause,

[43] As amended May 6, 1904.

MEXICO

approved by the House of Deputies, to whom the resignation shall be presented.[44]

ART. 83. The President, in entering upon his duties, shall make the following declaration, before Congress, or before the Permanent Committee in the recess of Congress:

> I promise, without reservation, to observe and to cause others to observe the political constitution of the United Mexican States, with its amendments, the laws of the reform, and all other laws emanating therefrom, and to perform faithfully and patriotically the duties of President of the Republic, which the people have conferred upon me, having always in view the welfare and prosperity of the Union.

The vice-president of the Republic, in the same session and in like terms, shall promise to perform the duties of the vice-presidency and when necessary, those of the President of the Republic; but if he should be prevented from making this promise in the same session, he may make it in another.[45]

ART. 84. The President and the vice-president of the Republic may not absent themselves from the national territory without the permission of the House of Deputies.[46]

ART. 85. The powers and duties of the President shall be the following:

I. To promulgate and execute the laws passed by the Congress of the Union, providing, within the executive sphere, for their exact observance.

II. To appoint and remove freely the secretaries of state, to remove the diplomatic agents, and superior officers of the treasury, and to appoint and to remove freely the other federal officers whose appointment or removal is not otherwise provided for by the constitution or the laws.

[44] As amended May 6, 1904. This article was also amended October 3, 1882, and April 24, 1896.

[45] As amended May 6, 1904. This article was also amended April 24, 1896.

[46] As amended May 6, 1904.

III. To appoint, with the approval of Congress, and, in its recess, of the Permanent Committee, ministers, diplomatic agents, and consuls-general.

IV. To appoint, with the approval of Congress, colonels and other superior officers of the national army and navy, and superior officers of the treasury.

V. To appoint all other officers of the national army and navy, in accordance with the laws.

VI. To dispose of the permanent land and naval forces for the internal security and external defense of the Federation.

VII. To dispose of the national guard for the same purposes, in the manner provided by Art. 72, clause XX.

VIII. To declare war in the name of the United Mexican States, after the passage of a law by the Congress of the Union.

IX. To grant letters of marque, upon the bases fixed by the Congress.

X. To conduct diplomatic negotiations and to make treaties with foreign powers, submitting them for the ratification of the Federal Congress.

XI. To receive ministers and other envoys from foreign powers.

XII. To convene Congress in extraordinary session when the Permanent Committee agrees thereto.

XIII. To give the judicial power the assistance which may be necessary for the prompt exercise of its functions.

XIV. To open all classes of ports, establish maritime and frontier custom-houses, and to designate their location.

XV. To grant, in accordance with law, pardons to criminals sentenced for offenses within the jurisdiction of the federal tribunals.

[XVI. To grant exclusive privileges, for a limited time, and in conformity with the proper law, to discoverers, inventors, or perfectors of some branch of industry.[47]]

[47] Added by amendment of June 2, 1882. This power had formerly belonged to the Congress.

ART. 86. For the transaction of the administrative business of the Federation there shall be the number of secretaries which the Congress may establish by law, such law to provide also for the distribution of business among the different secretaries.

ART. 87. No person shall be a secretary of state who is not a Mexican citizen by birth, in the exercise of his rights, and twenty-five years of age.

ART. 88. All rules, decrees, and orders of the President shall be signed by the secretary of the department to which the subject belongs. Without this requisite they shall not be obeyed.

ART. 89. The secretaries of state, as soon as the sessions of the first period are opened, shall render an account to the Congress of the state of their respective departments.

SECTION III. THE JUDICIAL POWER

ART. 90. The judicial power of the Federation shall be vested in a Supreme Court of Justice and in the district and circuit courts.

ART. 91. The Supreme Court of Justice shall be composed of fifteen judges, and shall act as a full court or in sections, in such manner as shall be determined by law.[45]

ART. 92. The justices of the Supreme Court of Justice shall serve for six years, and their election shall be indirect in the first degree, in the manner established by the election law.

ART. 93. No person shall be eligible to the position of member of the Supreme Court of Justice who is not in the judgment of the electors learned in the science of law, more than thirty-five years of age, and a Mexican citizen by birth, in the exercise of his rights.

ART. 94. The members of the Supreme Court of Justice, on entering upon the exercise of their functions, shall take an oath before Congress, and, in its recesses, before the Permanent

[45] As amended May 22, 1900.

Committee, in the following form: "Do you swear to perform loyally and patriotically the functions of magistrate of the Supreme Court of Justice which the people have conferred upon you, in conformity with the constitution, having always in view the welfare and prosperity of the Union?"

ART. 95. A member of the Supreme Court of Justice may resign his office only for grave cause, approved by Congress, to whom the resignation shall be presented. In the recesses of Congress, the approval shall be obtained from the Permanent Committee.

ART. 96. The law shall establish and organize the circuit courts, the district courts, and the staff of public prosecutors for the Federation.

The functionaries of the staff of public prosecutors, and the attorney-general of the Republic who is at their head, shall be appointed by the executive.[49]

ART. 97. The federal tribunals shall take cognizance of:

I. All controversies which may arise with respect to the execution and application of the federal laws [except when such application affects private interests only, in which case the regular local courts of the states, of the Federal District, and of the territory of Lower California shall have jurisdiction].[50]

II. All cases pertaining to maritime law.

III. All cases to which the Federation may be a party.

IV. All cases which may arise between two or more states.

V. All cases which may arise between a state and one or more citizens of another state.

VI. All civil or criminal cases that may arise out of treaties with foreign powers.

VII. All cases concerning diplomatic agents and consuls.

ART. 98. The Supreme Court of Justice shall have original jurisdiction of controversies which may arise between

[49] As amended May 22, 1900.

[50] As amended May 29, 1884.

one state and another, and of those to which the Union may be a party.

ART. 99. The Supreme Court of Justice shall also have power to determine questions of jurisdiction which may arise between the federal tribunals, between these tribunals and those of the states, or between the courts of one state and those of another.

ART. 100. In the other cases enumerated in Art. 97, the Supreme Court of Justice shall be a court of appeal or of last resort, according to the gradation which the law may establish in the jurisdictions of the circuit and district courts.

ART. 101. The courts of the Federation shall decide all questions arising out of:

I. Laws or acts of any authority violating individual guaranties.

II. Laws or acts of the federal authority encroaching upon or restricting the sovereignty of the states.

III. Laws or acts of the state authorities invading the sphere of the federal authority.

ART. 102. All the cases referred to in the preceding article shall be conducted, on petition of the aggrieved party, by means of judicial proceedings and forms which a special law shall establish. The decision shall always be such as to affect only the individuals concerned in the case, limiting itself to defend and protect them in the special case to which the proceedings refer, without making any general declaration respecting the law or the act which gave rise to the case.

TITLE IV. RESPONSIBILITY OF THE PUBLIC FUNCTIONARIES

ART. 103. Senators and deputies in the Congress of the Union, members of the Supreme Court of Justice, and the secretaries of state shall be responsible for the ordinary offenses committed by them during their term of office, and for the crimes, misdemeanors, or omissions which they may commit in the exercise of their functions. The governors of the states shall be responsible for the violation of the federal constitution and laws. The President and the vice-president of the Republic during the term of their offices may only be charged with the offenses of treason, express violation of the constitution, attacks upon the electoral liberty, and ordinary offenses of a grave character.

[The high functionaries of the Federation shall enjoy no constitutional immunities with respect to official crimes, misdemeanors, or omissions which they may commit while in the discharge of any public employment, office, or commission, which may have been accepted during the period in which, according to law, such immunities are to be enjoyed. This provision shall be applicable with respect to ordinary offenses which may be committed during the performance of such employment, office, or commission. In order that the proceedings may be instituted when the high functionary returns to the exercise of his proper functions, proceedings shall be undertaken in acordance with the provisions of Art. 104 of this constitution.[51]]

ART. 104. If the offense should be an ordinary one, the House of Deputies, resolving itself into a grand jury, shall determine by absolute majority whether or not there is sufficient ground to proceed against the accused. If the vote is in the negative, no further proceedings shall be had. If it is in the affirmative, the accused shall, by this fact, be deprived of his office and placed at the disposal of the ordinary courts.[52]

ART. 105. In cases of official crimes, the House of Deputies shall act as a jury of accusation, the Senate as a jury to try the matter.

The jury of accusation shall decide by an absolute majority of votes whether the accused is or is not culpable. If the decision should be favorable, the functionary shall continue in the

[51] As amended November 13, 1874, and May 6, 1904.
[52] As amended November 13, 1874.

exercise of his office. If it should be unfavorable, the accused official shall be immediately removed from his position and shall be placed at the disposal of the Senate. The Senate, resolving itself into a jury to try the matter, after hearing the accused and the accuser, if there should be one, shall, by absolute majority, impose the penalty provided by law.[53]

ART. 106. In cases of impeachment for crimes of an official character no pardon can be granted to the offender.

ART. 107. The responsibility for official crimes and misdemeanors may only be enforced during the period in which the functionary remains in office, and for one year thereafter.

ART. 108. In civil cases there shall be no privilege or immunity in favor of any public functionary.

TITLE V. STATES OF THE FEDERATION

ART. 109. The states shall adopt for their internal regulation the republican, representative, popular form of government [and shall provide in their respective constitutions for the re-election of their governors, in accordance with the provisions of Art. 78 relating to the President of the Republic].[54]

ART. 110. The states may fix among themselves, by friendly agreements, their respective boundaries; but such agreements shall not be carried into effect without the approval of the Congress of the Union.

ART. 111. The states shall not in any case have power:

I. To enter into alliances, treaties, or coalitions with another state, or with foreign powers. Coalitions between frontier states for offensive or defensive war against savages are excepted.

II. To grant letters of marque or of reprisal.

III. To coin money, issue paper money, [stamps], or stamped paper.[55]

[53] As amended November 13. 1874.

[54] As amended October 21, 1887. This clause was also amended May 5, 1878.

[55] Amended May 1, 1896.

[IV. To levy taxes upon persons or property which may pass through their territory.[56]]

[V. To prohibit or to tax, directly or indirectly, the entrance into their territory or the exit therefrom of any merchandise, foreign or domestic.[56]]

[VI. To burden the circulation or consumption of domestic or foreign merchandise with taxes or duties to be collected by local custom-houses, to subject such merchandise to inspection or registration, or to require that it be accompanied by special papers.[56]]

[VII. To enact or maintain in force laws or fiscal regulations discriminating, by means of taxation or otherwise, between merchandise, foreign or domestic, on account of its origin, whether this difference is established between similar productions of different origin, or because of similar local productions.[56]]

[VIII. To issue evidences of public debt, payable in foreign money or beyond the national territory; to contract directly or indirectly loans from foreign governments, or to contract obligations in favor of foreign societies or individuals in which there may be issued securities or bonds payable to bearer or transferrable by indorsement.[57]]

ART. 112. Neither shall they, without the consent of the Congress of the Union:

I. Establish tonnage duties, or any port duty, or impose taxes or duties upon imports or exports.

II. Have at any time permanent troops or vessels of war.

III. Make war by themselves on any foreign power, except in cases of invasion or of such imminent peril as to admit of no delay. In these cases the state shall give notice immediately to the President of the Republic.

ART. 113. Each state is bound to deliver criminals from

[56] Added by amendment of May 1, 1896.

[57] Added by amendment of December 18, 1901.

other states without delay to the authority which may claim them.

ART. 114. The governors of the state are bound to publish and enforce the federal laws.

ART. 115. In each state of the Federation full faith and credit shall be given to the public acts, records, and judicial proceedings of all the other states. The Congress may, by means of general laws, prescribe the manner of proving such acts, records, and proceedings, and the effect thereof.

ART. 116. The federal government is bound to protect the states against all invasion or external violence. In case of insurrection or internal disturbance it shall give them the same protection, provided that the legislature of the state, or the executive, if the legislature is not in session, shall request it.

TITLE VI. GENERAL PROVISIONS

ART. 117. The powers which are not expressly granted by this constitution to the federal authorities are understood to be reserved to the states.

ART. 118. No person shall hold at the same time two federal elective offices; but if elected to two, he may choose the one which he prefers.

ART. 119. No payment shall be made which is not included in the estimates, or authorized by a subsequent law.

ART. 120. The President of the Republic, the members of the Supreme Court of Justice, deputies, and all other public officers of the Federation, who are chosen by popular election, shall receive a compensation for their services, which shall be determined by law and paid from the federal treasury. This compensation may not be waived, and any law which may increase or diminish it shall not have effect during the period for which a functionary holds the office.

ART. 121. Every public officer, without any exception, before entering upon the discharge of his duties, shall take an oath to maintain this constitution and the laws emanating from it.

ART. 122. In time of peace no military authority shall exercise other functions than those having close connection with military discipline. No fixed and permanent military offices shall be established except in castles, fortresses, and arsenals depending immediately upon the government of the Union, or in camps, barracks, or depots which may be established outside of towns, for the stationing of troops.

ART. 123. The federal authorities shall have exclusive power to exercise, in matters of religious worship and external ecclesiastical discipline, the intervention which the laws may authorize.

ART. 124. The Federation shall have exclusive power to levy duties on merchandise imported, exported, or passing in transit through the national territory, as well as to regulate at all times and even to prohibit, for the sake of public safety or for police reasons, the circulation of any kind of goods in the interior of the Republic, whatever may be its origin; but the Federation shall have no power to establish or to enact in the Federal District and territories the taxes and laws referred to in clauses VI and VII or Art. III.[58]

ART. 125. The forts, barracks, arsenals, and other immovable property destined, by the government of the Union, to the public service or to the common use, shall be subject to the jurisdiction of the federal authorities, under provisions to be established by a law which the Congress of the Union shall enact; but for the acquisition of such property within the territory of any state, the consent of the legislature of such state shall hereafter be necessary.[59]

[58] As amended May 1, 1896. The original article and amendments to it of May 17, 1882, November 25, 1884, and November 22, 1886, related to the abolition of state customs and excise taxes and other taxes on internal commerce.

[59] As amended October 31, 1901.

ART. 126. This constitution, the laws of the Congress of the Union made in pursuance thereof, and all the treaties made or to be made by the President of the Republic, with the approval of Congress, shall be the supreme law of the whole Union. The judges of each state shall be bound by such constitution, laws, and treaties, any provision in the constitutions or laws of the states to the contrary notwithstanding.

TITLE VII. AMENDMENT OF THE CONSTITUTION

ART. 127. The present constitution may be amended or revised. No amendment shall become part of the constitution, if not agreed upon by the Congress of the Union, by a vote of two-thirds of the members present, and approved by a majority of the legislatures of the states. The Congress of the Union shall count the votes of the legislatures and make the declaration that the amendments have been adopted.

TITLE VIII. INVIOLABILITY OF THE CONSTITUTION

ART. 128. This constitution shall not lose its force and vigor even if its observance should be interrupted by a .rebellion. In case that by any public disturbance a government is established contrary to the principles which it sanctions, its efficiency shall be restored as soon as the people regain their liberty, and those who shall have figured in the government emanating from the rebellion, or have co-operated with it, shall be tried in accordance with the provisions of this constitution and of the laws made in pursuance thereof.

TEMPORARY PROVISION

This constitution shall be published at once and sworn to with the greatest solemnity throughout the whole Republic; but its provisions, except those relating to the election of the supreme powers, federal and state, shall not go into effect until the sixteenth of September next, when the first Congress under the constitution shall meet. On and after that date the President of the Republic and the Supreme Court of Justice, who shall continue in the exercise of their functions until their constitutionally elected successors enter upon the discharge of their duties, shall, in the exercise of their powers and duties, act in accordance with the provisions of this constitution.

ADDITIONS TO THE CONSTITUTION

ARTICLE 1. The church and the state shall be independent of each other. Congress shall not enact laws establishing or forbidding any religion.[60]

ART. 2. Marriage is a civil contract. Marriage and all other acts relating to the civil status of persons shall fall exclusively within the jurisdiction of the civil authorities, in the manner provided by law, and they shall have the force and validity given to them by such laws.[60]

ART. 3. No religious institutions shall acquire real estate or funds secured upon real estate, except in the case set forth in Art. 27 of the constitution.[60]

ART. 4. A simple promise to tell the truth and to comply with obligations entered into shall take the place of the religious oath, with its effects and penalties.[60]

[60] Added by amendment of September 25, 1873.

NETHERLANDS

Holland was occupied by French troops in 1794 and 1795, and by the treaty of the Hague of May 16, 1795, became the Batavian Republic, under the protection of France. After Napoleon became emperor of France, the Batavian Republic was in 1806 displaced by the kingdom of Holland with Louis Bonaparte as its ruler. But the king of Holland did not prove as subservient as Napoleon desired, and Holland was incorporated into the French empire in July, 1810. The French rule disappeared with the fall of Napoleon. Holland was restored to the Prince of Orange in 1814, and the kingdom of the Netherlands was created by the union of Holland and Belgium, as a barrier against subsequent French aggression.

On August 24, 1815, a constitution was promulgated for the united kingdom of the Netherlands. In 1840, after the settlement of all questions concerning the independence of Belgium, the constitution was revised, but without material alteration in the governmental organization. The constitution was revised in 1848 in such a manner as to establish more liberal principles of government; parliamentary government was substituted for the personal rule of the king; the Upper House became elective, and more extensive rights of self-government were conceded to the provinces and communes.

The amended constitution of 1848 restricted the suffrage to persons paying direct taxes of from twenty to one hundred and sixty florins. An extension of the electoral franchise was demanded by the Liberals as early as 1872, but it could only be accomplished by a constitutional amendment. The constitution was revised in 1887, and under its amended provisions the election law of 1896 was passed which brought about a fourfold increase in the number of qualified voters.

Until November 23, 1890, the king of the Netherlands was also grand duke of Luxemburg. The union of the two countries then came to an end because of the fact that only males may occupy the throne of the Grand Duchy of Luxemburg.

SELECT BIBLIOGRAPHY

Meijer. *Nederlandsche Staatswetten.* (9th ed., uitgegeven onder toezicht van H. J. Romeijn. (Sneek [1904]. 2 vols.) A collection of all important laws in the fields of constitutional and administrative law.

Buijs, J. T. *De Grondwet.* Toelichting en kritiek. (Arnhem, 1883–88. 3 vols.) The most elaborate commentary on the Dutch constitution; Vol. III is devoted to the amendments of 1887.

Helm, G. L. van den. *De Grondwet voor het koningrijk der Neder- landen.* (The Hague [1889].) Text annotated with special refer- ence to the revision of 1887.

Hartog, L. de. *Das Staatsrecht des Königreichs der Niederlande.* (Freiburg, 1886. Handbuch des oeffentlichen Rechts.)

Hasselt, W. J. C. van. *Verzameling van Nederlandsche staatsregelin- gen en grondwetten, 1789–1887.* (6th ed. by L. de Hartog, 1904.)

Sijbenga, T. *De grondwet van 1887 toegelicht.* (3d ed., The Hague, 1902.)

Lenting, L. E. *Schets van het Nederlandsch staatsbestuur.* (6th ed. by H. J. Romeijn, 1903.)

Lohman, A. F. de Savornin. *Onze Constitutie.* (2d ed., Utrecht, 1907.)

CONSTITUTION OF THE NETHERLANDS
(As amended November 6, 1887)

CHAPTER I. THE KINGDOM AND ITS INHABITANTS

ARTICLE 1. The Kingdom of the Netherlands comprises the territory in Europe as well as the colonies and possessions in other parts of the world.

ART. 2. The constitution is binding only for the Kingdom in Europe, except where it expresses the contrary.

Wherever the Kingdom is mentioned in the following articles, the Kingdom in Europe alone is referred to.

ART. 3. The law may unite and divide provinces and communes and form new ones.

The boundaries of the Kingdom, of the provinces, and of the communes may be changed by law.

Art. 4. All persons within the territory of the Kingdom shall have an equal right to protection of person and property.

The law shall regulate the admission and expulsion of foreigners and the general conditions under which treaties may be concluded with foreign powers regarding their extradition.

Art. 5. Every citizen of the Netherlands shall be admissible to any public employment.

No foreigner shall be admissible to such employment except in accordance with the provisions of the law.

Art. 6. The law shall determine who are citizens and who are residents.[1]

A foreigner shall not be naturalized except by virtue of a law.

The law shall regulate the consequences of naturalization with regard to the wife and minor children of the person naturalized.

Art. 7. No previous authorization shall be required in order that one may publish his thoughts or opinions through the press, except that every person shall be responsible according to law.

Art. 8. Every person shall have the right to present petitions, in writing, to the authorities.

Every petition must be signed by the petitioner. Signing in the name of others can only be done by virtue of a written power of attorney to accompany the petition.

Legally organized bodies may petition the authorities, but only upon matters pertaining to their particular sphere of activity.

Art. 9. The inhabitants have the rights of assembly and of association.

The law regulates and restricts the exercise of these rights in the interests of public order.

[1] "Residents" are those who have resided for eighteen months within the kingdom or in its colonies or possessions.

CHAPTER II. THE KING
SECTION I. THE SUCCESSION TO THE THRONE

ART. 10. The crown of the Netherlands is and remains bestowed upon His Majesty Willem Frederik, prince of Orange-Nassau, to be possessed heriditarily by him and his legitimate descendants in accordance with the following provisions.

ART. 11. The crown shall pass by succession to his sons and other male descendants on the male side, by right of primogeniture, provided that in case of the previous death of one entitled to the succession the latter's sons or other male descendants on the male side shall take his place in the same manner, and that the crown shall never pass to a younger line or to a younger branch as long as such a descendant is found in the older line or in the older branch.

ART. 12. In default of the successors indicated in the foregoing article, the crown shall pass to the living daughters of the last deceased king, by right of primogeniture.

ART. 13. In default also of the daughters referred to in the foregoing article, the crown shall pass to the daughters of the descending male lines of the last deceased king, and, failing also these and their descendants, the crown shall pass to the descending female lines.

In these cases the older line shall always have precedence over the younger, the male branch over the female, the older over the younger, and in each branch men shall have the precedence over women and older ones over younger ones.

ART. 14. In default of a successor entitled to the crown by virtue of the three preceding articles, the crown shall pass to the princess, belonging by birth to the house of Orange-Nassau, who stands nearest to the last deceased king in the line of descent from the late King Willem Frederik, prince of Orange-Nassau.

In case of equal degree of relationship the first born shall have the precedence.

If such blood relative of the King shall have died before the King, her descendants shall take her place, the male line taking precedence over the female and the older over the younger, and in every line the male branch over the female and the older over the younger, and in every branch men over women and older ones over younger ones.

ART. 15. In default of a successor entitled to the crown by virtue of one of the four preceding articles, it shall pass to the legitimate male descendants on the male side of the late Princess Caroline of Orange, sister of the late Prince Willem the Fifth and wife of the late prince of Nassau-Weilburg, in the same manner as is provided in Art. 11 with regard to the descendants of the late King Willem Frederik, prince of Orange-Nassau.

ART. 16. With respect to the succession, abdication of the crown shall have the same consequence as death.

ART. 17. A child with which a woman is pregnant at the time of the King's death shall be considered as being born as far as the right to the crown is concerned. If it is born dead it shall be considered as having never existed.

ART. 18. All children born of a marriage concluded by a king or by a queen without the consent of the States-General, or by a prince or princess of the reigning dynasty without the consent to be granted by a law, shall be excluded from the succession, both as regards themselves and their descendants.

By contracting such a marriage a queen shall abdicate the throne and a princess shall forfeit her right thereto.

When the crown has passed to another dynasty either by succession or in accordance with Arts. 15, 19, 20, or 21, the present provisions shall apply only to marriages concluded after the time when the crown so passed.

ART. 19. Whenever special circumstances render advisable any change in or provision regarding the order of succession, the King is authorized to make a recommendation to that effect.

The States-General, convened for this purpose in double number, shall deliberate and resolve thereon in joint session.

ART. 20. When no competent heir exists according to the constitution, one shall be appointed by a law, the draft of which shall be presented by the King.

The States-General, convened for this purpose in double number, shall deliberate and decide thereon in joint session.

ART. 21. When no competent successor exists according to the constitution, upon the death of the King, the appointment shall be made directly by the States-General in joint session. It shall be convened for this purpose in double number within a month after the King's death.

ART. 22. All provisions regarding the succession shall become applicable to the descendants of the first king to whom the crown passes by virtue of one of the two preceding articles, in such a manner that the new dynasty shall derive its origin from him, as far as succession is concerned, in the same manner and with the same effects as the house of Orange-Nassau, according to Article 10, derives its succession from the late King Willem Frederik, prince of Orange-Nassau.

The same principle shall apply, in the case of Art. 15, with regard to the therein mentioned descendants of the late Princess Caroline of Orange.

It shall likewise apply with regard to the descendants of the woman who is called to the throne by succession, provided that the crown shall pass only in case of entire absence of descendants in the succeeding line of the dynasty to which the woman belonged by birth.

ART. 23. The King shall wear no foreign crown, except that of Luxemburg.

In no case shall the seat of government be transferred beyond the kingdom.

SECTION 2.   THE REVENUE OF THE CROWN

ART. 24.   In addition to the revenue from the domains, ceded by the law of August 26, 1822, and restored to the state in 1848 by the late King Willem II as crown domains, the King shall enjoy a yearly income from the national treasury, the amount of which shall be fixed by law, upon each accession to the throne.

ART. 25.   Summer and winter residences shall be furnished for the King's use; however, no more than 50,000 florins per year shall be appropriated by the nation for their maintenance.

ART. 26.   The King and the Prince of Orange shall be exempt from all personal taxes.

They shall enjoy no exemption from any other tax.

ART. 27.   The King shall direct his household as he sees fit.

ART. 28.   During her widowhood, the annual income of a queen dowager from the national treasury shall be 150,000 florins.

ART. 29.   The oldest of the King's sons or of his other male descendants, who is the heir apparent to the throne, shall be the King's first subject and shall bear the title of Prince of Orange.

ART. 30.   The Prince of Orange shall enjoy, as such, an annual income of 100,000 florins from the national treasury, from the time he reaches his eighteenth year of age; this income shall be increased to 200,000 florins upon his contracting a marriage authorized by law.

SECTION 3.   GUARDIANSHIP OF THE KING

ART. 31.   The King shall be of age when he reaches his eighteenth year.

The same principle shall apply to the Prince of Orange in case he becomes regent.

Art. 32. The guardianship of the minor King shall be regulated, and the guardian or guardians appointed, by a law.

The draft of this law shall be discussed and agreed upon by the States-General in joint session.

Art. 33. This law shall be enacted during the life of the King for the event that his successor may be a minor. Should this not have been done, some of the nearest blood relatives of the minor King shall, if possible, be consulted concerning the establishment of the guardianship.

Art. 34. Before assuming the guardianship, every guardian shall take the following oath or promise in a joint session of the States-General, such oath to be administered to him by the president:

I swear (promise) allegiance to the King; I swear (promise) to fulfil sacredly all the duties imposed by the guardianship, and to take special care to inspire the King with affection for the constitution and love for his people! So truly help me God Almighty! (This I promise!)

Art. 35. Should the King become incapable of performing the duties of government, measures shall be taken for the necessary care of his person in accordance with the provisions contained in Art. 32, concerning the guardianship of a minor king.

The law shall determine the oath or promise to be taken by the guardian or guardians appointed for this purpose.

SECTION 4. THE REGENCY

Art. 36. During the minority of the King the royal authority shall be exercised by a regent.

Art. 37. The regent shall be appointed by a law, which may at the same time regulate the succession to the regency until the King attains his majority. This law shall be discussed and enacted by the States-General in joint session.

The law shall be enacted during the life of the King for the event that his successor may be a minor.

ART. 38. The royal authority shall likewise be conferred upon a regent in case the King becomes incapable of performing the duties of government.

Whenever the heads of the ministerial departments, assembled in council, conclude that this condition exists, they shall make their conclusion known to the Council of State and shall ask it to express its opinion within a fixed period.

ART. 39. If they still adhere to their opinion after the expiration of the fixed period, they shall convene the States-General in joint session and report the case to that body, presenting the opinion of the Council of State, if it has been received.

ART. 40. If the States-General in joint session is of opinion that the condition mentioned in the first paragraph of Art. 38 exists, it shall so declare in a resolution, which shall be promulgated by the president referred to in the second paragraph of Art. 108; such resolution shall go into effect on the day of its promulgation.

In default of such a president, one shall be appointed by the assembly.

ART. 41. In the case of Art. 40 the Prince of Orange shall become regent as of right upon attaining his eighteenth year.

ART. 42. If there is no Prince of Orange or if the Prince of Orange is not eighteen years of age, the regency shall be provided for in the manner prescribed by Art. 37; in the latter case until the time when the Prince of Orange reaches the age of eighteen years.

ART. 43. In assuming the regency the regent shall take the following oath or promise in a joint session of the States-General, the oath being administered by the president:

I swear (promise) allegiance to the King; I swear (promise) that, in exercising the royal authority while the King is in his minority (while the King remains incapable of performing the duties of government), I will constantly observe and maintain the constitution.

I swear (promise) that I will defend and preserve the independence and the territory of the kingdom with all my power; that I will protect public and individual liberty, and the rights of all of the King's subjects, and employ all the means which the laws place at my disposal for the preservation and promotion of the general and individual welfare, just as a good and faithful regent ought to do. So truly help me God Almighty! (This I promise!)

ART. 44. When a regent becomes incapable of exercising the regency, Arts. 38, second paragraph, 39, and 40 are applicable.

If the succession to the regency is not provided for, then the first paragraph of Art. 37 shall apply.

ART. 45. The royal authority shall be exercised by the Council of State:

1) Upon the death of the King, as long as the succession to the throne is not provided for according to Art. 21, or as long as no regent is appointed for the successor to the throne who is under age, or if the successor to the throne or regent is absent.

2) In the cases of Arts. 40 and 44, as long as there is no regent or the regent is absent; and in case of the death of the regent, as long as his successor has not been appointed or has not assumed the regency.

3) In case the succession to the throne is uncertain and there is no regent or the regent is absent.

The exercise of these duties shall cease as soon as the authorized successor or regent has assumed his authority.

Whenever the regency ought to be provided for, the Council of State shall introduce a bill for that purpose: in the cases mentioned under Nos. 1 and 2, within the period of one month after the Council has assumed the exercise of the royal authority; in the case mentioned under No. 3, within the period of one month after the succession to the throne has ceased to be uncertain.

Art. 46. Upon the appointment of a regent or the assumption of the regency by the Prince of Orange, a law shall determine the sum that shall be set aside from the annual revenue of the crown for the costs of the regency.

This provision shall not be changed during the regency.

Art. 47. As soon as the condition referred to in Art. 38 has ceased to exist, this fact shall be declared by the States-General in joint session by means of a resolution which shall be promulgated by order of the president mentioned in Art. 40.

Art. 48. This action shall be taken upon the recommendation of the regent or of at least twenty members of the States-General.

These members shall present their recommendation to the president of the Upper House who shall immediately convene the two houses in joint session.

If the session of the houses has closed, the members making the recommendation shall have authority to convene them.

Art. 49. The heads of the ministerial departments and the guardian or guardians shall be personally required to report to the houses of the States-General regarding the condition of the King or of the regent, as often as inquiry is made.

Paragraph 3 of Art. 94 is also applicable to the guardians in this case.

Art. 50. Immediately after the promulgation of the resolution mentioned in Art. 47, the King shall resume the exercise of his functions.

SECTION 5. THE INSTALLATION OF THE KING

Art. 51. Upon assuming the government, the King shall be solemnly sworn in and installed as soon as possible in a public joint session of the States-General in the city of Amsterdam.

ART. 52. At this session the following oath or promise shall be taken by the King, on the constitution.

I swear (promise) to the people of the Netherlands that I will always observe and maintain the constitution.

I swear (promise) that I will defend and preserve the independence and the territory of the kingdom with all my power, that I will protect public and individual liberty and the rights of all my subjects, and that I will employ all means which the laws place at my disposal for the preservation and promotion of the general and individual welfare, just as a good king ought to do. So truly help me God Almighty! (This I promise!)

ART. 53. After taking this oath or promise, the King shall be installed at the same session by the States-General; the president of the States-General shall pronounce the following solemn declaration, which shall thereupon be sworn to and confirmed by him and by each of the members separately:

In the name of the people of the Netherlands and by virtue of the constitution, we receive and swear allegiance to you as King; we swear (promise) that we will maintain your inviolability and the rights of your crown; we swear (promise) to do everything that a good and loyal States-General ought to do. So truly help us God Almighty! (This we promise!)

SECTION 6. THE POWERS OF THE KING

ART. 54. The King is inviolable; the ministers are responsible.

ART. 55. The executive power shall be vested in the King.

ART. 56. General administrative regulations shall be issued by the King.

Provisions to be enforced by penalties shall not be included among such regulations except by virtue of a law. The penalties to be imposed shall be regulated by law.

ART. 57. The King shall have supreme control of foreign relations.

ART. 58. The King declares war. He shall give immediate notice thereof to the two houses of the States-General, together with such additional information as he deems consistent with the interests of the state.

ART. 59. The King shall conclude and ratify all treaties with foreign powers. He shall also communicate the purport of these treaties to the two houses of the States-General, as soon as he considers that the interests of the state permit.

Treaties which contain modifications of the territory of the state, which impose pecuniary obligations upon the kingdom, or which contain any other provision concerning legal rights, shall not be ratified by the King until after approval by the States-General.

This approval is not required if the power has been reserved to the King by law to conclude such treaty.

ART. 60. The King shall have the supreme control over the land and naval forces.

The military officers shall be appointed by him. They shall be promoted, discharged, or retired by him in accordance with the rules prescribed by law.

Pensions shall be regulated by law.

ART. 61. The King shall have supreme control of the colonies and possessions of the kingdom in other parts of the world.

The regulations for the conduct of the government in the colonies and possessions shall be established by law.

The monetary system shall be regulated by law.

Other matters relating to these colonies and possessions shall be regulated by law as soon as the necessity therefor appears to exist.

ART. 62. The King shall cause a detailed report to be made annually to the States-General regarding the government and condition of the colonies and possessions.

The law shall regulate the manner in which the finances of the colonies are to be administered and accounted for.

ART. 63. The King shall have supreme control of the public finances. He shall regulate the salaries of all bodies and officials who are paid out of the national treasury.

The salaries of the Council of State, of the Court of Accounts, and of the judicial officers shall be regulated by law.

The King shall include the salaries in the estimates of expenses of the kingdom.

The pensions of officials shall be regulated by law.

ART. 64. The King shall have the right to coin money. He may have his likeness placed on the coins.

ART. 65. The King confers titles of nobility.

Foreign titles of nobility shall not be accepted by any citizen of the Netherlands.

ART. 66. Orders of knighthood may be established by law, upon the recommendation of the King.

ART. 67. The King, and with his consent the princes of his house, may accept foreign orders to which no obligations are attached.

In no case shall other citizens of the Netherlands, or foreigners in the governmental service of the Netherlands, accept foreign decorations, titles, ranks, or dignities, without the special permission of the King.

ART. 68. The King shall have the right to grant pardon in case of penalties imposed by judicial sentence.

He shall exercise this right after receiving the opinion of the judge designated for this purpose by a general administrative regulation.

Amnesty or exemptions from the legal consequences of crime shall be granted only by law.

ART. 69. Dispensation from legal provisions shall be granted by the King only under the authority of law.

The law conferring this authority shall specify the provisions to which the authorization to grant dispensation applies.

Dispensation from the provisions of general administrative regulations is permitted, provided this right has been expressly reserved to the King in the regulation in question.

ART. 70. The King shall settle differences arising between provinces, between provinces and communes, between communes, and between provinces or communes and *waterchappen*, *veenschappen*, and *veenpolders*,[2] which are not comprised among those mentioned in Art. 153 or among those the settlement of which is intrusted, by virtue of Art. 154, to the regular courts, or to a body vested with administrative jurisdiction.

ART. 71. The King shall recommend projects of law to the States-General and make such other recommendations to them as he considers proper.

He shall have the right to approve or to reject the laws adopted by the States-General.

ART. 72. The manner of promulgating laws and general administrative regulations, and the time when they shall go into force, shall be regulated by law.

The form for the promulgation of laws shall be as follows:

"We, etc., ... king of the Netherlands, etc., ...

"To all who shall see or hear these presents, greeting! make known:

"Whereas We have taken into consideration that, etc. (statement of the purpose of the law);

"Therefore We, having consulted the Council of State and in agreement with the States-General, have thought proper and enacted, and do hereby think proper and enact," etc. (text of the law).

"Given," etc.

In case a queen rules or the royal authority is exercised by a regent or by the Council of State, the changes rendered necessary thereby shall be made in the foregoing formula.

ART. 73. The King shall have the right to dissolve the

[2] See note to chap. ix, Arts. 188–91.

houses of the States-General, either separately or simultaneously.

The decree of dissolution shall at the same time contain an order for the election of new houses within fourteen days, and for the assembling of the newly elected houses within two months.

When the Council of State exercises the royal authority it shall not have the right of dissolution.

SECTION 7. THE COUNCIL OF STATE AND THE MINISTERIAL DEPARTMENTS

ART. 74. There shall be a Council of State whose composition and powers shall be regulated by law.

The King shall be president of the Council and shall appoint its members.

The Prince of Orange, upon reaching the age of eighteen years, shall be entitled, as of right, to a seat in the Council.

ART. 75. The King shall submit for discussion in the Council of State all matters to be presented by him to the States-General or which may be presented to him by the States-General, and all general administrative measures of the kingdom and of its colonies and possessions in other parts of the world.

At the head of decrees to be issued, it shall be stated that the Council of State has been consulted upon the matter.

The King shall also consult the Council of State upon all matters regarding which he thinks it proper to do so.

The King alone shall decide and shall always make known his decision to the Council of State.

ART. 76. The law may intrust the settlement of conflicts of jurisdiction to the Council of State or to a section thereof.

ART. 77. The King establishes ministerial departments and appoints and dismisses the heads thereof at his will.

The heads of the ministerial departments are charged with

the enforcement of the constitution and of the other laws in so far as such enforcement is within the power of the crown.

Their responsibility shall be regulated by law.

All royal decrees and orders shall be countersigned by the head of one of the ministerial departments.

CHAPTER III. THE STATES-GENERAL

SECTION I. COMPOSITION OF THE STATES-GENERAL

ART. 78. The States-General represents all the people of the Netherlands.

ART. 79. The States-General shall be divided into an Upper and a Lower House.

ART. 80. The members of the Lower House shall be elected directly by the male inhabitants, who are at the same time citizens of the Netherlands, and who fulfil the requirements of the election law as to aptitude and social condition and have attained the age prescribed by the law, which shall not be less than twenty-three years.[a]

The law shall determine to what extent the exercise of the right to vote is to be suspended in the case of private soldiers in the army or navy, during the time they are under arms.

From the exercise of the right to vote are excluded those who have been deprived of this right by judicial sentence; those who are in prison or custody; those who have lost the

[a] The right to vote for members of the Lower House of the States-General is granted to male inhabitants who are citizens and have attained the age of twenty-five years, provided they have during the preceding year paid a national property, business, income, or personal tax of one florin; those who do not pay this tax may vote (1) if they pay a certain annual rental; or, (2) receive a certain salary or pension, such rentals, salaries, and pensions varying for the different provinces and communes; (3) own government bonds to the value of 100 florins or have a deposit of 50 florins in a savings bank, or (4) have successfully passed an examination required by law or by general administrative regulation for admission to a public office or to a private occupation or employment. In September, 1907, a proposal was made for the amendment of the constitution, with a view to the reform of the electoral law and a further extension of the right to vote.

control or management of their property by judicial sentence; those who, during the civil year preceding the preparation of the electoral lists, have received assistance from a charitable institution or from a communal government; and those who have not paid a certain tax or taxes, should the electoral law require, as a condition of the right to vote, either the payment of a certain amount of one or more of the direct national taxes, or the possession of one or more of the sources of wealth upon which such taxes are based.

ART. 81. The Lower House shall be composed of one hundred members, who shall be elected in electoral districts.

The division of the kingdom into electoral districts, as well as everything pertaining to the right to vote and the manner of voting shall be regulated by law.

ART. 82. The Upper House shall be composed of fifty members.

They shall be elected by the provincial estates in the following proportions: North Brabant, 6; Gelderland, 6; South Holland 10; North Holland, 9; Zealand, 2; Utrecht, 2; Friesland, 4; Overijssel, 3; Groningen, 3; Drenthe, 2; Limberg, 3—50.

In case of the union, division, or change in boundaries of provinces, or of the formation of new ones, the law shall provide for the changes thereby rendered necessary in this apportionment.

ART. 83. When the States-General is convened in double number, there shall be added to the regular members of each house an equal number of extraordinary members, to be elected in the same manner as the regular members.

The decree of convocation shall also fix the day for the election.

SECTION 2.   THE LOWER HOUSE OF THE STATES-GENERAL

ART. 84. In order to be eligible to membership in the Lower House, the only requisites are to be a male citizen of the Netherlands, not to have lost the control or management of one's property or to have been rendered ineligible by a judicial sentence, and to have attained the age of thirty years.

ART. 85. The members of the Lower House shall be elected for four years.

They shall retire as a body and shall be immediately re-eligible.

ART. 86. The members shall vote without instructions from or conference with those who elect them.

ART. 87. Upon assuming their functions they shall take the following oath or promise:

I swear (promise) fidelity to the constitution. So truly help me God Almighty! (This I promise!)

Before being admitted to take this oath or promise, they shall take the following oath (declaration and promise):

I swear (declare) that, in order to be elected a member of the States-General, I have not promised or given, directly or indirectly, any gift or present to any person under any name or pretext whatever.

I swear (promise) that I will not accept, directly or indirectly, any promises or gifts from any person, to do or to refrain from doing anything in this office. So truly help me God Almighty! (This I declare and promise!)

These oaths (promises and declaration) shall be administered by the King, or, at a meeting of the Lower House, by the president authorized for this purpose by the King.

ART. 88. The president shall be appointed by the King, for the period of one session, from a list of three members submitted by the House.

ART. 89. The members shall receive for traveling expenses, in going to and returning from each session, a sum to be regulated by the law in accordance with the distances.

As further compensation they shall be allowed a sum of 2,000 florins per year.

Members who hold the office of Minister, and during the period of the session, those who have been absent during the whole session shall not receive this compensation.

SECTION 3.   THE UPPER HOUSE OF THE STATES-GENERAL

ART. 90.   In order to be eligible to membership in the Upper House, the requirements for membership in the Lower House must be fulfilled, besides which it is necessary either to be one of the highest taxpayers to the national direct taxes, or to hold or to have held one or more of the important public offices designated by law.

The number of the above-mentioned highest taxpayers is limited in each province to one for every 1,500 persons, who also possess the general qualifications for membership in the States-General.

ART. 91.   The members of the Upper House shall be chosen for nine years.   Art. 86 is applicable to them.

Upon assuming their office they shall take the same oaths (promises and declaration) as are prescribed for the members of the Lower House, to be administered by the King, or, at a meeting of the Upper House, by the president authorized for the purpose by the King.

They shall receive traveling expenses and expenses of residence according to law.[4]

One-third shall retire every three years in accordance with a list prepared for this purpose.   The retiring members are immediately re-eligible.

ART. 92.   The president shall be appointed by the King from among the members for the period of one session.

SECTION 4.   PROVISIONS COMMON TO BOTH HOUSES

ART. 93.   No one shall be a member of both houses at the same time.

Any person who is at the same time elected in more than one district as a member of either the Upper or Lower House,

---

[4] In accordance with the law of May 4, 1889, members of the Upper House who do not reside in the place of meeting receive ten florins per diem during the session.

or as a member of both houses, shall declare which of these elections he accepts.

ART. 94. The heads of the ministerial departments shall have seats in both houses. They shall have only a deliberative voice, unless they have been elected members of the house in which they sit.

They shall furnish the houses, orally or in writing, such information, as is requested and the furnishing of which is not considered detrimental to the interests of the state.

They may be summoned by either of the two houses to attend its meetings for this purpose.

ART. 95. Both houses shall have the right to investigate the conduct of public affairs, either separately or in joint session, in the manner provided by law.

ART. 96. A member of the States-General shall not at the same time be vice-president or member of the Council of State; president, vice-president, member, attorney-general, or advocate-general of the High Court; president or member of the Court of Accounts, or commissioner of the King in a province.

The law shall regulate, as far as necessary, the consequences of a person's being a member of either house and at the same time holding any office paid from the national treasury, and not mentioned in the foregoing paragraph.

Soldiers in active service who become members of either house shall, *ipso facto*, remain on the inactive list during such membership. When they cease to be members, they shall return to active service.

Persons who, after election as members of the States-General, accept a salaried office which they did not hold at the time of election, shall forfeit their membership by such acceptance, but are re-eligible.

ART. 97. The members of the States-General shall not be liable to judicial prosecution for anything which they may have said in its sessions or which they may have presented to it in writing.

ART. 98. Each house shall examine the credentials of its newly elected members and settle any contests that may arise concerning such credentials or concerning the election itself.

ART. 99. Each house shall appoint its clerk.

Such clerk shall not at the same time be a member of either house.

ART. 100. The States-General shall meet at least once each year.

Its regular session shall commence on the third Tuesday in September.

The King may call an extraordinary session as often as he thinks proper.

ART. 101. The separate sessions of the two houses, as well as their joint sessions, shall be held publicly.

The doors shall be closed whenever one-tenth of the members present so demand or when the president considers it necessary.

The assembly shall decide whether the deliberations are to take place with closed doors.

Matters considered in secret session may also be decided therein.

ART. 102. In case the King dies or abdicates the throne when the States-General is not in session, that body shall assemble without being called.

Such extraordinary session shall meet on the fifth day after the King's death or abdication. If the houses are dissolved, this period shall begin at the conclusion of the new elections.

ART. 103. The session of the States-General shall be opened, in a joint meeting of the two houses, by the King or by a committee acting on his behalf. It shall be closed in the same manner whenever he thinks that the interests of the state no longer require its continuance.

The regular annual session shall last at least twenty days, unless the King makes use of the right mentioned in Art. 73.

ART. 104. Upon the dissolution of one or both of the houses, the King shall also close the session of the States-General.

ART. 105. The houses shall not deliberate or take any action, either separately or in joint session, unless more than half their members are present.

ART. 106. All final action upon matters shall be taken by an absolute majority of the voting members.

In case of a tie in the votes, the decision shall be postponed to a subsequent meeting.

If there is an equality of votes at such meeting or at any meeting in which all members are present, the proposition is considered as rejected.

The vote shall be taken by the calling of names, whenever one of the members so demands, and in such a case shall be viva voce.

ART. 107. The voting on persons for the appointments or presentations mentioned in the constitution shall be done by means of secret unsigned ballots.

An absolute majority of the voting members shall decide; in case of a tie the decision shall be reached by lot.

ART. 108. In a joint session the two houses shall be regarded as one, and their members shall sit where they please.

The president of the Upper House shall preside over the meeting.

SECTION 5. THE LEGISLATIVE POWER

ART. 109. The legislative power shall be exercised jointly by the King and the States-General.

ART. 110. The King shall send his recommendations, whether of laws or of other matters, to the Lower House in a written message or by a committee.

He may instruct special commissioners, designated by him, to support the ministers during the consideration of such measures in the meetings of the States-General.

ART. 111. Any measure recommended by the King shall always first be examined before being submitted to a public discussion.

The House shall determine in its Rules of Order in what manner this examination shall be made.

ART. 112. The Lower House, as well as a joint session of the States-General, shall have the right to amend a measure proposed by the King.

ART. 113. Whenever the Lower House decides to adopt a proposition, either unchanged or amended, it shall send it to the Upper House with the following message:

"The Lower House of the States-General sends to the Upper House the inclosed measure recommended by the King, and is of the opinion that it should be adopted by the States-General as it stands."

When the Lower House decides not to adopt a proposition, it shall make the fact known to the King in the following words:

"The Lower House of the States-General expresses its thanks to the King for his zeal in promoting the interests of the state, and respectfully requests him to take his proposition under further consideration."

ART. 114. The Upper House, in accordance with Art. 111, shall consider the proposition as it is adopted by the Lower House.

When it decides to adopt the proposition, it shall make the fact known to the King and to the Lower House in the following terms:

"To the King:

"The States-General expresses its thanks to the King for his zeal in promoting the interests of the state, and agrees to the proposition as it stands."

"To the Lower House:

"The Upper House of the States-General makes known to

the Lower House that it has agreed to the proposition regarding . . . . sent to it on . . . . by the Lower House."

When the Upper House decides not to adopt the proposition, it shall make known the fact to the King and to the Lower House in the following terms:

"To the King:

"The Upper House of the States-General expresses its thanks to the King for his zeal in promoting the interests of the state, and respectfully requests him to take his proposition under further consideration."

"To the Lower House:

"The Upper House of the States-General makes known to the Lower House that it has respectfully requested the King to take under further consideration the proposition regarding . . . . sent to it by the Lower House on . . . . ."

ART. 115. Until the Upper House takes action upon it, the King shall have the power to withdraw the proposition made by him.

ART. 116. The States-General shall have the power to present projects of law to the King.

ART. 117. The initiative in this regard shall belong exclusively to the Lower House, which shall consider the proposed measure in the same manner as prescribed for measures proposed by the King, sending it, after adoption, to the Upper House with the following message:

"The Lower House of the States-General sends the following proposed measure to the Upper House, and is of the opinion that the States-General ought to request the King's consent thereto."

It is authorized to intrust one or more of its members with the written or oral defense of its measure in the Upper House.

ART. 118. When the Upper House, after having deliberated on the measure in the usual manner, shall have approved it, it shall send the measure to the King with the following statement:

"The States-General, believing that the accompanying measure will tend to promote the interests of the state, respectfully requests the King's consent thereto."

It shall also notify the Lower House of its action, in the following manner:

"The Upper House of the States-General makes known to the Lower House that it has agreed to the measure received by it on . . . . concerning . . . . and has requested the King's consent thereto in the name of the States-General."

When the Upper House does not approve the measure, it shall make the fact known to the Lower House in the following manner:

"The Upper House of the States-General has not thought proper to request the King's consent to the proposed measure returned herewith."

ART. 119. Other recommendations than projects of laws may be presented to the King by either of the houses separately.

ART. 120. The King shall make known to the States-General as soon as possible whether or not he approves a project of law adopted by that body. The notification shall be given in the following manner:

"The King consents to the proposed measure" or, "The King is taking the proposed measure under consideration."

ART. 121. All bills adopted by the States-General and approved by the King shall acquire the force of law and shall be promulgated by the King.

The laws are inviolable.

ART. 122. The laws shall be binding only for the kingdom unless it is expressed therein that they are binding for the colonies and possessions in other parts of the world.

SECTION 6. THE BUDGET

ART. 123. The estimates of all the expenses of the kingdom shall be fixed and the means of meeting such expenses provided by law.

ART. 124. The projects of the general budgetary laws shall be annually presented to the Lower House in the name of the King, immediately after the opening of the regular session of the States-General, before the beginning of the year for which the budget is to serve.

ART. 125. No chapter of the estimates of expenses shall relate to more than one of the general administrative departments.

Each chapter shall form the subject of one or more projects of law.

Transfers may be permitted by the budgetary law.

ART. 126. An account of the receipts and expenditures of the kingdom for each year shall, after approval by the Court of Accounts, be presented to the legislative bodies in the manner provided by law.

CHAPTER IV. THE PROVINCIAL ESTATES AND THE COMMUNAL GOVERNMENTS

SECTION I. COMPOSITION OF THE PROVINCIAL ESTATES

ART. 127. The members of the Provincial Estates shall be chosen directly for six years by the male inhabitants of the province, who are citizens of the Netherlands, and who fulfil the requirements of the law as to aptitude and social condition and have reached the age prescribed by the law, which shall not be under twenty-three years.

The second and third paragraphs of Art. 80 are applicable to these elections.

Half of the members shall retire every three years.

In order to be eligible to membership in the Provincial Estates it is necessary to be a male citizen of the Netherlands and a resident of the province, not to have lost the control or management of one's property or have been deprived of the right to vote by judicial sentence, and to have attained the age of twenty-five years.

The election of the members of the Provincial Estates shall take place in the manner prescribed by law.

ART. 128.   No one shall at the same time be a member of the Upper House of the States-General and of the Estates of a province, nor a member of the Estates of more than one province.

ART. 129.   The members of the Estates shall take the following oath or promise upon assuming office:

I swear (promise) fidelity to the constitution and to the laws of the kingdom. So truly help me God Almighty! (This I promise!)

They shall be admitted to take this oath (promise) after having first taken an oath (declaration and promise) similar to the one hereinbefore prescribed by Art. 87 for members of the Lower House of the States-General.

ART. 130.   The Estates shall meet as often during the year as the law provides, and also whenever they are convened in extraordinary session by the King.

The meetings shall be public, with the same reservation as that contained in Art. 101 with regard to the sessions of the houses of the States-General.

ART. 131.   The members of the Estates shall vote without instructions from or conference with those who elect them.

ART. 132.   With regard to the deliberations and voting, the rules prescribed in Arts. 105, 106, and 107 for the houses of the States-General shall apply.

SECTION 2.   THE POWERS OF THE PROVINCIAL ESTATES

ART. 133.   The authority and powers of the Estates shall be regulated by law, regard being had for the provisions contained in the following articles of this section.

ART. 134.   The Estates shall be intrusted with the regulation and administration of the affairs of the province.

They may enact such ordinances as they consider necessary for the interests of the province.

Such ordinances shall require the approval of the King. This approval shall not be refused except by a decree giving the reasons therefor, after consultation with the Council of State.

ART. 135. When the laws or general administrative regulations require it, the Estates shall co-operate in the execution of such laws and regulations.

ART. 136. Every resolution of the Estates establishing, altering, or abolishing a provincial tax shall require the approval of the King.

The law shall prescribe general rules with regard to provincial taxes.

Such taxes shall not obstruct transit, or the export to or import from other provinces.

ART. 137. The budget of the provincial receipts and expenditures, to be prepared annually by the Estates, shall require the approval of the King.

The preparation of the provincial accounts shall be regulated by law.

ART. 138. The Estates may defend the interests of the province and of its inhabitants before the King and the States-General.

ART. 139. The Estates shall appoint from their own members a Committee of the Estates, to which, in accordance with rules to be established by law, the daily administration of affairs shall be intrusted, and this whether the Estates are or are not in session.

ART. 140. The power of the King to suspend or annul the decisions of Provincial Estates or of the Committee of the Estates which conflict with the law or with public interests shall be regulated by law.

ART. 141. The King shall appoint a commissioner in each province, who shall be charged with the execution of royal orders and with supervision over the acts of the Estates.

This commissioner shall be president of the Provincial Estates and of the Committee of the Estates, and shall have a vote in the latter body.

His salary and the expenses of his residence shall be paid from the national treasury. The law shall determine whether any other expenses of the provincial government are to be borne by the kingdom.

SECTION 3. THE COMMUNAL GOVERNMENTS

ART. 142. The composition, organization, and powers of the communal governments shall be regulated by law, regard being had for the provisions contained in the following articles of this section.

ART. 143. At the head of the commune shall be a council, the members of which shall be directly elected for a certain number of years by the male inhabitants of the commune who are citizens of the Netherlands, who fulfil the requirements of the law as to aptitude and social condition, and who have attained the age prescribed by the law, which shall not be less than twenty-three years.

The second and third paragraphs of Art. 80 are applicable to these elections.

In order to be eligible to membership in the council it is necessary to be a male citizen of the Netherlands and a resident of the commune, not to have lost the control or management of one's property or have been deprived of the right to vote by judicial sentence, and to have attained the age of twenty-three years.

The election of the council shall take place in the manner prescribed by law.

The president shall be appointed by the King, from among or from without the members of the council, and may be dismissed by him.

ART. 144. The council shall be intrusted with the regulation and administration of the local affairs of the commune.

It may adopt such ordinances as it considers necessary for the interests of the commune.

When the laws, general administrative regulations, or provincial ordinances require it, the communal governments shall co-operate in enforcing such laws, regulations, or ordinances.

A law may provide the manner in which the administration of the commune shall be conducted, in a manner differing from the provisions of the first two paragraphs of this article, when the regulation and administration of the local affairs of a commune are grossly neglected by the communal council.

The law shall determine what authority takes the place of the communal government when the latter fails to execute the laws, the general administrative measures, or the provincial ordinances.

ART. 145. A law shall regulate the power of the King to suspend or to annul the resolutions of communal governments which conflict with the law or with public interests.

This power is unlimited in the case of local ordinances and regulations.

ART. 146. The decisions of communal governments concerning such control over communal property or such other civil acts as the law prescribes and concerning the budgets of receipts and expenditures shall be submitted to the approval of the Committee of the Provincial Estates.

The preparation of the budgets and of the accounts shall be regulated by law.

ART. 147. The resolution of a communal government establishing, altering, or abolishing a local tax shall be presented to the Committee of the Provincial Estates, which shall report thereon to the King, without whose approval no action shall be taken in the matter.

The law shall prescribe general rules with regard to local taxes.

These taxes shall not obstruct transit, or the export to or import from other communes.

ART. 148. The communal government may represent the interests of the commune and of its inhabitants before the

King, the States-General, and the Estates of the province to which it belongs.

CHAPTER V. JUSTICE

SECTION I. GENERAL PROVISIONS

ART. 149. Justice shall be administered throughout the kingdom in the name of the King.

ART. 150. Civil and commercial law, criminal law, military criminal law, the administration of justice, and the organization of the courts shall be regulated by law in general codes, saving the right of the legislative power to regulate particular subjects by separate laws.

ART. 151. No one shall be deprived of his property without a previous declaration by law that the public utility requires that it be taken, and without receiving a compensation previously paid or determined, both in accordance with the provisions of a general law.

This general law shall also determine the cases in which the previous declaration by law is not required.

The requirement that the compensation be paid or determined in advance shall not apply when war, danger of war, revolt, fire, or inundation renders necessary the immediate taking of possession.

ART. 152. When the public interest requires that property be destroyed by the public authorities or rendered temporarily or permanently useless, this shall be done upon payment of a compensation, unless the law otherwise provides.[5]

The use of property for the preparation and execution of military inundations, when rendered necessary by war or by danger of war, shall be regulated by law.

ART. 153. All controversies regarding property or the rights arising therefrom, regarding debts, and regarding other civil rights shall belong exclusively to the jurisdiction of the courts.

[5] See additional Art. V.

ART. 154. The law may intrust either to the regular courts or to a body invested with administrative jurisdiction the settlement of controversies not included among those mentioned in Art. 153; the law shall regulate the procedure and the effects of the decision.

ART. 155. The judicial power shall be exercised only by the courts established by law.

ART. 156. No one shall be removed against his will from the jurisdiction of the judge before whom he is entitled to be tried by law.

The law shall determine the manner of deciding conflicts of competence which may arise between the administrative and the judicial authorities.

ART. 157. Except in the cases provided by law, no one shall be taken into custody except upon a warrant from a judge, stating the reasons for the arrest. This warrant must be shown to the person against whom it is issued, either at the time of or as soon as possible after the arrest.

The law shall prescribe the form of this warrant and the period within which the persons arrested must be given a hearing.

ART. 158. The entrance of a dwelling against the will of the occupant shall only be allowed in the cases determined by law and by virtue of a special or general warrant from an authority designated by law.

The law shall prescribe the formalities to be complied with in exercising this authority.

ART. 159. The secrecy of letters intrusted to the mail or to other public carriers is inviolable, except by order of a judge in the cases prescribed by law.

ART. 160. General confiscation of the property of the guilty person shall not be imposed as a penalty for any offense.

ART. 161. All judgments shall indicate the reasons upon which they are based, and, in criminal cases, the provisions of law upon which the sentence is based.

Judgments shall be pronounced in public session.

Saving the exceptions provided by law, the sessions of courts shall be public.

A judge may depart from this rule in the interests of public order and morals.

SECTION 2.   THE COURTS

ART. 162.   There shall be a supreme court called the High Court of the Netherlands, the members of which shall be appointed by the King in conformity with the following article.

ART. 163.   When a vacancy occurs the fact shall be made known by the High Court to the Lower House of the States-General, which, in order to fill it, shall present a list of three persons from which the King shall choose one.

The King shall appoint the president and the vice-president from among the members of the High Court.

ART. 164.   Members of the States-General, heads of the ministerial departments, governors-general, and higher officers who under different titles are clothed with the same power in the colonies or possessions in other parts of the world, members of the Council of State, and commissioners of the King in the provinces shall, even after their retirement from office, be subject to prosecution before the High Court, either by the King or by the Lower House, because of offenses committed in the exercise of these offices.

The law may provide that still other officers and members of higher bodies shall be tried before the High Court for official misconduct.

ART. 165.   The High Court shall see that suits are properly tried and decided, and that the judicial officers comply with the laws.

When judicial proceedings, decrees, or judgments are in conflict with the laws, the High Court may annul them and set them aside, in accordance with the regulations established by law in this matter and saving the exceptions established by law.

The other powers of the High Court shall be determined by law.

Art. 166. Judicial officers shall be appointed by the King.

Judicial officers who are vested with the power to try cases, and the attorney-general of the High Court shall be appointed for life.

They may be dismissed or relieved of their duties by judgment of the High Court in the cases prescribed by law.

They may at their own request be relieved of their duties by the King.

If a body is vested with administrative jurisdiction in the last resort for the kingdom, the first, second, and fourth paragraphs of this article shall apply to its members.

They may be dismissed or relieved of their duties in the manner and in the cases prescribed by law.

This article is not applicable to those who are exclusively vested with jurisdiction over persons belonging to the army and navy or to any other armed force, or who are intrusted with the decision of disciplinary cases.

CHAPTER VI. RELIGIOUS WORSHIP

Art. 167. Every person shall be absolutely free to profess his religious opinions, except that society and its members shall be protected against violations of the criminal law.

Art. 168. Equal protection shall be granted to all religious denominations in the kingdom.

Art. 169. The adherents of the various religious denominations shall all enjoy the same civil and political rights and shall have an equal right to hold dignities, offices, and employments.

Art. 170. All public religious worship inside of buildings and inclosures shall be permitted, except that the necessary measures may be taken to preserve the public peace and order.

Under the same reservation, public religious worship shall

be allowed outside of buildings and inclosures, wherever it is now permitted according to the laws and regulations.

ART. 171. The salaries, pensions, and other incomes of any kind, which are at present enjoyed by the various religious denominations or by their ministers, are guaranteed to such denominations.

Ministers who have hitherto drawn no salary or have drawn an insufficient one from the national treasury may be allowed a salary or have their present salary increased.

ART. 172. The King shall see that all religious denominations remain obedient to the laws of the state.

ART. 173. The government shall not interfere in the correspondence with heads of the various churches, nor in the promulgation of ecclesiastical regulations, saving the responsibility in accordance with law.

CHAPTER VII. FINANCES

ART. 174. No taxes shall be levied for the benefit of the national treasury except by virtue of law.

This provision is also applicable to taxes levied for the benefit of national works and institutions, in so far as the right to regulate these taxes is not reserved to the King.

ART. 175. No exemptions shall be granted in the matter of taxation.

ART. 176. The state guarantees the fulfilment of its obligations toward its creditors. The debt shall be taken under consideration annually for the purpose of protecting the interests of the creditors of the state.

ART. 177. The weight, standard, and value of the coin shall be regulated by law.

ART. 178. The supervision and management of affairs relating to the mint, and the settlement of controversies regarding the alloy, assay, and other matters relating to coinage shall be regulated by law.

ART. 179. There shall be a Court of Accounts, the composition and duties of which shall be regulated by law.

Upon a vacancy occurring in this court, the Lower House of the States-General shall present a list of three persons from which the King shall make the appointment.

The members of the Court of Accounts shall be appointed for life.

The third and fourth paragraphs of Art. 166 are applicable to them.

CHAPTER VIII. DEFENSE

ART. 180. All citizens of the Netherlands who are able to do so are obliged to assist in maintaining the independence of the kingdom and in defending its territory.

This obligation may also be imposed upon residents who are not citizens.

ART. 181. For the protection of the interests of the state there shall be an army and a navy composed of volunteers and of those who are required to perform military service.

Compulsory military service shall be regulated by law. The obligations which may be imposed, with regard to national defense, upon those who do not belong to the army or navy, shall also be regulated by law.

ART. 182. Foreign troops shall not be taken into the service of the state except by virtue of a law.

ART. 183. Persons required to serve in the navy may be assigned to service either in or out of Europe. Advantages shall be attached by law to the service to be performed by them in the colonies and possessions in other parts of the world.

ART. 184. Persons required to serve in the army shall not without their consent be sent to the colonies or possessions of the kingdom in other parts of the world.

ART. 185. When, in case of war, danger of war, or other extraordinary circumstances, all or part of those not in active service are called to arms in a special case by the King, a bill shall be immediately introduced in the States-General to provide as far as necessary for their remaining under arms.

ART. 186.   All the expenses of the armies of the kingdom shall be borne by the national treasury.

The quartering and maintenance of the troops and the transportation and furnishing of supplies of every kind required for the armies or for the defensive works of the kingdom may be imposed upon one or more inhabitants or communes only in accordance with general rules established by law and upon payment of compensation.

The exceptions from these general rules in case of war, danger of war, or other extraordinary circumstances shall be determined by law.

The King shall decide whether "danger of war" exists in the sense in which that phrase is used in the laws of the kingdom.

ART. 187.   For the maintenance of external or internal security any part of the territory of the kingdom may be declared by or on behalf of the King to be in a state of war or of siege.   The law shall determine the manner and the cases in which this may be done and shall regulate the effects of such a declaration.

In these regulations it may be provided that the constitutional powers of the civil officers to maintain public order and to enforce police regulations shall be wholly or partly transferred to the military authorities, and that the civil officers shall be subordinate to the military authorities.

In this case Arts. 7, 9, 158, and 159 of the constitution may, in addition, be disregarded.

In case of war paragraph 1 of Art. 156 may also be disregarded.

CHAPTER IX.   WATERSTAAT*

ART. 188.   The law shall prescribe rules regarding the administration of the *waterstaat*, including the supreme and

* Under *waterstaat* are included all works for protection against the

immediate control thereof, regard being had for the provisions contained in the following articles of this chapter.

ART. 189. The King shall exercise supreme control over everything relating to the *waterstaat*, regardless of whether the costs thereof are defrayed from the national treasury or in some other manner.

ART. 190. The Provincial Estates shall have the immediate control over all works pertaining to the *waterstaat*, *waterschappen, veenschappen,* and *veenpolders.* Nevertheless the law may assign the control over these works to others.

The Estates are authorized, with the consent of the King, to make changes in the existing arrangements and regulations of *waterschappen, veenschappen,* and *veenpolders,* to abolish *waterschappen, veenschappen,* and *veenpolders,* to establish new ones, and to adopt new regulations for such institutions. The administrations of such institutions may propose to the Provincial Estates modifications of their organization or rules.

ART. 191. The governments of *waterschappen, veenschappen,* and *veenpolders* may, according to rules established by law, make ordinances in the local interests of these institutions.

CHAPTER X. PUBLIC INSTRUCTION AND THE RELIEF OF THE POOR

ART. 192. Public instruction shall be an object of constant care on the part of the government.

The organization of public instruction shall be regulated by law, the religious convictions of everyone being respected.

sea, dunes, dikes, dams, rivers, bridges, railways, other public works in general, and the exploitation of peat bogs.

Waterschappen are associations formed for the purpose of protecting lands against the sea, and for drainage or irrigation.

Veenschappen are peat bogs, and *veenpolders* are districts whose owners are grouped into associations for the administration and exploitation of peat bogs.

Adequate public primary instruction shall be provided by the government throughout the kingdom.

The imparting of instruction shall be free, except that it shall be under the supervision of the authorities, and that, as far as intermediate and primary instruction is concerned, the teachers shall be subject to examination as to their ability and moral character; all to be regulated by law.

The King shall cause a detailed report to be made annually to the States-General on the condition of the higher, intermediate, and primary schools.

ART. 193. The relief of the poor shall be an object of constant care on the part of the government, and shall be regulated by law.

The King shall cause a detailed report to be made annually to the States-General concerning the measures taken in this matter.

CHAPTER XI. AMENDMENTS

ART. 194. In every project to amend the constitution the proposed amendment shall be expressly indicated. A law shall declare that there is a reason for taking under consideration the proposed amendment as set forth in it.

ART. 195. After the promulgation of this law the houses shall be dissolved. The new houses shall consider the proposed amendment, and two-thirds of the votes cast shall be necessary to adopt the amendment as presented to them in accordance with the aforementioned law.

ART. 196. No change shall be made in the succession to the throne during a regency.

ART. 197. Amendments to the constitution, adopted by the King and the States-General, shall be solemnly promulgated and added to the constitution.

ADDITIONAL ARTICLES

ART. I. All existing authorities shall continue until superseded by others, in conformity with this constitution.

ART. II. All laws, regulations, and decrees in force at the time of the promulgation of the amendments to the constitution shall remain in force until superseded by others.

ART. III. The seigniorial rights relative to the nomination or appointment of persons to public offices are abolished.

The abolition of other seigniorial rights and the indemnification of the persons enjoying them may be provided for and regulated by law.

ART. IV. Art. 151 of the constitution shall not apply to excavations when the materials are taken from ground which by virtue of customs or ordinance or by any other authority, was in 1886 liable to use for such purposes with or without compensation.

ART. V. The first paragraph of Art. 152 of the constitution shall remain inapplicable until the law has gone into force, prescribing the cases in which no compensation shall be allowed for destroying property or rendering it permanently or temporarily useless.

ART. VI. Without prejudice to the right of the King to dissolve one or both of the houses of the States-General, the two houses shall remain as they are composed on the date of the promulgation of the laws containing amendments to the constitution, until the day of opening of the new houses. If elections are necessary before this day in order to fill places rendered vacant by dismissal, death, or other cause, such elections shall be held in accordance with the regulations in force on the day of such promulgation. The King shall fix the date of opening of the new houses, as soon as possible after the elections referred to in Article IX.

ART. XII. The King is authorized to have the text of the revised constitution made known, and to make such changes in numbers as may appear necessary in articles that refer to other articles.[7]

[7] Additional Arts. VII–XI related to the first elections under the amended constitution and to the revision of the election law; they have now ceased to be of any importance.

NORWAY

From 1397 to 1814 Norway was united with Denmark, and since the seventeenth century it had been absolutely governed from the latter country. In the later Napoleonic wars Denmark sided with France, and Sweden obtained in 1812 and 1813 the agreement that it might seize Norway as a reward for its assistance in overthrowing Napoleon.

Danish resistance was easily overcome by Bernadotte, Crown Prince of Sweden since 1810, and Norway was ceded to Sweden by the treaty of Kiel of January 14, 1814. Norway objected to the forced union with Sweden; the Norwegians adopted a liberal constitution on May 17, 1814, and elected as king the Danish prince, Christian Frederick. But their resistance was unavailing; the Norwegian forces were defeated; Christian Frederick abdicated, and the Storthing gave its consent to the union with Sweden.

The Eidsvold constitution of May 17 was revised on November 4, 1814, and Charles XIII of Sweden was chosen king of Norway. Norway retained its independent government; the changes in the constitution were such as were made necessary by the fact that the ruler of Sweden became king of Norway. The constitution of 1814, frequently amended, is still the constitution of Norway. Of the amendments the most important are: (1) that of April 24, 1869, establishing annual sessions of the Storthing; (2) that of July 4, 1884, extending the right to vote; (3) that of April 3, 1898, establishing universal male suffrage; (4) that of May 25, 1905, providing for the direct election of members of the Storthing.

From the first the union with Sweden hung heavily on Norway, and a constant struggle was maintained by the latter country to gain absolute political equality with the sister kingdom. In 1891 began the Norwegian contest for a separate consular service, a contest which finally ended in the rupture of the Union. Sweden was willing to concede a separate consular service, but not on the terms demanded by Norway. On February 8, 1905, the Norwegian prime minister announced to the Storthing that negotiations with Sweden regarding the consular service had been broken off. On April 5, the Prince Regent, who had assumed the government because of the ill-health of the King, appealed to Norway to resume negotiations upon the basis of a joint control of foreign relations. To this appeal the Norwegian government replied on April 17, 1905, that it was obliged "to advise against entering into new negotiations regarding the affairs of the Union until after a Norwegian consular service has been established." The Norwegian government required furthermore that an agreement be made in advance permitting each country to act freely regarding its future relations, before further negotiations would be opened with reference to the continuance of the Union.

The Norwegian demands were refused by the Prince Regent on April 25, 1905. On May 24, 1905, the Storthing passed a law organizing a separate Norwegian consular service, which was vetoed by the King on May 27. The Norwegian Council had on May 26 indicated its intention to resign if the King should not approve the consular law, but the King had refused to accept the resignations because of his inability to form a new government. On June 6 the members of the Council formally withdrew from office, and the Storthing resolved on June 7, 1905, "to empower the resigning Council of State until further notice to exercise as the Norwegian government the powers belonging to the King in accordance with the constitution of the kingdom of Norway and with existing laws, with the changes rendered necessary by the fact that the union with Sweden which provides that there shall be a common king, is dissolved in consequence of the fact that the King has ceased to act as king of Norway." On November 18, 1905, the Norwegian constitution was revised so as to omit all reference to the union with Sweden.

Prince Carl of Denmark was elected king of independent Norway and was crowned as Haakon VII at Trondhjem on June 22, 1906.

SELECT BIBLIOGRAPHY

ASCHEHOUG, T. H. *Norges Nuvaerende Statsforfatning.* (2d ed., Christiania, 1891-93. 3 vols.) The standard treatise on the Norwegian government.

Aschehoug, T. H. *Das Staatsrecht der vereinigten Königreiche Schweden und Norwegen.* (Freiburg, 1886. Handbuch des oeffentlichen Rechts.) Contains brief studies on the constitutional law of Norway and Sweden.

Morgenstierne, Bredo. *Laerbog i den Norske statsforfatningsret.* (Christiania, 1900.)

CONSTITUTION OF NORWAY[1]
(November 4, 1814)

A. FORM OF GOVERNMENT AND RELIGION

Article 1. The Kingdom of Norway is a free, independent, indivisible, and inalienable state. Its form of government is that of a limited hereditary monarchy.

Art. 2. The Evangelical Lutheran religion shall remain the public religion of the state. Such inhabitants as profess this religion are required to educate their children therein. Jesuits shall not be admitted.

B. THE EXECUTIVE POWER, THE KING, AND THE ROYAL FAMILY

Art. 3. The executive power shall be vested in the King.

Art. 4. The King shall always profess, maintain, and defend the Evangelical Lutheran religion.

Art. 5. The King's person shall be sacred; he shall not be censured or impeached; the responsibility shall rest upon his council.

Art. 6. The order of succession shall be lineal and agnatic in the legitimate descendants from male to male, the nearer line being preferred to the more remote, and within the same line the older descendant being preferred to the younger.

---

[1] In the preparation of this text assistance has been received from the translations issued by Knute Nelson (Chicago, 1899), and by H. L. Brækstad (London, 1905). Numerous articles of the Norwegian constitution have been repealed; on this account the articles in force are not numbered consecutively.

A posthumous child shall also be considered in the line of succession and shall take his proper place therein as soon as he is born.

When a prince in the line of succession to the Norwegian crown is born, his name and the time of his birth shall be reported to the Storthing at its next succeeding session and be entered in its journal.

Art. 7. If there be no prince entitled to the succession, the King may propose a successor to the Storthing, which shall have the right to choose another person if it does not approve of the one proposed by the King.

Art. 8. The age of the majority of the King shall be fixed by law.

As soon as the King has attained the age prescribed by law he shall publicly declare himself of full age.

Art. 9. As soon as the King, upon coming of age, assumes the government, he shall take the following oath before the Storthing:

I promise and swear that I will govern the Kingdom of Norway in conformity with its constitution and laws; so truly help me God and his holy Word!

If the Storthing is not in session at the time, the oath shall be deposited in writing with the Council of State, and shall be solemnly renewed by the King at the next Storthing, either verbally, or in writing through the person whom he may appoint for that purpose.

Art. 10. When he becomes of age, the King shall be crowned and anointed in the Cathedral of Trondhjem, at such time and with such ceremonies as he may prescribe.

Art. 12. The King shall personally appoint a Council of State of Norwegian citizens, who shall be not less than thirty years of age. This Council shall consist of one Minister of State and of at least seven other members.

The King shall apportion the business among the members of the Council of State in such manner as he considers proper.

Upon extraordinary occasions the King may, in addition to the regular members of the Council, summon other Norwegian citizens who are not members of the Storthing, to sit in the Council of State.

Father and son or two brothers shall not at the same time have seats in the Council of State.

ART. 13. When the King is absent from the capital of the kingdom, he shall commit the internal administration of the kingdom, in such matters as he may prescribe, to the Minister of State together with at least five other members of the Council of State.

They shall carry on the government in the King's name and on his behalf. They shall inviolably observe the provisions of this constitution and also the several instructions in conformity therewith which the King may communicate to them. They shall present to the King a respectful report concerning the matters upon which they take action.

Matters of business shall be acted upon by vote, and in case of an equality of votes the Minister of State, or in his absence the first member of the Council of State shall have two votes.

ART. 16. The King shall regulate all public religious and church service, all meetings and assemblies relating to religious matters, and shall see that the public teachers of religion follow the rules prescribed for their guidance.

ART. 17. The King may issue and repeal regulations concerning commerce, customs, industrial pursuits, and public order; however, they shall not be in conflict with the constitution, or with the laws passed by the Storthing in pursuance of Arts. 77, 78, and 79 of this constitution. Such regulations shall be in force provisionally until the next Storthing.

ART. 18. The King shall, in general, cause to be collected the taxes and duties imposed by the Storthing.

ART. 19. The King shall take care that the crown estates and regalia are used and managed in the manner provided by the Storthing, and for the greatest advantage of the public.

ART. 20. The King in Council shall have power to pardon offenders after conviction. The offender shall have the option to accept the King's pardon or to suffer the punishment imposed upon him.

No pardon or reprieve, except remission from the death penalty, shall be granted in the cases which the Odelsthing prosecutes in the Court of Impeachment.

ART. 21. The King, with the advice of the Council of State, shall choose and appoint all civil, ecclesiastical, and military officers. These officers shall swear, or if by law freed from the taking of an oath, shall solemnly promise obedience and fidelity to the constitution and to the King. The royal princes shall not hold civil offices.

ART. 22. The Minister of State and the other members of the Council of State, officers of the departments, ambassadors, and consuls, the higher civil and ecclesiastical officers, commanders of regiments and of other military corps, commanders of fortresses, and commanding officers of vessels of war, may be removed by the King upon the advice of the Council of State, without previous judicial sentence. How far pensions shall be granted to the officers thus removed shall be determined by the next Storthing. In the meantime they shall receive two-thirds of their former salary.

Other officers may only be suspended by the King, and shall immediately be proceeded against before the courts, but shall not be dismissed except after judicial sentence; nor shall they be transferred without their consent.

ART. 23. The King may, at his pleasure, confer orders in recognition of distinguished services, which shall be publicly announced; but he shall confer no other rank or title than that which each office carries with it. Such orders shall relieve no one from the duties and burdens common to all citizens, nor shall they carry with them any preference in securing appointment to public office. Officers who are honorably discharged shall retain the title and rank of the offices which they held.

No personal or mixed hereditary privileges shall hereafter be granted to anyone.

ART. 24. The King may, at pleasure, appoint and dismiss his royal household and the attendants of the court.

ART. 25. The King shall be commander-in-chief of the land and naval forces of the kingdom. These forces shall not be increased or diminished without the consent of the Storthing. They shall not be placed in the service of a foreign power, nor shall troops of a foreign power, except auxiliary troops to repel hostile attack, be brought into the kingdom without the consent of the Storthing.

In time of peace no other than Norwegian troops shall be stationed in Norway.

The Norwegian troops and flotilla shall not be employed in offensive war without the consent of the Storthing.

The Norwegian navy shall have its dock-yards and in time of peace its stations or harbors in Norway.

The militia and the other Norwegian troops, not classed as troops of the line, shall never be employed beyond the borders of Norway.

ART. 26. The King shall have power to mobilize troops, to commence war and conclude peace, to enter into and to withdraw from alliances, to send and to receive ambassadors.

ART. 27. All members of the Council of State shall, unless they have a lawful excuse, attend the meetings of the Council of State, and no action shall be taken in that body unless more than half of the members are present.

ART. 28. Reports upon appointments to office and upon other matters of importance, with the exception of diplomatic affairs and of matters relating to military command, shall be presented to the Council of State by the member to whose department the matter belongs, and the matter shall be disposed of by him in accordance with the decision of the Council of State.

ART. 29. If a councilor of state is prevented, by a lawful

excuse, from attending the meeting and presenting the matters which belong to his department, such matters shall be presented by another councilor of state, whom the King shall designate for that purpose.

If, for valid cause, so many are absent from the meeting that not more than half of the members are present, other officers shall in like manner be designated to sit in the Council of State.

ART. 30. Minutes shall be kept of all matters acted upon by the Council of State. It shall be the duty of everyone who has a seat in the Council of State to express his opinions frankly; the King shall listen to such opinions, but it shall remain with him to decide according to his own judgment. If any member of the Council of State thinks that the King's decision is in conflict with the constitution or the laws or is clearly injurious to the kingdom, it shall be his duty vigorously to protest against such decision and to enter his opinion in the minutes. A member who has not thus protested shall be regarded as having concurred with the King, and shall be responsible therefor in the manner hereinafter provided, and may be impeached by the Odelsthing before the Court of Impeachment.

ART. 31. All orders issued by the King, with the exception of matters of military command, shall be countersigned by the Minister of State.

ART. 32. All actions taken by the government during the King's absence shall be issued in the King's name and signed by the Council of State.

ART. 33. All reports and all despatches connected therewith shall be written in the Norwegian language.

ART. 34. The next heir to the throne, if he is a son of the reigning King, shall bear the title of Crown Prince. Other persons in the line of succession to the throne shall be called princes, and the daughters of the royal house, princesses.

ART. 35. As soon as the heir to the throne has attained

his eighteenth year, he shall be entitled to a seat in the Council of State, but without vote or responsibility.

ART. 36. No prince of the blood may marry without the consent of the King. If he violates this rule, he shall forfeit his right to the crown of Norway.

ART. 37. The royal princes and princesses shall not personally be answerable to any other person than the King, or to such person as the King may appoint to be judge over them.

ART. 39. If the King dies and his successor is still under age, the Council of State shall immediately summon the Storthing.

ART. 40. Until the Storthing is assembled and has provided for the government during the King's minority, the Council of State shall conduct the government of the kingdom in conformity with the constitution.

ART. 41. When the King is absent from the kingdom without being engaged in warfare or if he be prevented by illness from conducting the government, the prince entitled to the succession, provided he has attained the age fixed for the King's majority, shall conduct the government as the person in the temporary exercise of royal power. Otherwise the Council of State shall conduct the government of the kingdom.

ART. 43. The election of a regency to conduct the government during the King's minority shall devolve upon the Storthing.

ART. 44. Those who conduct the government in the cases referred to by Arts. 40 and 41, shall take the following oath before the Storthing:

I promise and swear that I will conduct the government in accordance with the constitution and the laws, so truly help me God and his holy Word!

If the Storthing is not in session at the time, the oath shall be deposited in writing with the Council of State and shall be renewed before the next session of the Storthing.

ART. 45. As soon as their administration of the state comes to an end they shall render an account of the same to the King and the Storthing.

ART. 46. If the proper authorities neglect immediately to summon the Storthing, in accordance with Art. 39, it shall become the absolute duty of the Supreme Court, as soon as four weeks have elapsed, to issue such summons.

ART. 47. The management of the King's education during his minority shall be determined by the Storthing, if his father has not left written instructions concerning this matter.

It shall be the invariable rule that the King during his minority be given sufficient instruction in the Norwegian language.

ART. 48. If the royal family becomes extinct in the male line and no successor has been elected, a new King shall be elected by the Storthing. Meanwhile the executive power shall be exercised in accordance with Art. 40.

C. CITIZENSHIP AND THE LEGISLATIVE POWER

ART. 49. The people exercise the legislative power through the Storthing, which shall be composed of two bodies, the Lagthing and the Odelsthing.

ART. 50. Every Norwegian citizen dwelling within the kingdom, who has attained the age of twenty-five years and has been a resident of the country for five years, shall be entitled to vote.[2]

ART. 51. Regulations regarding the registrar's duties and the registration of qualified voters shall be established by law.

[2] Universal male suffrage was introduced by an amendment of 1898. On June 15, 1907, a constitutional amendment was voted granting the right to vote for members of the Storthing to all Norwegian women twenty-five years of age or over, who themselves or whose husbands pay a tax upon an annual income of 400 kroner in cities or upon 300 kroner in the country. Women had before the passage of this law the right to vote in communal elections under similar conditions. Under the new constitutional provision about 300,000 of the 550,000 Norwegian women above the age of twenty-five will enjoy the right to vote.

ART. 52. The right to vote is suspended:

a) By indictment for a criminal offense entailing loss of the right to vote.

b) By being placed under guardianship.

c) By insolvency or bankruptcy, so long as the debtor's property is under administration.

d) By being or having been in the receipt of poor relief during the year immediately preceding the election.

ART. 53. The right to vote is lost:

a) By conviction of criminal offenses in accordance with the provisions of the law.

b) By entering the service of a foreign power without the consent of the government.

c) By acquiring citizenship in a foreign state.

d) By conviction of buying votes, selling one's own vote, or of having voted in more than one election precinct.

ART. 54. The electoral assemblies shall be held every third year. They shall be concluded before the end of the month of September.

ART. 55. The electoral assemblies shall proceed in the manner provided by law. Disputes regarding the right to vote shall be settled by the managers of the election, from whose decision there may be an appeal to the Storthing.

ART. 56. Before the elections begin, Arts. 50–64 of the constitution shall be read aloud by the officer who presides at the election.

ART. 57. The number of representatives in the Storthing to be elected by the cities is fixed at forty-one. Of these there shall be elected from Aalesund and Molde together, one; from Arendal and Grimstad together, one; from Bergen, four; from Bodö, one; from Brevik, one; from Dramen, two; from Flekkefjord, one; from Frederikshald, one; from Frederikstad, one; from Hammerfest, Vardö, and Vadsö together, one; from Haugesund, one; from Holmestrand, one; from Kongsberg and Hönefoss together, one; from Kragerö, one; from

Christiania, five; from Christiansand, two; from Christiansund, one; from Larvik and Sandefjord together, one; from Lillehammer, Hamar, Gjövik and Kongsvinger together, one; from Moss and Dröbak together, one; from Porsgrund, one; from Sarpsborg, one; from Skien, one; from Stavanger, two; from Tromsö, one; from Trondhjem and Levanger together, four; from Tönsberg, one, and from Österrisör, one.

A city not named here or to be founded hereafter, shall be included with the electoral district of such city as may be provided by law.

ART. 58. The number of representatives in the Storthing to be elected by the country districts is fixed at eighty-two. Of these, five shall be chosen from the county of Akerhus, five from the county of North Bergenhus, six from the county of South Bergenhus, four from the county of Bratsberg, four from the county of Buskerud, two from the county of Finmarken, six from the County of Hedemarken, four from the county of Jarlsberg and Larvik, five from the county of Christian, four from the county of Lister and Mandal, four from the county of Nedenes, six from the county of Nordland, five from the county of Romsdal, five from the county of Smaalenene, five from the county of Stavanger, three from the county of Tromsö, four from the county of North Trondhjem, five from the county of South Trondhjem.

ART. 59. Each district, for which several representatives to the Storthing are to be elected, shall be divided into as many election districts as there are representatives to be elected. These divisions and the rules for the electoral procedure shall be determined by law. The following rules shall be observed in addition to the other provisions of the constitution with respect to this matter:

a) Each city, and in the country districts each parish, and each small seaport town with separate municipal government, shall form a separate voting precinct. If a city contains two or more election districts, each district shall form a separate

voting precinct. Likewise shall a part of a city form a separate
voting precinct, when united with another city or cities into
one election district. As regards country districts the election
districts shall be composed of the same or of adjacent voting
precincts. A change in the division of an electoral district
which is not rendered necessary by changes in the general
administrative divisions of the kingdom, shall not apply to the
first general election of representatives to the Storthing held
after such change has been made.

b) The electoral assemblies shall be held separately in each
voting precinct. A representative of the election district in the
Storthing and a substitute shall be voted for directly by the
electoral assemblies. If, in the election of the representative,
no one receives more than half of all the votes cast and found
valid in the election district, a new election shall be held in
which a plurality shall suffice for election; in case of a tie
a decision shall be reached by lot.[3]

ART. 60. The qualified voters within the kingdom who
are not able to be present because of illness, military service,
or for other lawful reason, may send their votes in writing
to the officers of the electoral assembly before the voting is
finished.

How far and in what manner qualified voters sojourning
outside of the kingdom may be allowed to send their votes in
writing to the officers of the electoral assembly, shall be determined by law.

ART. 61. No one shall be elected a representative unless
he is thirty years of age, has resided ten years in the kingdom,
and is a qualified voter in the election district for which he
is chosen.

However, anyone who has been minister of state or
councilor of state may be elected a representative in an election

[3] The direct election of members of the Storthing was first introduced
by an amendment of May 25, 1905, which amended Arts. 54–61, 63, and 64
of the constitution.

district of which he is not a qualified voter, provided he is otherwise eligible.

ART. 62. Members of the Council of State, officers employed in the departments of the government, officers and pensioners of the Court shall not be eligible as representatives.

ART. 63. Everyone who is elected a representative shall be bound to accept the election, unless he is elected under the terms of the second paragraph of Art. 61, or is prevented by reasons which the Storthing considers lawful. Anyone who has served as representative in the three regular sessions of the Storthing after one election, shall not be bound to accept election to the succeeding Storthing.

If a person is elected a representative without being obliged to accept such election, he shall declare, in the time and manner provided by law, whether or not he accepts such election.

It shall also be provided by law, within what time and in what manner a person elected for two or more constituencies within the district of which he is a qualified voter, shall declare which election he will accept.

ART. 64. The elected representative shall be furnished with a certificate of election, the validity of which shall be determined by the Storthing.

ART. 65. Each representative shall be entitled to compensation from the treasury of the state for traveling expenses to and from the Storthing and for subsistence during the time of his attendance.

ART. 66. Except when apprehended in the commission of an open offense, representatives shall be privileged from arrest during their attendance at the Storthing and in going to and returning from the same; and they shall not be held responsible outside of the Storthing for opinions expressed therein. Every representative is bound to conform to the established rules of procedure.

ART. 67. The representatives elected in the manner aforesaid shall constitute the Storthing of the kingdom of Norway.

Art. 68. The Storthing shall, as a rule, assemble on the first week day after the tenth of October of each year, at the capital of the kingdom, unless the King, on account of extraordinary circumstances, such as hostile invasion or contagious disease, shall designate another city of the kingdom for the purpose. Such designation shall then be publicly announced in time.

Art. 69. In extraordinary cases the King may convene the Storthing at another than the usual time. In such a case the King shall issue a proclamation, which shall be read in all the churches of the episcopal towns at least fourteen days before the members of the Storthing are to assemble at the appointed place.

Art. 70. Such extraordinary session of the Storthing may be adjourned by the King whenever he thinks proper.

Art. 71. The members of the Storthing shall serve as such for three successive years, in all extraordinary and regular sessions of the Storthing which are held during that time.

Art. 72. If the Storthing is in extraordinary session at the time when the regular session should commence, the extraordinary session shall be adjourned before the regular session begins.

Art. 73. The Storthing shall select one-fourth part of its members to constitute the Lagthing; the remaining three-fourths shall form the Odelsthing. This selection shall take place at the first regular session of the Storthing which convenes after a new election, and thereafter the Lagthing shall remain unchanged for all sessions of the Storthing assembled after the same election, except that vacancies occurring among its members shall be filled by special selection.

Each house shall hold its meetings separately and elect its own president and secretary. Neither house shall hold meetings unless two-thirds of its members are present.

Art. 74. As soon as the Storthing is organized, the King,

or the one appointed by him for the purpose, shall open its proceedings with a speech, in which he shall give information regarding the conditions of the kingdom and concerning matters to which he particularly desires to direct the attention of the Storthing. No deliberations shall take place in the presence of the King.

When the proceedings of the Storthing are opened the Minister of State and the councilors of state shall have the right to attend in the Storthing and in both branches thereof, and upon an equality with its members but without vote, to take part in the proceedings, in so far as they are conducted publicly, but in secret sessions, only so far as the body in question may grant permission.

ART. 75.   The Storthing shall have power:

a) To enact and to repeal laws; to impose taxes, imposts, duties, and other public burdens, which, however, shall not remain in force beyond the first day of April of the year after the one in which a new regular session of the Storthing has met, unless they are expressly renewed in such session.

b) To borrow money on the credit of the kingdom.

c) To regulate the currency of the kingdom.

d) To appropriate the money necessary to meet the expenditures of the state.

e) To determine the amount which shall annually be paid to the King for the maintenance of his royal household, and to settle the appanage of the royal family, which shall not, however, consist of real property.

f) To have laid before it the minutes of the Council of State and all public reports and papers (exclusive of those relating particularly to matters of military command).

g) To have submitted to it the alliances and treaties which the King has entered into with foreign powers on behalf of the state, except secret articles, which shall not, however, conflict with those that are public.

h) To summon before it, upon public affairs, anyone

except the King and the royal family; this exception, however, shall not apply to royal princes if they hold office.

i) To revise temporary salary and pension lists, and to make such changes therein as it considers necessary.

k) To appoint five auditors who shall annually audit the accounts of the state, and issue printed abstracts thereof; for this purpose such accounts shall be submitted to the auditors within six months after the expiration of the year for which the appropriations of the Storthing were made.

l) To naturalize foreigners.

ART. 76. Every bill shall be first presented in the Odels-thing, either by one of its members or by the government, through a councilor of state. If adopted in that house the bill shall be sent to the Lagthing which may either approve or reject it, and in the latter case shall return it with objections. Such objections shall be considered by the Odelsthing, which may either drop the bill or send it again to the Lagthing with or without alteration. When a bill from the Odelsthing has been twice presented to the Lagthing and has been a second time rejected, the entire Storthing shall meet and act upon the bill by a two-thirds vote. Three days at least shall intervene between each such deliberation.

ART. 77. When a measure passed by the Odelsthing is approved by the Lagthing or by the united Storthing it shall be sent to the King with a request for his approval.

ART. 78. If the King approves the measure he shall affix his signature thereto, whereby it becomes law.

If he does not assent to it he shall return it to the Odels-thing with a statement that he does not at the time think proper to approve it. In this case the measure shall not again be submitted to the King by the Storthing then in session.

ART. 79. If a measure has been passed without change by three regular Storthings convened after three separate successive elections, and separated from each other by at least two intervening regular sessions, without any conflicting action having in the meantime been taken in any session between its first and last passage, and is then presented to the King with the request that his majesty will not refuse his approval to a measure which the Storthing, after the most mature deliberation, considers beneficial, such measure shall become law even though the King fails to approve it before the adjournment of the Storthing.

ART. 80. The Storthing shall remain in session as long as it considers proper, but not beyond two months without the King's consent. When, having finished its business or having been in session for the appointed time, it is adjourned by the King, he shall signify his action upon the measures not already disposed of, either by approving or rejecting them. All measures which he does not expressly approve shall be considered rejected.

ART. 81. All laws shall be promulgated in the Norwegian language and (with the exception of those referred to in Art. 79) in the King's name, under the seal of the kingdom of Norway, and in the following terms: "We, N. N., make it publicly known that the following act of the Storthing of such a date has been presented to us in the following terms: (here follows the act), which act we have assented to and approved and do hereby assent to and approve as law, under our hand and the seal of the state."

ART. 82. The approval of the King is not required for resolutions of the Storthing, by which:

a) It declares itself assembled as Storthing, in accordance with the constitution.

b) It determines its own rules of procedure.

c) It approves or rejects the credentials of the members present.

d) It affirms or reverses decisions in election controversies.

e) It naturalizes foreigners.

f) And finally, the action by which the Odelsthing impeaches councilors of state or others.

ART. 83. The Storthing may procure the opinion of the Supreme Court upon questions of law.

ART. 84. The Storthing shall sit in public session, and its proceedings shall be printed and published, except in the cases where a majority decides to the contrary.

ART. 85. Whoever obeys an order the purpose of which is to disturb the liberty and safety of the Storthing, is thereby guilty of treason against his country.

D. THE JUDICIAL POWER

ART. 86. The members of the Lagthing together with the Supreme Court shall constitute the Court of Impeachment (Rigsret), which shall try, without appeal, cases instituted by the Odelsthing against members of the Council of State or of the Supreme Court for misconduct in office, or against members of the Storthing for offenses committed by them in their official capacity.

The president of the Lagthing shall preside in the Court of Impeachment.

ART. 87. The accused may, without assigning any reason therefor, challenge as many as one-third of the members of the Court of Impeachment, provided however, that the court shall not consist of less than fifteen persons.

ART. 88. The Supreme Court shall be the court of last resort. It shall consist of not less than one chief justice and six associates.

This article shall not prevent the final disposal of criminal cases, in accordance with law, without the co-operation of the Supreme Court.

ART. 89. In time of peace the Supreme Court, with two military officers of high rank designated by the King, shall be a court of appeal and of last instance in all military cases which involve life, honor, or loss of liberty for a longer period than three months.

ART. 90.   The decisions of the Supreme Court shall in no case be appealed or reviewed.

ART. 91.   No one shall become a member of the Supreme Court before he is thirty years of age.

E.   GENERAL PROVISIONS

ART. 92.   Public offices of the state shall only be filled by Norwegian citizens, who speak the language of the country and:

a) Were either born in the kingdom of parents who were then subjects of the state;

b) Or were born in a foreign country of Norwegian parents, who at the time were not subjects of another state;

c) Or shall hereafter reside ten years in the kingdom;

d) Or are naturalized by the Storthing.

Others, however, may be appointed as teachers in the University and colleges, as physicians, and as consuls in foreign places.

No one shall be appointed as chief magistrate[4] before he is thirty years of age, or as magistrate, inferior judge, or sheriff, before he is twenty-five years of age.

Only those who profess the public religion of the state may be members of the Council of State. As to the other officers of the state, the necessary rules shall be established by law.

It shall be determined by law to what extent women, who fulfil the requirements prescribed for men by the constitution, may be appointed to public offices.

ART. 94.   Steps shall be taken to enact a new civil and criminal code of general application, at the first, and if this is not possible, at the second regular session of the Storthing. In the meantime the existing laws of the state shall remain in force in so far as they are not in conflict with this constitution or with the provisional ordinances which may be issued in the meantime.

[4] The leading administrative officer of the county.

The existing permanent taxes shall likewise continue until the next session of the Storthing.

ART. 95. No dispensations, writs of protection, or letters of respite or reparation shall be granted after the new general code takes effect.

ART. 96. No one shall be tried except in accordance with law or punished except by virtue of a judicial sentence. Examination by means of torture is forbidden.

ART. 97. No law shall have retroactive effect.

ART. 98. Fees paid to officers of the courts of justice shall not be subject to any tax.

ART. 99. No one shall be arrested except in the cases and in the manner provided by law. Whoever causes unjustifiable arrest or illegal detention shall be responsible to the person arrested.

The government shall have no right to employ military force against citizens of the state, except in accordance with the forms provided by law, unless an assembly should disturb the public peace and not immediately disperse after the civil magistrate has three times read aloud to it the articles of the law relating to riots.

ART. 100. There shall be liberty of the press. No one shall be punished for any writing which he has caused to be printed or published, whatever its contents may be, unless he has intentionally or clearly shown or incited others to show disobedience of the laws, contempt of religion or morality, or of the constitutional authorities or resistance to their orders, or has made false and defamatory charges against any person. Everyone shall be at liberty freely to express his opinions concerning the administration of public affairs or upon any other subject.

ART. 101. No new and permanent privileges placing restrictions upon the freedom of industry shall hereafter be granted to anyone.

ART. 102.   Searches of houses shall not be made except in criminal cases.

ART. 103.   Immunity shall not be granted to those who hereafter become bankrupt.

ART. 104.   Real and personal property shall in no case be confiscated.

ART. 105.   If the welfare of the state requires that any person be deprived of his real or personal property for a public purpose, he shall receive full compensation from the public treasury.

ART. 106.   The proceeds and income of church estates shall be devoted exclusively to the benefit of the clergy and the promotion of education.   The property of charitable institutions shall be devoted exclusively to their own use.

ART. 107.   The Odel[5] and Aasaede[6] rights shall not be abolished.   The specific conditions under which these rights shall continue, to the greatest benefit of the state and of the country population, shall be determined by the next or the next following session of the Storthing.

ART. 108.   No earldoms, baronies, entails, or trusts in real property shall hereafter be established.

ART. 109.   Every citizen of the state, without regard to birth or fortune, shall be equally bound to render military service to his country for a limited time.   The application of this principle, the limitations to be placed upon it, and the determination of whether it will be for the good of the country that liability to military service shall terminate at the age of twenty-five years, shall be left to the decision of the first regular session of the Storthing, after a committee has gathered full information.   In the meantime the existing regulations shall remain in force.

---

[5] Odelsret is the right of a family to redeem property within a certain time after it has been sold.

[6] Aasaedesret is the right of the eldest son to acquire possession of the estate at a moderate price.

ART. 110. Norway retains its own bank and its own currency and coinage, and these institutions shall be established by law.

ART. 111. The form and colors of the Norwegian flag shall be established by law.

ART. 112. If experience should show that any part of the constitution of the kingdom of Norway ought to be altered, the proposed amendment shall be presented in one of the regular sessions of the Storthing after a new election, and published in the press. But it is only within the power of the Storthing at one of its regular sessions after the next election to decide whether the proposed change shall or shall not be made. However, such an amendment shall never contravene the principles of this constitution, but shall only relate to such modifications in particular provisions as will not change the spirit of this constitution, and the alteration must be concurred in by two-thirds of the Storthing.

PORTUGAL

The Portuguese royal family took refuge in Brazil in 1807, when Portugal was invaded by French troops. King John VI remained in Brazil until 1821 when he was called home by the Portuguese insurrection which had broken out in the previous year. The revolutionary forces were in control of the country and John assented to a liberal constitution which was promulgated on September 23, 1822. This constitution was of short duration; the absolutist party soon gained the ascendency and in 1824 it was withdrawn.

Upon the death of John VI the Portuguese crown passed to his son, Dom Pedro, emperor of Brazil. Dom Pedro issued the constitutional charter of April 29, 1826, and abdicated in favor of his daughter. The regent, Miguel, seized the throne in 1828, and from that date until 1834, when the queen was restored, the government was conducted without reference to constitutional forms.

The charter of 1826 was restored in 1834. A popular uprising took place in 1836 in favor of the more liberal constitution of 1822, which was declared in force until a new constitution should be adopted. The new constitution was issued on April 4, 1838. Direct elections were introduced, the moderative power disappeared, and in place of the House of Peers an elected Senate was established.

A counter-revolution of 1842 restored the charter of 1826 which has continued in force since that date and has been amended in 1852, 1885, and 1896. The most important amendment to the charter was that of 1852 establishing direct elections for the House of Deputies.

The Portuguese constitution is a close copy of English institutions. However, parliamentary government has never been very successful, and for a number of years financial and administrative mismanagement has reduced the country almost to a condition of bankruptcy. A strong man came to the presidency of the Council in May, 1907, and proposed to carry through a number of much-needed reforms. The Cortes refused to sanction these measures and was dissolved; from May, 1907, to April, 1908, the country was governed by a dictator, without the participation of the Cortes. During this time the king by decrees altered the local administration of the country and changed the provision of the constitution which relates to the appointment of life peers. A change of ministry was brought about by the assassination of the king and crown prince on February 1, 1908, and one of the first acts of the new ministry was to withdraw the decrees of the dictatorial government. Members of a new Cortes were elected on April 5, 1908. With the new ministry all of the reforms of the dictatorship came to an end.

SELECT BIBLIOGRAPHY

PORTUGAL. *Carta constitucional da Monarchia Portugueza . . . . e diplomas correlativos.* (Lisboa, 1890.)

PORTUGAL. *Codigo administrativo approvado por carta de lei de 4 de Maio de 1896.* (Lisboa, 1904.)

TAVARES DE MEDEIROS, J. J. *Das Staatsrecht des Königreichs Portugal.* (Freiburg, 1892. Handbuch des oeffentlichen Rechts.)

CONSTITUTIONAL CHARTER OF PORTUGAL

(April 29, 1826)

TITLE I. THE KINGDOM OF PORTUGAL, ITS TERRITORY, GOVERNMENT, DYNASTY, AND RELIGION

ARTICLE 1. The Kingdom of Portugal is the political association of all the Portuguese citizens. They form a free and independent nation.

ART. 2. The territory of the Kingdom of Portugal and of Algarves comprises:

1) In Europe, the Kingdom of Portugal, which is composed of the provinces of Minho, Traz-os-Montes, Beira, Estremadura, Além-Tejo, the Kingdom of Algarve, and the adjacent islands of Madeira, Porto Santo, and the Azores.

2) In West Africa, Bissau and Cacheu; the Costa da Mina, the fort of S. João Baptista de Ajudá, Angola, Benguela and its dependencies, Cabinda, Molembo, the Cape Verde Islands and the islands of S. Thomé and Principe and their dependen-

cies; on the East Coast, Moçambique, Rio de Senna, Sofalla, Inhambane, Quelimane, and the Islands of Cape Delgado.

3) In Asia, Salsette, Bardez, Goa, Damão, Diu, the settlements of Macao, and the islands of Solor and Timôr.

ART. 3. The nation does not renounce rights which it may have in any portion of territory in the three parts of the world, not included in the preceding article.

ART. 4. The government of the nation is monarchical, hereditary, representative.

ART. 5. The reigning dynasty shall continue to be that of the house of Braganza, in the person of the princess Dona Maria da Gloria, in consequence of the abdication and cession of her august father, Dom Pedro I, emperor of Brazil, the legitimate heir and successor of Dom João VI.

ART. 6. The Apostolic Roman Catholic religion shall continue to be the religion of the kingdom. All other religions shall be permitted to foreigners, who may hold domestic or private services in houses intended for that purpose; such houses shall not have the external appearance of churches.

TITLE II. PORTUGUESE CITIZENS

ART. 7. The following are Portuguese citizens:

1) Those born in Portuguese territory or its dominions, and who are not now Brazilian citizens, even though the father may have been a foreigner, provided he did not reside in Portugal in the service of his country.

2) Children of a Portuguese father or the illegitimate children of a Portuguese mother, born in a foreign country, if they should establish their residence within the kingdom.

3) The children of a Portuguese father who is in a foreign country in the service of the kingdom, even though they have not established a residence within the kingdom.

4) Naturalized foreigners, whatever may be their religion. A law shall determine what conditions are necessary in order to obtain naturalization papers.

ART. 8. The rights of Portuguese citizenship are lost:

1) By naturalization in a foreign country.

2) By accepting office, pension, or decoration from any foreign government, without the permission of the King.

3) By banishment under sentence.

ART. 9. The exercise of political rights is suspended:

1) For physical or moral incapacity.

2) By sentence condemning to prison or degradation, as long as the effects of such sentence may last.

TITLE III. THE POWERS AND THE NATIONAL REPRESENTATION

ART. 10. The division and harmony of the public powers is a principle necessary for the maintenance of the rights of the citizens, and is the surest means of making effective the guaranties contained in this constitution.

ART. 11. The public powers recognized by the constitution of the Kingdom of Portugal are four: the legislative power, the moderative power, the executive power, and the judicial power.

ART. 12. The representatives of the Portuguese nation shall be the King and the General Cortes.

TITLE IV. THE LEGISLATIVE POWER

CHAPTER I. THE DIVISIONS OF THE LEGISLATIVE POWER AND THEIR POWERS

ART. 13. The legislative power shall belong to the Cortes, with the approval of the King.

ART. 14. The Cortes shall be composed of two houses: The House of Peers and the House of Deputies.

[The peers and deputies shall represent the nation, and not the King who may appoint them, nor the bodies or districts which may elect them.[1]]

[The constitution does not recognize instructions binding upon peers or deputies.[1]]

[1] Amendment of July 24, 1885.

Art. 15. The Cortes shall have the following powers:

1) To receive the oath of the King, Prince royal, regent, or regency.

2) The Cortes shall have power to recognize the regent, to elect the regency of the kingdom in the cases provided by Art. 93 of the constitution, and to define the limits of the regency's power.

The provisions of this article shall in no way alter those established by the law of April 7, 1846, in dispensation of Arts. 92 and 93 of the constitutional charter of the Monarchy.[2]

3) To recognize the Prince royal as the successor to the throne, in the first session immediately following his birth.

4) To name the guardian of the minor King, in case his father did not name a guardian in his will.

5) Upon the death of the King or the vacancy of the throne, to conduct an examination of the administration which had ended, and to reform the abuses introduced by it.

6) To make, interpret, suspend, and repeal laws.

7) To see that the constitution is observed, and to promote the general welfare of the nation.

8) To determine annually the public expenses and to levy the direct taxes.

9) To permit or to prohibit the entrance of foreign land or naval forces into the kingdom or into its ports.

10) To determine annually, upon the information of the government, the ordinary and extraordinary land and naval forces.

11) To authorize the government to contract loans.

12) To establish suitable means for the payment of the public debt.

13) To regulate the administration and sale of state property.

[2] As amended by Art. 1 of additional act of July 5, 1852.

14) To create or suppress public offices and to establish the salaries thereof.

15) To determine the weight, value, inscription, type. and denomination of money, and the standard of weights and measures.

ART. 16.   The members of the House of Peers shall have the title Worthy Peers of the Kingdom, and the members of the House of Deputies, Messieurs Deputies of the Portuguese Nation.

ART. 17.   Each legislature shall continue three years and each annual session shall last three months.[8]

[No session lasting less than three months shall be taken into account with reference to the duration of the legislature unless there should be another session during the same year which lasts a sufficient time to complete the three months.[8]]

ART. 18.   The King shall open the session every year on the second day of January.

ART. 19.   The King shall also close the session; the opening and closing ceremonies shall take place in the General Cortes, with the houses in joint session, the peers sitting on the right and the deputies on the left.

ART. 20.   The forms to be observed on these occasions and upon receiving royal communications shall be established by regulations of the houses.

ART. 21.   The King shall appoint the president and vice-president of the House of Peers; the president and vice-president of the House of Deputies shall be chosen by the King from a list of five members presented by that house; each house shall adopt its own rules regarding the choice of its secretaries, the determination of the qualifications of its members, their oaths, and regarding its rules of procedure.

ART. 22.   In a joint session of the two houses, the president of the House of Peers shall preside; the members of the

[8] As amended July 24, 1885..

two houses shall occupy the same positions as at the opening of the Cortes.

ART. 23. The sessions of both houses shall be public except in the cases when the welfare of the state requires that they be secret.

ART. 24. Business shall be transacted by majority of votes of the members present.

ART. 25. The members of the two houses shall be inviolable for opinions which they may express in the discharge of their duties.

ART. 26. No life peer or deputy, from the time of their being declared such in their respective houses, shall be arrested by any authority whatever, except by the order of their respective houses, unless they be taken in the commission of an act punished by the heaviest penalty.

This provision shall likewise apply to temporary peers from the time of their election until the end of their term of office.[4]

ART. 27. Should any peer or deputy be accused of or indicted for an offense, the judge, suspending all further proceedings, shall report the matter to the proper house, which shall decide whether the peer or deputy should be suspended, or whether the judicial proceedings shall continue during the recess of the houses or only after the end of the term of office of the accused.[5]

ART. 28. Peers or deputies may be appointed to the offices of minister of state or councilor of state, without thereby forfeiting their seats in their respective houses, and may perform the duties of the two offices at the same time.[6]

[The deputy who, after his election, accepts honorary reward, remunerative employment, or a salaried commission, the appointment to which depends upon the free choice of the

[4] As amended, July 24, 1885. Altered by amendment of Art. 39, of April 3, 1896, which abolishes elective peerages.

[5] As amended July 24, 1885.

[6] As amended July 24, 1885.

government, shall lose his place as deputy; and, for his re-election, shall be subject to the conditions which regulate the eligibility of public officers, according to the provisions of Art. 9 of the present additional act.[7]]

[No one shall lose the position of deputy who leaves the house in conformity with article 33 of the charter.[7]]

ART. 29. He may likewise hold the two offices if he held one of them when elected.

ART. 30. No one shall be a member of both houses at the same time.

ART. 31. The exercise of any office other than those of councilor of state and minister of state shall cease during the term of its occupant as peer or deputy.

[In case of urgent necessity of the public service either house may, upon the request of the government, permit any of its members, who hold a public office in the capital, to perform the duties of such office in addition to their legislative functions.[8]]

ART. 32. In the interval of the sessions the King shall not employ a deputy beyond the kingdom, nor shall a deputy exercise any office which would make it impossible for him to be present at the time of a regular or extraordinary session of the General Cortes.

ART. 33. If, in an unforeseen case, the public security or the good of the state should make it necessary that a deputy be employed upon some other function, the House itself shall have power to decide the matter.

CHAPTER II.   THE HOUSE OF DEPUTIES

ART. 34. The House of Deputies shall be elective and temporary.

[7] Added by Art. 2 of additional act of July 5, 1852. Arts. 4–9 of the additional act are inserted after Art. 62.

[8] Added by Art. 3 of additional act of July 5, 1852. This addition also amends Art. 33.

ART. 35. The House of Deputies alone shall have the initiative:

1) Concerning taxes.

2) Concerning the recruiting the troops.

ART. 36. The House of Deputies shall also take the initiative:

1) In the examination of an administration that has ended, and in the reform of abuses introduced by it.[9]

2) In the discussion of propositions submitted by the executive power.

ART. 37. The House of Deputies shall have the exclusive power to impeach ministers of state and councilors of state.

ART. 38. During the sessions the deputies shall receive a pecuniary compensation, fixed at the end of the last session of the preceding legislature. In addition to this, they may be reimbursed for the expenses of going to and returning from the sessions.

CHAPTER III. THE HOUSE OF PEERS

[ARTICLE 1. Besides the peers in their own right mentioned in Art. 40 of the constitutional charter and in sec. 2 of Art. 6 of the law of July 24, 1885, the House of Peers shall be composed of life peers, not exceeding ninety in number, appointed by the King.]

[Sec. 1. Actual peers of the kingdom by hereditary right and, by the same title, those who are comprised within the provisions of sec. 7 of Art. 6 of the law of July 24, 1885, shall continue to form part of the House of Peers.]

[Sec. 2. Within the number of ninety peers of the kingdom fixed by the present article shall be included the present peers of royal appointment, but not the peers by hereditary right.]

[ART. 2. Citizens who are less than forty years of age or who are absolutely ineligible to the House of Deputies shall not be appointed peers of the kingdom.]

[9] Amended by Art. 14 of the additional act of July 5, 1852. See Art. 139.

[Sec. 1. The following are not included in the preceding part of this article:

1) Heads of diplomatic missions.

2) Royal commissaries in the provinces beyond the sea, and the governors of such provinces.

3) The higher employees of the royal household.]

[Sec. 2. The appointment of a peer of the kingdom shall be officially communicated to the House of Peers, and upon the proposition of any of its members may be objected to, upon the sole basis of a violation of this article, within a period of five days after the communication, such objection to be acted upon by the House within a period of ten days after its presentation.]

[Sec. 3. In default of objection or of action thereon in the manner and time provided by the preceding paragraph, the president of the House of Peers shall admit the appointee to take the oath and to a seat in the House.]

[Art. 3. Peers of the kingdom who at present or in the future occupy places in the administrative councils, directorates, or offices of enterprises or companies organized by contract or special concession from the state, or which have a privilege from the state not conferred by general law, subsidy, or guaranty of income, except those who by the delegation of the government represent the interests of the state in such enterprises or companies, and peers of the kingdom who are concessionaries, bidders, or contractors of public works are forbidden to exercise the rights of the peerage, nor may they be permitted to take part in the discussions or to vote unless they prove that the occasion of such incompatibility has ceased.]

[The violation of this article shall be punished by the suspension of political rights for three years, and shall render void all acts in which the offending peer took part, either alone or with others, in the service of such companies, enterprises, concessions, bids, or contracts.]

ART. 6. Sec. 1. The peers of the kingdom who are members of the House of Peers at the time of the publication of this law shall continue to sit therein as life peers.

Sec. 2. The Patriarch of Lisbon and the archbishops and bishops of the continental territory of the kingdom shall likewise have seats in the House of Peers, as life members.

Sec. 7. The next heirs of deceased peers and of peers living at the date of the publication of this law are entitled to sit in the House of Peers by virtue of their hereditary right, provided they comply with the provisions of the law of May 3, 1878. This provision does not in any way alter that contained in sec. 4 of this article.[10]

ART. 40. The Prince royal and the Infants shall be peers by right, and shall take their seats as soon as they attain the age of twenty-five years.

ART. 41. The House of Peers shall have the exclusive power:

1) To take cognizance of personal offenses committed by members of the royal family, ministers of state, councilors of state, and peers, and of the offenses of deputies during the period of the legislature.

2) To take cognizance of matters involving the responsibility of secretaries and of councilors of state.

3) Upon the death of the King, to convene the Cortes for the election of a regency, when a regency is to be elected; if the provisional regency does not convene the Cortes.

ART. 42. In the trial of crimes, where the power of impeachment does not belong to the House of Deputies, the

[10] Fifty elective peerages were established on July 24, 1885, but were abolished by Arts. 1-3 of the constitutional amendment of April 3, 1896, which are inserted above. Art. 39 of the constitution is now composed entirely of provisions introduced in 1885 and 1896. Persons who were peers in 1885 and their immediate successors continue to be members of the House of Peers by virtue of their hereditary right, but upon the death of such members the House of Peers will be composed entirely of life peers appointed by the king, of the clerical peers mentioned above, and of the peers indicated in Art. 40.

accusation shall be made by the attorney-general of the crown.

ART. 43.   The sessions of the House of Peers shall begin and end at the same time as those of the House of Deputies.

ART. 44.   Every meeting of the House of Peers at a time when the House of Deputies is not in session is illegal and void, except in the cases provided by the constitution.

CHAPTER IV.   THE INITIATION, DISCUSSION, APPROVAL, AND
PROMULGATION OF LAWS

ART. 45.   Each house shall have the right to initiate, reject, or approve bills.

ART. 46.   The initiative of the executive power in the preparation of laws may be exercised by any of the ministers of state; their proposals shall not be converted into bills until after they have been examined by a committee of the House of Deputies, to which such proposals shall be first submitted.

ART. 47.   The ministers may attend and discuss their proposals, after the report of the committee, but they shall not vote or be present when the vote is taken, unless they are peers or deputies.

[The ministers may appoint, from among the superior officers of the administration of the state, special delegates to take part in the discussion of specified projects of law before the legislative houses.]

[Such appointment shall be communicated to the president of the proper house, in which the delegate shall have a seat during the discussion of the project for which he is designated.[11]]

ART. 48.   If the House of Deputies adopts the proposals it shall send them to the Peers with the following message: "The House of Deputies sends to the House of Peers the attached proposals of the executive power (with or without amendments), and thinks that they should be adopted."

ART. 49.   If the House of Deputies does not adopt the

[11] Added by amendment of April 3, 1896.

proposals it shall inform the King, by a deputation of seven members, in the following manner: "The House of Deputies expresses to the King its recognition of the zeal which he displays in guarding the interests of the kingdom, and respectfully requests that he be pleased to take under further consideration the proposals of the government."

ART. 50. In general the proposals which the House of Deputies considers and approves shall be sent to the House of Peers with the following message: "The House of Deputies sends to the House of Peers the attached proposition, and thinks that it should be forwarded to the King for his approval."

ART. 51. If, however, the House of Peers does not adopt in full the bill submitted by the House of Deputies, but alters or amends it, the bill shall be returned in the following manner: "The House of Peers sends to the House of Deputies its proposition as amended, and thinks that with such amendments it should be presented to the King for royal approval."

ART. 52. If the House of Peers, after consideration, should decide that it cannot approve the proposition or bill, it shall use the folowing terms: "The House of Peers returns to the House of Deputies the proposition to which it cannot give its consent."

ART. 53. The House of Deputies shall follow the same practice with the House of Peers when it does not agree to a bill which originated in that house.

ART. 54. When either of the legislative houses does not approve, in whole or in part, any project of law emanating from the other house, or does not approve amendments made by the other house of any project of law, a committee of an equal number of peers and deputies shall be appointed when either house proposes it, and such committee shall decide by a majority vote whether the project shall be immediately reduced into a decree of the General Cortes or whether it shall be rejected.[12]

[Sec. 1. Should there be a tie in the voting upon a project, upon any of its articles, or upon any of its amendments, or when the committee has not reached any result concerning the matter submitted to it, either house may request a joint session of the General Cortes, presenting such request to the moderative power.[12]]

[Sec. 2. The General Cortes shall be convened and shall assemble in joint session within thirty days, in the hall of the House of Deputies, under the direction of the president of the House of Peers, the first secretaries of the two houses acting as secretaries.[12]]

[Sec. 3. If on the day for the meeting of the General Cortes a majority of the members of each house does not assemble, the session shall be adjourned to the next working day, when action shall be taken, no matter what may be the number of peers and deputies who appear. The object of the disagreement shall be voted upon without discussion.[12]]

ART. 55. If either of the two houses, after the conclusion of its discussion, adopts in full the bill submitted to it by the other house, such bill shall be changed into the form of a decree, and after being read in the session, it shall be forwarded to the King in duplicate signed by the president and two secretaries. The King's approval shall be requested in the following form: "The General Cortes forwards to the King the inclosed decree, which it thinks advantageous and beneficial to the kingdom, and requests that His Majesty may be pleased to give it his approval."

ART. 56. This message shall be sent by a deputation of seven members from the house having the bill under final consideration; this house shall, at the same time, notify the other house in which the bill originated that the measure has been adopted and forwarded to the King for his approval.

ART. 57. If the King withholds his consent, he shall

[12] As amended April 13, 1896.

reply in the following terms: "The King wishes to consider the bill in order to decide upon it in his own time." To this the House shall reply: "It returns thanks to His Majesty for the interest which he takes in the nation."

ART. 58. This disapproval shall be final.

ART. 59. The King shall give or refuse his approval to every decree, within a month after it is presented to him.

ART. 60. If the King approves the bill of the General Cortes he shall speak thus, "The King consents." As soon as it has been approved the bill is in form for promulgation as a law of the kingdom. One of the two autograph copies, after being signed by the King, shall be sent to the archives of the house from which it was forwarded; the other copy shall be used by the proper secretary of state in promulgating the law, and shall then be deposited in the public archives.

ART. 61. The promulgation of the law shall be made in the following terms: "D. (F.), by the grace of God, King of Portugal and of Algarves, etc. We make known to all our subjects that the General Cortes enacts and that we approve the following law (full text of the law in the language of the enactment). We command, therefore, all authorities who should know and execute this law, that they comply and make others comply with all of its provisions. The secretary of state for the affairs of . . . . (the competent department) shall print, publish, and distribute this law."

ART. 62. When the law is signed by the King and countersigned by the proper secretary of state, and sealed with the royal seal, the original shall be preserved among the public archives, and printed copies shall be sent to all legislative bodies of the kingdom, to the courts, and to other places where it may be proper that the law be made public.

CHAPTER V. THE ELECTIONS [13]

ART. 4. Deputies shall be chosen by direct election.

ART. 5. Every Portuguese citizen in the enjoyment of

[13] Chap. v (Arts. 63 to 70) was displaced by Arts. 4 to 9 of the additional act of July 5, 1852, which are here inserted. By the original provisions of

his civil and political rights shall be an elector, provided that
he show:

I. That he has a clear annual income of one hundred
milreis, derived from real property, capital, commerce, industry, or permanent employment.

II. That he has attained his legal majority.

Persons of twenty-one belonging to either of the following classes shall be considered as of age:

1) Priests of the sacred orders.

2) Married men.

3) Officers of the army and navy.

4) Possessors of literary titles, in conformity with law.
Possessors of literary titles shall not be required to make any
proof of their income.

ART. 6.   The following shall be excluded from voting:

1) Servants, exclusive of bookkeepers and clerks in commercial houses, of servants of the royal house who are not of
the white lace, and of managers of farms and factories.

2) Persons who are not allowed the administration of their
property and those charged with crime or under trial.

3) Freed slaves.

ART. 7.   All persons having the right to vote may also be
elected as deputies, without conditions as to permanent or
temporary residence, or place of birth.

The following are excepted:

1) Naturalized foreigners.

2) Those who do not have a clear annual income of four
hundred milreis derived from the sources enumerated in Art.
5 of the present additional act, or who do not possess the

the constitution deputies were elected indirectly by provincial electors chosen
in parochial assemblies. The election of deputies is now further regulated
by the law of August 8, 1901. A system of minority or proportional representation prevails. In each circle which elects more than one deputy, each person votes for one or two less than the number to be chosen; e. g., in the
eastern circle of Lisbon seven deputies are chosen, but each person votes
for only five candidates.

qualifications and literary titles referred to in the second clause of that article.

ART. 8. Those who do not have the right to vote in the election of deputies shall not have the right to vote in the elections of any other public officers.

ART. 9. The electoral law shall determine:

1) The electoral procedure, and the number of deputies to be apportioned to the population of the kingdom.

2) The offices which are incompatible with the position of deputy.

3) The cases in which, by reason of the exercise of public functions, certain citizens shall respectively be ineligible.

4) The manner and form in which proof of income may be made in the various continental provinces of the kingdom, in the adjacent islands, and beyond the seas.

5) The literary titles which supplement age and which relieve from proof of income.

TITLE V. THE KING

CHAPTES I. THE MODERATIVE POWER

ART. 71. The moderative power is the keystone of the whole political organization and shall belong exclusively to the King as the supreme head of the nation, for he constantly watches over the maintenance of the independence, equilibrium, and harmony of the other public powers.

ART. 72. The person of the King is sacred and inviolable. He shall be subject to no responsibility whatever.

ART. 73. His titles are: King of Portugal, and of Algarves on both sides of the sea, in Africa, Lord of Guinea, and of the conquest, navigation, and commerce of Ethiopia, Arabia, Persia, and India, etc. He shall be addressed as Most Faithful Majesty.

ART. 74. The King shall exercise the moderative power under the responsibility of his ministers:[14]

[14] As amended July 24, 1885.

1) Appointing peers to the number of ninety, without other restriction than that provided by article 2 of the present law.[15]

2) Convening the General Cortes in extraordinary session, when the interests of the kingdom require it.

3) Approving the decrees and resolutions of the General Cortes, in order that they may have the force of law (Art. 55).

4) Proroguing or adjourning the General Cortes, and dissolving the House of Deputies in the cases in which the safety of the state may require it, convening immediately a new House.

[Proroguing or adjourning the General Cortes, and in the terms of paragraph 4 of Art. 74 of the constitutional charter, dissolving the House of Deputies and convening another to replace it.[16]]

5) Appointing and dismissing without restraint the ministers of state.

6) Suspending judges, in the cases referred to by Art. 121.

7) Remitting or reducing penalties imposed upon criminals condemned by virtue of a judicial sentence, with the exception of ministers of state sentenced for crimes committed in the exercise of their functions; with respect to ministers the royal prerogative shall be exercised only upon petition of one of the legislative houses.[17]

8) Granting amnesty in urgent cases, when the interests of humanity and the welfare of the state should make it advisable.

CHAPTER II.   THE EXECUTIVE POWER

ART. 75. The King shall be the head of the executive power, and shall exercise it through his ministers of state.

His principal powers shall be:

1) To call the elections for the new regular General Cortes on the second day of March of the fourth year of the existing

[15] As amended April 3, 1896.
[16] Idem.
[17] Idem.

Cortes; in the Portuguese possessions the elections shall be held a year earlier.

2) To appoint bishops and to bestow ecclesiastical benefices.

3) To appoint judges.

4) To appoint other civil and political officers.

5) To appoint the commanders of the land and naval forces and to remove them, when the welfare of the state requires it.

6) To appoint ambassadors and other diplomatic and commercial agents.

7) To conduct political negotiations with foreign powers.

8) To make treaties of offensive and defensive alliance, of subsidy and of commerce, bringing them to the knowledge of the General Cortes, after they have been concluded, when the interests and security of the state permit. Treaties concluded in time of peace, which involve the cession or exchange of territory of the kingdom or of possessions belonging to the kingdom, shall not be ratified until after they have been approved by the General Cortes.

[Every treaty, concordat, or convention which the government may conclude with any foreign power shall, before ratification, be approved by the Cortes in secret session.[18]]

9) To declare war and to make peace, giving to the assembly such information as may be compatible with the interests and security of the state.

10) To grant naturalization papers, in the manner provided by law.

11) To bestow titles, honors, distinctions, and military orders in recompense for services rendered to the state; the granting of pecuniary rewards shall be subject to the approval of the assembly, unless they may have been already determined upon and fixed by law.

[18] Added by Art. 10 of the additional act of July 5, 1852.

12) To issue decrees, instructions, and regulations necessary for the proper execution of the laws.

13) To determine the application of revenue voted by the Cortes for the various branches of the public administration.

14) To give or to refuse his assent to decrees of council, apostolic letters, and to any other ecclesiastical constitutions, which are not in conflict with this constitution, the approval of the Cortes also being necessary, if such ecclesiastical acts contain provisions of general application.[19]

15) To look after all things which bear upon the internal and external security of the state, in conformity with this constitution.

ART. 76. The King, before being proclaimed, shall take the following oath, before the two houses in joint session, the president of the House of Peers administering the oath:

I swear to maintain the Apostolic Roman Catholic religion and the integrity of the kingdom, to observe and to cause others to observe the political constitution of the Portuguese nation and the other laws of the kingdom, and to look out for the general welfare of the nation, in so far as I am able.

ART. 77. The King shall not absent himself from the kingdom for more than three months without the consent of the Cortes.[20]

CHAPTER III.   THE ROYAL FAMILY AND ITS REVENUE

ART. 78. The heir apparent to the throne shall bear the title of Prince royal; his eldest son shall bear the title of Prince of Beira, and his other children that of Infants. The heir apparent and the Prince of Beira shall be addressed as Royal Highness, the Infants as Highness.

ART. 79. The heir apparent upon reaching the age of fourteen years shall take the following oath before the two

[19] Amended by Art. 10 of the additional act of July 5, 1852. See number 8 of this article.

[20] As amended July 24, 1885.

houses in joint session, the president of the House of Peers administering the oath:

> I swear to maintain the Apostolic Roman Catholic religion, to observe the political constitution of the Portuguese nation, and to be obedient to the laws and to the King.

Art. 80.   As soon as the King succeeds to the throne, the General Cortes shall assign to him and to the queen, his wife, a revenue sufficient for the maintenance of their high position.

Art. 81.   The Cortes shall also assign revenues for the support of the Prince royal and of the Infants, when they are born.

Art. 82.   When the princesses or infantas marry, the Cortes shall grant them dower, and after the granting of dower, the revenue paid for their support shall cease.

Art. 83.   The Infants who marry and reside outside of the kingdom shall be granted a sum of money to be fixed by the Cortes, and thereafter they shall receive no further revenue for their support.

Art. 84.   The revenues and dower referred to in the preceding articles shall be paid by the public treasury to a steward named by the King, who shall conduct all business affairs concerning the interests of the royal house.

Art. 85.   The royal palaces and lands now in the possession of the King shall continue to belong to his successors, and the Cortes shall provide for the acquisition of property and the construction of buildings which it may consider proper for the convenience and recreation of the King.

CHAPTER IV.   THE SUCCESSION TO THE THRONE

Art. 86.   Dona Maria II, queen by the grace of God and by the formal abdication and cession of Dom Pedro I, emperor of Brazil, shall continue to reign in Portugal.

Art. 87.   Her legitimate descendants shall succeed to the throne according to the regular order of primogeniture and representation, the elder line being always preferred to the younger, in the same line or grade the nearer degree of kinship to the more remote, in the same grade the male to the female, and in the same sex the older to the younger.

Art. 88. Should the line of legitimate descendants of Dona Maria II fail, the crown shall pass to the collateral lines.

Art. 89. No foreigner shall succeed to the throne of Portugal.

Art. 90. The marriage of the presumptive heiress to the crown shall be contracted with the consent of the King, and shall never be with a foreigner; if there be no King at the time to give his consent, no marriage shall be contracted without the approval of the General Cortes. The prince-consort shall not take part in the government and shall not be called King until after the Queen shall have had a son or a daughter.

CHAPTER V. THE REGENCY DURING THE MINORITY OR INCAPACITY OF THE KING

Art. 91. The King is a minor until he attains the age of eighteen years.

Art. 92. During his minority the kingdom shall be governed by a regency, which shall belong to the nearest relative of the King, according to the order of succession, provided he be over twenty-five years of age.

Art. 93. If the King have no such relative, the kingdom shall be governed by a permanent regency appointed by the General Cortes, and composed of three members, of whom the oldest shall be president.

Art. 94. During the interval before this regency is elected a provisional regency shall govern the kingdom; this regency shall be composed of the minister of state for the kingdom, of the minister of justice, and of the two senior councilors of state, and shall be presided over by the widow of the deceased king, or if there be none, by the senior councilor of state.

ART. 95. In case of the death of the reigning queen, her husband shall preside over the regency.

ART. 96. If the King, for physical or moral cause clearly apparent to a majority of each of the houses of the Cortes, should be rendered incapable of governing, the Prince royal, if over eighteen years of age, shall govern in his place as regent.

ART. 97. The regent or regency shall take the oath mentioned in Art. 76, adding to it an oath of fidelity to the King and a promise to surrender the government to him when he attains his majority or when his disability is removed.

ART. 98. The acts of the regency or of the regent shall be published in the name of the King, with the following formula: "The regency commands in the name of the King," or "The Prince royal, regent, commands in the name of the King."

ART. 99. Neither the regency nor the regent shall be responsible.

ART. 100. During his minority the successor to the throne shall be under the guardian named in his father's will; if there were no such appointment the Queen mother shall be guardian; failing this, the General Cortes shall name a guardian, with the restriction that no one shall be guardian of the minor King who would succeed to the throne in case of the King's death.

CHAPTER VI. THE MINISTRY

ART. 101. There shall be several secretaries of state. A law shall determine their number and the duties of each of them; their number may be increased or diminished in any manner that may seem most convenient.

ART. 102. The ministers shall sign or countersign all acts of the executive power; without ministerial signature such acts shall not be executed.

ART. 103.   The ministers of state shall be responsible:

1) For treason.

2) For giving or taking bribes, or for extortion.

3) For abuse of power.

4) For failure to observe the law.

5) For actions infringing upon the liberty, security, or property of citizens.

6) For any misuse of public property.

ART. 104.   A special law shall define the nature of these offenses, and the method of procedure against them.

ART. 105.   No verbal or written order of the King shall relieve the ministers of their responsibility.

ART. 106.   Foreigners, even though naturalized, shall not be ministers of state.

CHAPTER VII.   THE COUNCIL OF STATE

ART. 107.   There shall be a Council of State composed of councilors appointed for life by the King.

ART. 108.   Foreigners, even though naturalized, shall not be councilors of state.

ART. 109.   Councilors of state before exercising their functions shall take an oath, administered by the King, to maintain the Apostolic Roman Catholic religion, to observe the constitution and the laws, to be faithful to the King, to counsel him according to their consciences, having only in view the welfare of the nation.

ART. 110.   The councilors shall be consulted in all important affairs and in general measures of public administration, especially concerning the declaration of war, conclusion of peace, and negotiations with foreign powers; as well as upon all occasions when the King proposes to exercise any of the powers granted to the moderative power by Art. 74, with the exception of the power mentioned in clause 5.

ART. 111.   Councilors of state shall be responsible for

advice given, in evident bad faith, in opposition to the laws and to the interests of the state.

ART. 112. The Prince royal, as soon as he attains the age of eighteen years, shall enter, by right, the Council of State; the other princes of the royal house may not become members of the Council of State except by appointment of the King.

CHAPTER VIII. THE MILITARY FORCE

ART. 113. All Portuguese shall be under obligation to take up arms in order to maintain the independence and integrity of the kingdom, and to defend it against internal and external enemies.

ART. 114. Should the General Cortes not fix the permanent military force by land and sea, it shall remain as it was until it shall be increased or diminished by that body.

ART. 115. The military force is by its nature obedient; it shall never assemble without having been ordered to do so by a competent authority.

ART. 116. The power to employ the military forces by land and sea and to dispose of them in the manner considered best for the security and defense of the kingdom, shall belong exclusively to the executive power.

ART. 117. Special ordinances shall regulate the organization of the army and navy, their promotions, pay, and discipline.

TITLE VI. THE JUDICIAL POWER

THE JUDGES AND THE COURTS OF JUSTICE

ART. 118. The judicial power shall be independent and shall be composed of judges and juries which shall act in civil and criminal cases, in the manner which the codes shall determine.

ART. 119. The juries shall determine the facts and the judges shall apply the law.

ART. 120. The inferior judges shall be irremovable, but

this shall not imply that they may not be transferred from one place to another, in the time and manner determined by law.

ART. 121. The King may suspend them because of charges brought against them, after first having heard such judges and after consulting the Council of State. The papers in such a case shall be sent to the higher court of the proper district, in order that there may be a trial in accordance with law.

ART. 122. Such judges may be removed only after judicial sentence.

ART. 123. All judges of inferior courts and officers of justice shall be responsible for abuses of power and malversation committed in the exercise of their functions; this responsibility shall be made effective by law.

ART. 124. For giving or taking bribes, peculation, or extortion there shall be a popular action against such judges, which may be commenced by anyone within a year and a day after the offense, in the manner to be established by law.

ART. 125. In order to determine cases upon appeal and in last instance, there shall be in the provinces of the kingdom such superior courts as may be necessary for the convenience of the people.

ART. 126. In criminal cases the taking of evidence and all other proceedings until judgment, shall hereafter be public.

ART. 127. In civil cases and in penal cases civilly prosecuted the parties may name referees. The judgments of such referees shall be executed without appeal, if the parties have agreed to that effect.

ART. 128. No suit shall be commenced until after an attempt has been made to settle the matter in dispute by compromise.

ART. 129. For this purpose there shall be justices of the peace, who shall be elected at the same time and in the same manner as members of the municipal councils. Their powers and districts shall be regulated by law.

ART. 130.   In the capital of the kingdom there shall be, in addition to the superior court which shall be established here as in the other provinces, a court with the title of Supreme Court of Justice.   This court shall be composed of learned judges taken from the superior courts in order of seniority; such judges shall be given the title of councilors.   In its first organization, the judges of the abolished courts shall be employed in this court.

ART. 131.   The Supreme Court shall have jurisdiction:

1) To grant or to deny appeals in the cases and in the manner determined by law.

2) To try offenses and breaches of duty which may be committed by its members, by the judges of the superior courts, or by the members of the diplomatic corps.

3) To hear and to decide conflicts of jurisdiction between the provincial superior courts.

TITLE VII. THE ADMINISTRATION AND THE GOVERNMENT OF THE PROVINCES

CHAPTER I. THE ADMINISTRATION

ART. 132.   The administration of the provinces shall remain as at present until altered by law.[81]

[81] The province has not been an area for governmental purposes since 1836. The local government of Portugal is now regulated by the administrative code of May 4, 1896. For administrative purposes the territory of the country is divided into districts, the districts into communes (concelhos), and the communes into parishes. In the cities of Lisbon and Oporto the communes are divided into wards and the wards into parishes. Each district is governed by a district committee composed of two appointed members and of three members (vogaes) elected triennially by delegates from the communal councils. The civil governor of the district, who is also president of the committee, is appointed by the central government. The District Committee, its appointed legal member, or the inferior judges of the district form an administrative court of first instance. In each commune there is an elected council, all of the members of which are chosen on one ticket; the number of members of the communal council varies from five in the smaller communes to fifteen in Lisbon. At the head of each commune is an adminis-

[The provinces beyond the sea shall be governed by special laws, according as the circumstances of each of them may require.[22]]

[Sec. 1. When the Cortes is not in session, the government, after hearing and consulting the proper authorities, may issue in council such legislative measures as may be considered urgent.[22]]

[Sec. 2. So likewise the governor general of a province beyond the sea, may, after consulting his council of government, take such steps as may be indispensable to provide for any necessity so urgent that the matter cannot be delayed for the decision of the Cortes or of the government.[22]]

[Sec. 3. In both cases the government shall submit to the Cortes, as soon as it assembles, the measures so taken.[22]]

CHAPTER II.   THE COMMUNAL COUNCILS

ART. 11. In each commune there shall be a communal council elected directly by the people, which shall have the economic administration of the corporation, in conformity with the law.[23]

ART. 135. The exercise of municipal functions, the passage of police ordinances, the application of local revenues, and the use by the municipal council of all other local and proper powers shall be regulated by law.

CHAPTER III.   THE PUBLIC REVENUE

ART. 136. The receipt and expenditure of public funds shall be intrusted to an office called the Public Treasury; the

trator appointed by the central government upon the nomination of the civil governor of the district. The parish is governed by an elective council or junta, over which the parish priest presides. The circle is simply an election district and has no administrative functions.

[22] Added by additional act of July 5, 1852.

[23] Arts. 133 and 134 of the Constitutional Charter were displaced by Art. 11 of the additional act of July 5, 1852, which is here inserted. See note to Art. 132.

various departments of this office, established by law, shall
have charge of the collection and administration of public
funds and of the accounts.

ART. 137. All direct taxes, with the exception of those
applied to the interest and amortisation of the public debt, shall
be established annually by the General Cortes, but existing
taxes shall continue until they have been repealed or replaced
by others.

ART. 138. The minister of state for the treasury, having
received from the other ministers the accounts and estimates
of their expenses, shall annually present to the House of Deputies, as soon as the Cortes convenes, a general account of the
receipts and expenses for the preceding year, and also a general
estimate of the public expenses for the succeeding year, with
a statement of the amounts received from all taxes and public
revenues.

[ART. 12. Taxes shall be voted annually; the laws which
establish them are binding for one year only.]

[Sec. 1. Sums voted for any public expenditure shall not
be applied for other purposes, except by a special law which
authorizes the transfer.]

[Sec. 2. The administration and collection of the revenues of the state shall be the functions of the Public Treasury,
except in the cases specified by law.]

[Sec. 3. There shall be a court of accounts, the organization and powers of which shall be determined by law.]

[ART. 13. Within the first fifteen days after the organization of the House of Deputies, the government shall present
to it the estimates of receipts and expenditures for the succeeding year, the proposal fixing the land and naval forces, and
that for the recruiting of the contingents of the public force.
If at the end of the financial year the Cortes should not have
voted these laws, the last legal provisions concerning these
matters shall remain in force during the next year, until a new
action by the legislative power. If, however, the Cortes should

not have been in session, it shall be convened in extraordinary session and assembled within a period of three months, for the sole purpose of deliberating concerning the matters referred to in this article; if it should be in session, it shall not be closed without having deliberated concerning these matters, except in case of dissolution; in case of dissolution, the Cortes shall be convened and assembled in ordinary or extraordinary session, for this purpose only, within the period above indicated.[24]]

TITLE VIII. GENERAL PROVISIONS, AND GUARANTIES OF THE CIVIL AND POLITICAL RIGHTS OF PORTUGUESE CITIZENS

ART. 139. The General Cortes, at the beginning of its session, shall examine as to whether the political constitution of the kingdom has been exactly observed, and shall adopt such measures as it thinks proper.

[Each house of the Cortes shall have the right to proceed, by means of commissions of inquiry, to the investigation of any matter within its competence.[25]]

ART. 140. If, four years after the amendment of any article of the constitution of the kingdom, it is thought that a further reform of the constitution is desirable, the proposed amendment shall be presented in writing in the House of Deputies and must be supported by one-third of the members of that house.[26]

ART. 141. The proposal of amendment shall be read three times, with an interval of six days between each reading; after the third reading the House of Deputies shall consider whether it shall be admitted to discussion, and if it is admitted

[24] Arts. 12 and 13 of the additional act of July 5, 1852, are here inserted. They amend Arts. 136–38 of the constitution but do not entirely repeal them; Art. 13 was amended on April 3, 1896, and is here given as amended.

[25] Added by Art. 14 of the additional act of July 5, 1852. This clause also amends clause 1 of Art. 36.

[26] As amended July 24, 1885.

to discussion the same procedure shall be followed as in the passage of a law.

ART. 142. If the proposal is admitted to discussion and the necessity of the amendment is recognized, a law shall be passed, approved, and promulgated by the King in the regular form, authorizing the electors of deputies to the succeeding legislature to confer upon the deputies special power to adopt the proposed amendment.

ART. 143. In the first session of the succeeding legislature the proposed amendment shall be discussed, and if adopted it shall become a part of the constitution and shall be solemnly promulgated.

ART. 144. Matters of a constitutional character are those which relate to the limits and respective powers of the several departments of government, and to the political and individual rights of citizens. All laws not of a constitutional character may be altered by the regular legislature, without the formality referred to above.

ART. 145. The inviolability of the civil and political rights of Portuguese citizens, which have as a basis liberty, personal security, and property, is guaranteed by the constitution of the kingdom, in the following manner:

1) No citizen shall be obliged to do or to refrain from doing anything, except by virtue of law.

2) The provisions of law shall never have a retroactive effect.

3) Everyone may express his opinions by word or in writing, and may make them public through the press, without their being submitted to censorship, provided, however, that he shall be answerable for the abuses which he may commit in the exercise of this right, in the cases and in the manner to be determined by law.

4) No one shall be prosecuted because of religion, provided that he respects the religion of the state and does not offend public morals.

5) Everyone may remain within or depart from the kingdom, as he may wish, carrying his goods with him, if he conforms to the police laws and his going does not injure a third person.

6) The house of every citizen is an inviolable refuge. At night no one shall enter it except with his consent, or in case of request from within it, or to protect it from fire or flood; during the day no house shall be entered, except in the cases and in the manner provided by law.

7) No one shall be arrested unless for an offense already committed, except in the cases specified by law; in every case the judge, in a note signed by himself, shall make known to the accused the reasons for his imprisonment, the names of his accusers, and the evidence against him, within twenty-four hours after his arrest if it takes place within a city, town, or other place near the residence of the judge, or if the arrest occurs in a remote place, within a reasonable time to be fixed by law, having in view the extent of territory.

8) In the case of offenses already committed no one shall be taken to prison, or being in prison, shall be retained there, if he will furnish proper bail, in the cases where the law permits bail; in general the accused may obtain liberty without bail if charged with an offense for which the punishment does not exceed six months of imprisonment, or banishment from the district.

9) Except when an offender is taken in the act, no one shall be arrested unless upon the written order of the proper authority. In case of arbitrary arrest, the judge who ordered it and the person who made the complaint shall be subject to such penalties as the law shall provide.

The provision regarding imprisonment before the commission of an offense shall not apply to military regulations established as necessary for the discipline and recruiting of the army, nor to the cases, not purely criminal, in which the law provides, nevertheless, for the imprisonment of any person for disobedience of the orders of the courts, or for not complying with certain obligations within a specified time.

10) No person shall be sentenced except by a competent authority, in virtue of a pre-existing law, and in the form prescribed by such law.

11) The independence of the judicial power shall be maintained. No authority may remove pending cases to a higher court without cause, withhold cases from final decision, or revive cases in which final judgment has been rendered

12) The law shall be equal for all, and shall protect, punish, and recompense each one in proportion to his merits.

13) Every citizen shall be admissible to public offices, civil, political, or military, without other distinctions than those resulting from his talents and morals.

14) No one shall be exempt from contributing toward the expenses of the state in proportion to his property.

15) All privileges not essential to and connected with offices of public utility are abolished.

16) With the exception of cases which by their nature belong to special courts, in conformity with law, there shall be no extraordinary tribunals nor special commissions for the trial of civil or criminal cases.

17) Civil and criminal codes, founded upon the solid basis of justice and equity, shall be adopted as soon as possible.

18) Whipping, torture, branding, and all other inhuman penalties are abolished for the future.

[The penalty of death for political offenses is abolished; such offenses shall be defined by law.[27]]

19) No penalty shall extend beyond the person of the offender; therefore there shall be no confiscation of goods in any case, nor shall the infamy of the offender extend to his relatives of any degree.

20) The prisons shall be secure, clean, and well ventilated, having different apartments for the separation of criminals,

---

* Added by Art. 16 of additional act of July 5, 1852.

with reference to their circumstances and the nature of their crimes.

21) The right of property is guaranteed in its entirety. If the public good, legally proven, should require the use or application of the property of a citizen, he shall first be paid the value of such property. A law shall determine when property may be taken for a public purpose, and shall establish rules for the ascertainment of the compensation.

22) The public debt is also guaranteed.

23) No kind of labor, culture, industry, or commerce shall be prohibited unless it is opposed to public policy or to the security and health of the citizens.

24) Inventors shall have the property of their discoveries or products. The law shall secure to them a temporary exclusive privilege, or shall remunerate them for the loss which they may suffer through the making public of their discoveries.

25) The secrecy of letters in inviolable. The postal administration shall be held strictly responsible for any violation of this section.

26) Recompenses conferred for civil or military services rendered to the state, and the rights acquired in them in conformity with law, are guaranteed.

27) State employees shall be strictly responsible for the abuses or omissions of which they may be guilty in the exercise of their functions; they shall not make their subordinates responsible.

28) Every citizen may present in writing to the legislative or executive authorities, claims, complaints, or petitions, and may expose any violation of the constitution, requiring that the proper authorities make effective the responsibility of the offenders. [The right of association is also guaranteed; the exercise of this right shall be regulated by a general law.[28]]

29) The constitution also guarantees public relief of the poor.

[28] As amended July 24, 1885.

30) Primary instruction shall be free to all citizens.

31) The constitution guarantees hereditary nobility and its privileges.

32) There shall be colleges and universities in which shall be taught the elements of the sciences, belles lettres, and arts.

33) The constitutional authorities shall not suspend the constitution nor the individual rights guaranteed by it, except in the cases and under the circumstances specified in the following section.

34) In case of rebellion or of invasion by an enemy, if the security of the state should require the suspension, for a limited time, of any of the guaranties which protect individual liberty, such guaranties may be suspended by a special act of the legislative power. However, if the Cortes be not in session and the country is in imminent danger, the government may exercise the same power as a temporary and indispensable measure, ceasing to exercise it as soon as the urgent necessity ceases; in the latter case, however, the government shall present to the Cortes, as soon as it convenes, a detailed report of the arrests and other preventive measures taken; and all officers receiving orders to execute such measures shall be responsible for abuses committed by them in this respect.

RUSSIA

On August 19, 1905, the Russian emperor issued regulations for the election of a national representative body, upon a restricted suffrage. This concession did not satisfy the liberal elements, and on October 30 an imperial manifesto was issued, promising:

1) To grant to the population the immutable guaranties of civil liberty, upon the basis of real inviolability of person, of liberty of conscience, of speech, of assembly, and of association.

2) To permit the participation in the Duma of the Empire, as far as possible within the brief period of time remaining before the convocation of the Duma and without interrupting the progress of the elections to that assembly, of those classes of the population who are now completely deprived of electoral rights, leaving the further development of the principle of universal suffrage to the newly established legislative procedure.

3) To establish, as an immutable rule, that no law shall become effective without the approval of the Imperial Duma, and that the representatives of the people be guaranteed the possibility of exercising an effective supervision as to the legality of the acts of the Imperial authorities.[1]

The liberal election law of December 24, 1905, and the fundamental laws of May 6, 1906, were steps toward the execution of these promises. A note to Art. 59 of the Fundamental Laws indicates developments since the first convention of the Duma.

SELECT BIBLIOGRAPHY

ENGELMANN, J. *Das Staatsrecht des Kaiserthums Russland.* (Freiburg, 1889. Handbuch des oeffentlichen Rechts.)

OETTINGEN, MAX VON. *Abriss des russischen Staatsrechts.* (Berlin, 1899.)

WALLACE, DONALD MACKENZIE. *Russia.* (New ed., New York, 1905.) An authoritative work which discusses to some extent the Russian local and imperial government.

[1] This text is a free translation of the French text published in the *Journal de St. Petersbourg* of November 4, 1905.

LEROY-BEAULIEU, ANATOLE. *The Empire of the Tsars and the Russians.* Translated from the 3d French ed. by Zénaïde A. Ragozin. (New York, 1893–96. 3 vols.) The best work on Russia in the English language.

MILYOUKOV, PAUL. *Russia and Its Crisis.* (Chicago, 1905.)

HARPER, SAMUEL N. *The New Electoral Law for the Russian Duma.* (Chicago, 1908.) An excellent study of the present election law of Russia.

PARES, BERNARD. *Russia and Reform.* (London, 1907.) Perhaps the best book in English upon present political conditions in Russia.

THE FUNDAMENTAL LAWS OF THE RUSSIAN EMPIRE

(May 6, 1906)

1. The Russian Empire is one and indivisible.

2. The Grand Duchy of Finland, forming an inalienable part of the Russian Empire, shall be governed in its internal affairs by special regulations established on the basis of a special legislature.[1]

[1] When Finland was annexed to Russia in 1809, the emperor Alexander I guaranteed the religion and the fundamental laws of the country. The fundamental laws thus guaranteed were the Swedish laws of 1772 and 1789, under which there existed a general Swedish diet of four estates. A local Finnish diet, containing representatives of the four estates, was at once convened, and accepted the Russian emperor as Grand Duke of Finland. For about ninety years Finland retained its local institutions almost unimpaired, although the diet was infrequently in session. According to a law approved by the Russian emperor in 1869, no fundamental law could be enacted or altered without the consent of the Estates.

For some time before 1899 there had been a strong feeling among Russian officials that Finnish institutions should be assimilated to those of the rest of the empire. When difficulty was apprehended in obtaining the passage of laws reorganizing the Finnish army and incorporating it with that of the empire, the emperor, on February 16, 1899, issued a manifesto by which he withdrew from the Finnish diet all power to legislate upon matters of "general interest and importance for the empire."

This step and others during the several succeeding years, tending to destroy the independence of the grand duchy, were vigorously opposed by the Finnish people. In consequence of a general strike in October, 1905,

3. The Russian language is the official language of the Empire and its use is obligatory in the army, the navy, and in all governmental and public institutions. The use of local languages and dialects in governmental and public institutions shall be regulated by special laws.

CHAPTER I. THE NATURE OF THE SUPREME AUTOCRATIC POWER

4. The Emperor of all the Russias wields the supreme autocratic power. To obey his authority, not only through fear but for the sake of conscience, is ordered by God himself.

5. The person of the Emperor is sacred and inviolable.

6. The same supreme autocratic power shall belong likewise to the Empress when the succession to the throne falls to a person of the female sex according to the established order; but her consort shall not be considered an emperor; he shall enjoy the rights and privileges similar to those of the consorts of emperors but without the title.

7. The Emperor is vested with the legislative power jointly with the Council of the Empire and the Imperial Duma.

8. The initiative in all legislative measures[2] belongs to the Emperor. Only through his initiative may fundamental laws be submitted to the Council of the Empire and the Imperial Duma for discussion.

the Russian government was forced to yield. An imperial manifesto of November 4, 1905, annulled the obnoxious laws, and convened the Finnish diet. On May 10, 1906, a bill for the reform of representation in the Finnish diet was approved by the emperor and adopted by the diet. By this law the diet is organized into a single chamber of two hundred delegates, of whom sixty form a Grand Committee, somewhat similar to the Norwegian Lagthing. Members of the diet are elected by direct universal suffrage, the right to vote being given to men and women who have attained the age of twenty-four years. The diet holds annual sessions and its members are elected for three years upon a system of proportional representation.

[2] But not the exclusive power of initiation with respect to ordinary legislation. See No. 65 of this law, p. 192.

9. The Emperor sanctions the laws and without his approval no law shall be put into execution.

10. The executive power in all its extent shall belong to the Emperor within the limits of the entire Russian Empire. The Emperor acts directly in matters of supreme government; in subordinate governmental matters a certain degree of power may be intrusted by him, in accordance with the law, to the competent officers and persons acting in his name and by his orders.

11. The Emperor in the exercise of the supreme powers of government issues, in conformity with the laws, ukases for the organization and the putting into execution of various parts of the governmental administration, as well as orders necessary for the execution of the laws.

12. The Emperor has supreme control of all relations of the Russian Empire with foreign powers. He likewise determines the course of the international policy of the Russian Empire.

13. The Emperor declares war and concludes peace, as well as other treaties with foreign countries.

14. The Emperor is the supreme chief of the Russian army and navy. He is vested with the supreme command of all land and naval forces of the Russian Empire. He determines the organization of the army and of the navy, and issues ukases and orders concerning: the disposition of the troops, the placing of troops on war footing, their instruction, the course of military service in the army and the navy, and in general concerning everything bearing on the organization of the armed forces and the defense of the Russian Empire. The Emperor likewise, in the exercise of his supreme power, determines limitations with regard to right of residence and acquisition of real property in localities forming part of fortified regions and points of support for the army and the navy.

15. The Emperor declares localities to be in a state of war or any other special and exceptional state.

16. The Emperor has the right to coin money and to determine its form.

17. The Emperor appoints and dismisses the president of the Council of Ministers, the ministers and the chiefs of separate departments, as well as other officials for whose appointment and dismissal no other mode of procedure has been established.

18. The Emperor, in the exercise of supreme power, establishes limitations with regard to officials, as demanded by the needs of the government service.

19. The Emperor grants titles, decorations, and other official distinctions, as well as rights of ownership. He determines the conditions and procedure for the granting of titles, decorations, and distinctions.

20. The Emperor issues directly ukases and orders with regard to property forming his own personal possessions, as well as with regard to property, known as the Emperor's possessions, which belongs always to the reigning Emperor and which cannot be willed, divided, or alienated in any way. The former as well as the latter possessions are not subject to taxation or to any other charges.

21. To the Emperor, as head of the imperial family, belongs the right, in accordance with the rules governing the imperial house, to manage appanages assigned to the imperial family (*Udel*). He likewise determines the organization of the establishments and institutions belonging to the ministry of the court, as well as the manner of their administration.

22. The judicial power shall be exercised in the name of the Emperor by courts, established by law, and their decisions shall be issued in the name of his Imperial Majesty.

23. The Emperor has the right to pardon condemned persons, to commute punishments, and to pardon completely persons who have committed misdemeanors or crimes, stopping proceedings against them and freeing them from trial and punishment, as well as to free them from government dues,

through his sovereign mercy, and in general to grant privileges in special cases, which are not covered by general laws, in case no interests or private rights protected by the law suffer through such action.

24. The provisions of the Code (Vol. I, Part 1, edition of 1892): on the order of succession to the throne (Arts. 3–17), on the coming of age of the Emperor, on the regency and guardianship (Arts. 18–30), on the accession to the throne and the oath of allegiance (Arts. 31–34 and Appendix V), on the holy coronation and the anointment (Arts. 35 and 36), on the title of his Imperial Majesty and the arms of the Empire (Arts. 37–39 and Appendix I), and on the religion (Arts. 40–46) maintain the force of fundamental laws.

25. The provisions concerning the imperial family (Code, Vol. I, Part 1, ed. of 1892, Arts. 82–179, and Appendices II–IV and VI), continuing to have the force of fundamental laws, may be amended and supplemented only by the Emperor himself in accordance with the procedure established by him, if the amendments and supplements to such provisions do not encroach upon general laws and do not require any new expenditures from the public treasury.

26. The ukases and orders of the Emperor, issued directly by him or according to the procedure of the higher administration, shall be countersigned by the president of the Council of Ministers or by the competent minister, or by the chief of an independent institution, and shall be published by the Senate.

CHAPTER II. THE RIGHTS AND DUTIES OF RUSSIAN SUBJECTS

27. The conditions under which Russian citizenship may be acquired, as well as those under which it is forfeited, shall be determined by law.

28. The defense of the throne and of the country is the sacred duty of every Russian subject. The entire male population without distinction of classes is liable to military service in accordance with the terms of the law.

29. All Russian subjects are under the obligation to pay

the taxes and dues established by law, and to fulfil all other obligations imposed by law.

30. No one shall be prosecuted for criminal offenses in any other manner than that established by law.

31. No one shall be arrested except in the cases determined by law.

32. No one shall be tried and punished except for criminal offenses provided by laws in force at the time they were committed, unless new laws exclude the actions committed by the culprit from the category of criminal offenses.

33. The domicile of everyone is inviolable. Searches or sequestrations in a domicile without the consent of the owner shall take place only in the cases and in the manner provided by law.

34. Every Russian subject shall have the right to select his place of abode and his occupation, to buy and sell property, and to depart from the territory of the Empire without molestation; limitations upon these rights are established by law.

35. Property is inviolable. The forced taking of real property, when such is necessary for governmental or public interests, shall take place only for an equitable and adequate compensation.

36. Russian subjects shall have the right to assemble peacefully and without arms, for purposes allowed by the law. The law determines the conditions under which meetings may be held, the manner of closing them, and likewise the limitation as to the localities where they may take place.

37. Everyone shall have the right, within the limits prescribed by law, to express his thoughts orally or in writing, and also to disseminate them through the press or by other means.

38. Russian subjects shall have the right to form societies and associations for purposes which are not forbidden by law. The conditions for the formation of such societies and associa-

tions, the course of their activity, the conditions and the procedure by which they obtain the rights of juridical persons, as well as the manner of dissolving societies and associations, shall be determined by law.

39. The Russian subjects shall enjoy liberty of conscience. The conditions under which this liberty is enjoyed shall be determined by law.

40. All foreigners residing in Russia shall enjoy the same rights as Russian subjects, within certain limitations established by law.

41. Exceptions from the provisions of this chapter, with regard to localities in a state of war or in other exceptional state, shall be determined by the law.

CHAPTER III. THE LAWS

42. The Russian Empire shall be governed in accordance with the immutable principles of law, promulgated according to the established procedure.

43. The laws are binding upon all Russian subjects as well as upon all foreigners residing in the Russian Empire.

44. No new law shall be promulgated without the approval of the Council of the Empire and of the Imperial Duma, and no law shall become effective until after the approval of the Emperor.

45. During the recess of the Imperial Duma, if extraordinary circumstances require the adoption of a measure which should be made the subject of legislative deliberation, the Council of Ministers may present such a measure directly to the Emperor. Such a measure shall not, however, introduce any changes in the fundamental laws of the Empire, or in the organization of the Council of the Empire or of the Imperial Duma, or regulations concerning the elections to the Council of the Empire or to the Imperial Duma. The legal force of such a measure ceases if it is not submitted to the Imperial Duma within two months after that body has resumed its

work, by the competent minister or by the head of an independent institution, in the form of a project of law; or if such measure is rejected by the Imperial Duma or by the Council of the Empire.

46. Laws enacted for a certain locality or for a certain part of the population are not repealed by new general laws unless such new laws specifically repeal them.

47. Every law shall have force only for the future, except in the cases when it is stated in the law itself that it is retroactive, or that it is only a confirmation or explanation of the sense of a former law.

48. The custody of the laws is intrusted to the Senate. For this reason every law shall be sent in the original or in a certified copy to the Imperial Senate.

49. The laws are published by the Senate in the established order, and are not in force until such publication.

50. Legislative measures shall not be published if the procedure in enacting them does not correspond with the requirements of these fundamental laws.

51. After its publication, the law becomes effective from the date fixed in the law itself and, should such a date not be fixed, from the day the publication of the Senate, in which the law is printed, reaches the various localities of the Empire. It may be provided in the law itself that, until its publication, it may be put into execution by telegraph or by couriers.

52. A law shall not be abrogated in any other way except by a new law. Therefore, until the existing law has been repealed by a new law, it remains in force.

53. No one may plead ignorance of the law after the law has been published in acordance with the established order.

54. Regulations concerning building, technical, and economic departments as well as orders and regulations issued to institutions and officers of the military and naval departments, after having been examined by the Military Council or the Admiralty Council, shall be submitted directly to the Emperor,

if such regulations, orders, and measures concerning the above-mentioned departments do not encroach upon the general laws and do not require new expenditures, or if the expenditures required are covered by the expected economies realized in the military and naval budgets respectively. In the case when the new expenditure cannot be covered by the above-mentioned economies, such orders, regulations, and measures shall be submitted to the Emperor only after the necessary credit has been demanded in accordance with the established forms.

55. Regulations regarding military and naval courts shall be issued in accordance with the forms established in the military and naval law.

CHAPTER IV. THE COUNCIL OF THE EMPIRE, THE IMPERIAL DUMA, AND THE COURSE OF THEIR ACTIVITY

56. The Council of the Empire and the Imperial Duma shall be convened annually by ukase of the Emperor.

57. The duration of the annual session of the Council of the Empire and of the Imperial Duma and the dates for adjournments during the year shall be fixed by ukase of the Emperor.

58. The Council of the Empire shall be composed of members appointed by the Emperor and members chosen by election. The total number of members of the Council of the Empire, appointed by the Emperor and summoned to the Council, shall not exceed the number of members chosen by election.[3]

[3] The Council of the Empire as a legislative body was instituted by imperial ukase of March 5, 1906, superseded by the ukase of May 7, 1906. The elected members of the Council are chosen by: (1) the clergy of the Greek Orthodox church; (2) the provincial zemstvos; (3) the assemblies of the nobility; (4) the Imperial Academy of Science and the imperial universities; (5) the Council of Trade and Commerce, the Moscow section of such Council, the local Committees of Commerce and Manufactures, Committees of Exchange, and Boards of Trade. The Greek Orthodox church chooses six members; each provincial zemstvo, one; the assemblies of the nobility, eighteen; the Imperial Academy of Science and the universities together, six; the Council of Trade and Commerce together

59. The Imperial Duma shall be composed of members elected by the population of the Russian Empire for a term of five years, in accordance with the principles established by the laws regulating the elections to the Imperial Duma.[4]

60. The Council of the Empire examines the credentials of its members chosen by election. The Imperial Duma examines in a like manner the credentials of its members.

61. The same person shall not at the same time be a member of the Imperial Duma and a member of the Council of the Empire.

62. The part of the Council of the Empire, chosen by election, may be dissolved before the expiration of its term, by ukase of the Emperor, which shall at the same time order new elections of members to the Council of the Empire.

63. The Imperial Duma may be dissolved by ukase of the Emperor before the expiration of the term for which its mem-

with Committees of Commerce and Boards of Trade elect twelve members. All of these elections take place indirectly by means of electoral colleges for each of the five classes of electors, each class choosing its members in a separate electoral body.

The elected members of the Council of the Empire are chosen for nine years, in such a manner that one-third of each class shall retire every third year.

[4] The Duma was instituted by imperial ukase of August 19, 1905, and the first election regulations were issued on the same day. These regulations provided for indirect elections with a limited suffrage. By manifesto of October 30, 1905, the emperor promised an extension of the suffrage, and such extension was accomplished by the ukase of December 24, 1905. By this instrument the right to vote for electors in the urban electoral colleges was extended: (1) to all persons who for one year had owned or possessed a life estate in real property assessed for state or municipal taxes. Under the August regulations there had been a tax qualification of from 500 to 3,000 rubles for this class of voters; (2) to all persons who for one year had conducted a commercial enterprise for which an industrial certificate was required; (3) to persons who had resided within the town and paid a lodging tax for one year; (4) to persons who for one year had paid a tax on personal industry; (5) to persons occupying, for the period of one year, an apartment rented in their own names; (6) to persons receiving certain state or local pensions. Laborers who, by the election regulations of August 19, 1905, were practically excluded from the right to vote, were permitted by the

bers have been elected. The same ukase shall order new elections of members to the Imperial Duma, and shall fix the time of its meeting.

64. The Imperial Duma and the Council of the Empire enjoy equal rights in matters of legislation.

65. The Council of the Empire and the Imperial Duma, in the course of their functions as determined by the laws establishing them, have the right to propose the amendment or repeal of existing laws or the enactment of new laws, with the exception of the fundamental laws of the Empire, the initiative for the revision of which belongs exclusively to the Emperor.

66. The Council of the Empire and the Imperial Duma, in the course of their functions as determined by the laws establishing them, have the right to demand explanations from the ministers and from the heads of independent departments, subordinate to the Senate, with regard to actions of apparent

ukase of December 24, to choose electors to the provincial and urban electoral colleges. As the peasants had already been granted the right to vote, the December regulations went far toward establishing universal male suffrage. The system of indirect elections was retained and was extended in the case of the new electoral class of laborers. An ukase of March 5, 1906, provided for the internal organization and procedure of the Duma.

Under the above-mentioned provisions the first Duma assembled on May 10, 1906; it was dissolved on July 21, 1906. The second Duma met on March 5, 1907; it was dissolved on June 16, 1907, because of its failure immediately to surrender, upon the demand of the government, fifty-five Social Democratic members accused of plotting against the government; the third Duma met on November 14, 1907. In violation of the Fundamental Laws, the emperor, at the time of dissolving the second Duma, issued a new election law. By this law elections will hereafter be by distinct classes of voters, in a manner somewhat similar to the system recently abandoned in Austria. The classes are: (1) landed proprietors; (2) urban electors, divided into two classes according to the amount of taxes which they pay; (3) peasants; (4) laborers. The landed proprietors and the richer classes gain an increased influence in the elections; the influence of peasants and laborers is reduced. The large industrial centers lose their special representation. The total number of representatives is reduced from 524 to 442, the curtailment being principally in the non-Russian portions of the empire; the Polish representation is reduced from 36 to 14.

illegality on their part or on the part of officers subordinate
to them or to their offices.

67. The Council of the Empire and the Imperial Duma
shall have power, in the order of procedure prescribed for
these institutions, to deliberate concerning all matters placed
within their authority by the laws creating these bodies.

68. Projects of law shall be discussed in the Imperial
Duma, and upon its approval shall be submitted to the Council
of the Empire. Projects of law, elaborated by the Council of
the Empire shall be discussed in the Council and upon its
approval shall be submitted to the Imperial Duma.

69. Projects of law not adopted by the Council of the
Empire or by the Imperial Duma shall be considered as
rejected.

70. Projects of law, elaborated by the Council of the
Empire or by the Imperial Duma, and not approved by the
Emperor, shall not again be presented in either of these bodies
for consideration during the same session. Projects of law,
elaborated by the Council of the Empire or by the Imperial
Duma and rejected by one of these bodies, may be again
presented to these bodies for consideration during the same
session, if the Emperor should order it.

71. Projects of law, presented to the Imperial Duma and
approved by the latter and by the Council of the Empire, and
projects of law, elaborated by the Council of the Empire and
approved by the latter and by the Imperial Duma, shall be
submitted to the Emperor by the president of the Council of
the Empire.

72. In the revision of the budget, the sums destined for the
covering of government loans and other indebtedness contracted by the Russian Empire shall not be excluded or
curtailed.

73. Credits for the expenses of the ministry of the imperial
court as well as those for the institutions subordinate thereto,
in sums not exceeding those assigned in the budget of 1906,

shall not be submitted for discussion before the Imperial Duma or the Council of the Empire. Likewise, changes made in the above-mentioned credits by virtue of the regulations regarding the imperial family, on account of changes made in such regulations, shall not be subject to discussion either in the Imperial Duma or in the Council of the Empire.

74. Should the budget not be approved before the beginning of the fiscal year, the last budget approved according to the legal forms shall remain in force with only the modifications introduced by laws passed since its establishment. Until the publication of the new budget, credits may be gradually opened by order of the Council of Ministers and placed at the disposal of the various ministers and principal institutions in amounts absolutely necessary, which shall, however, not exceed one-twelfth of the total amount of the expenditures fixed by the budget.

75. Extraordinary credits for the needs in time of war and for special preparation preceding war may be opened in all branches of the government, by virtue of the powers of the supreme administration, in the manner prescribed by law.

76. Government loans to cover ordinary budgetary and extraordinary expenditures may be granted in accordance with the procedure established for the approval of the budget of expenditures and revenues of the Empire. Government loans for the purpose of covering expenditures, in cases and within the limits provided by Art. 74, as well as loans for the purpose of covering expenditures mentioned in Art. 75, may be authorized by the Emperor, in the exercise of the supreme power.

77. If the project giving the number of men necessary for the recruiting of the army and the navy has been submitted in time to the Imperial Duma and a law regarding this matter shall not have been enacted in the regular manner by May 1, the Emperor may, by ukase, call to the colors the necessary number of men; this number, however, shall not exceed that recruited in the previous year.

CHAPTER V.   THE COUNCIL OF MINISTERS, THE MINISTERS,
AND THE HEADS OF INDEPENDENT INSTITUTIONS

78. The direction and unification of the actions of the ministers and of the heads of independent institutions in matters bearing upon legislation as well as in the higher governmental administration shall belong to the Council of Ministers and shall be based on principles determined by law.[5]

79. The ministers and heads of independent institutions have the right to vote in the Council of the Empire and in the Imperial Duma only if they are members of these bodies.

80. The obligatory orders, instructions, and regulations, issued by the Council of Ministers, by the ministers and the heads of independent institutions, as well as by other persons authorized by law to take such action, shall not be in violation of the law.

81. The president of the Council of Ministers, the ministers, and the heads of independent institutions shall be responsible to the Emperor for the general course of the governmental administration.   Each of them shall be individually responsible for his actions and orders.

82. The president of the Council of Ministers, the ministers, and heads of independent institutions incur the civil and criminal responsibility, in accordance with the provisions of the law, for all criminal offenses committed in the discharge of their duties.

[5] The Council of Ministers was organized by imperial ukase of November 1, 1905. The president of the Council has the right to require information from all other ministers, and to represent the general administration in the Duma and in the Council of the Empire. No general administrative measure can be adopted without the action of the Council of Ministers.

SPAIN

The Spanish constitutional régime begins with the year 1808; in that year Ferdinand VII and his father, Charles IV, under pressure of Napoleon, abdicated in favor of the French, and Joseph Bonaparte became king of Spain. Napoleon convened at Bayonne an assembly of Spanish notables, to which was submitted the project of a constitution; this constitution was adopted almost without change and was published on July 6, 1808.

The people of Spain did not submit to French domination as tamely as did their legitimate rulers. Provincial juntas were organized to resist the foreigners; an independent national government was established, and a general Cortes was convened in 1810; the liberal constitution of March 18, 1812, was adopted by this Cortes.

When Ferdinand VII was restored to the Spanish throne in 1814 he refused to submit to a constitutional government, and restored as far as possible the absolutist system which had existed before 1808. But the Spanish people had gained some experience in self-government from 1808 to 1814; contact with people from other countries had made them familiar with liberal principles; this was particularly true of the military officers who had come in contact with the advanced political thought of France and England. The military insurrection of 1820 forced Ferdinand to accept the constitution of 1812, but the French intervention of 1823 overthrew the constitution, and restored the system of absolutism, which continued until Ferdinand's death in 1833.

Ferdinand's wife, who became regent after his death, issued on April 10, 1834, a constitution by which a legislature with limited power was created. Further concessions were necessary in order to obtain support in the civil war against the Carlists; the constitution of 1812 was re-established in 1836 and a constituent Cortes was convened which adopted the constitution of June 17, 1837, which was modeled after the constitution of 1812. A more conservative constitution was adopted on May 23, 1845.

A constituent Cortes was again convened in 1854, and a liberal constitution was drawn up in 1856 but was not adopted; by a royal decree of 1856 the constitution of 1845 was amended and re-established; this constitution was amended in several important respects in a reactionary direction in 1857 but these amendments were repealed in 1864.

In 1868 a revolution occurred which drove Queen Isabel II from the throne. A new Cortes, elected by universal suffrage, adopted the constitution of June 1, 1869; the monarchical system was continued, but for some time no one could be persuaded to accept the vacant throne. Amadeo, the son of Victor Emmanuel of Italy, was finally chosen king, but governed only a little over two years.

After Amadeo's resignation the republic was proclaimed, and in 1873 a republican constitution, with a federal system of government, was drawn up, but was not adopted. The republic did not rest upon the solid basis of popular support; the people turned again to the Bourbon rulers who had been so recently driven from the country. The monarchy was re-established in December, 1874, and Alfonso XII was proclaimed king. A constituent Cortes was convened in February, 1876, and the constitution now in force was adopted on June 30 of the same year; this constitution has remained unaltered until the present day.

SELECT BIBLIOGRAPHY

SPAIN. *Constitución política de la monarchía Española y leyes complementarias.* (4th ed., Madrid, 1901.)

————. *Constituciones de España y de las demas naciones de Europa.* . . . . Por una Sociedad de jurisconsultos. (Madrid, 1886. 2 vols.) Contains text of all the Spanish constitutions.

MARTÍNEZ ALCUBILLA, MARCELO. *Diccionario de la administración Española.* (5th ed., 1892-94. 9 vols.) An invaluable collection of laws relating to Spanish public administration. Since 1892 the collection has been continued by an annual appendix.

SANTAMARIA DE PAREDES, VICENTE. *Curso de derecho político.* (6th ed., Madrid, 1898.) A general work which contains an excellent sketch of Spanish constitutional history and constitutional law.

COLMEIRO, MANUEL. *Elementos del derecho político y administrativo de España.* (7th ed., Madrid, 1887.)

Santamaria de Paredes, Vicente. *Curso de derecho administrativo.* (5th ed., Madrid, 1898.) The best brief treatise on Spanish administrative law.

Posada, Adolfo. *Tratado de derecho administrativo.* (Madrid, 1897–98. 2 vols.)

Torres Campos, Manuel. *Das Staatsrecht des Königreichs Spanien.* (Freiburg, 1889. Handbuch des oeffentlichen Rechts.)

Gmelin, Hans. *Studien zur spanischen Verfassungsgeschichte des neunzehnten Jahrhunderts.* (Stuttgart, 1905.) A useful study of Spanish constitutional development.

Publicaciónes Parlamentarias. An ambitious work which is to include Spanish constitutional texts, a treatise on Spanish constitutional law, and a collection of foreign constitutions. The first volume, which contains texts of Spanish constitutional documents, has been issued (*Constituciónes y reglamentos.* Madrid, 1906).

Pons y Umbert, A. *Organización y funcionamento de las cortes según las constituciónes españolas y reglamentación de dicho cuerpo colegislador.* (Madrid, 1906.)

POLITICAL CONSTITUTION OF THE SPANISH MONARCHY[1]

(June 30, 1876)

TITLE I. SPANIARDS AND THEIR RIGHTS

ARTICLE 1. The following are Spaniards:

1) Persons born in Spanish territory.

2) Children of a Spanish father or mother, although born outside of Spain.

3) Foreigners who have obtained papers of naturalization.

4) Foreigners who without such papers have acquired a residence in any town of the kingdom.

Spaniards lose their nationality by becoming naturalized in a foreign country, or by entering the service of another government without the permission of the King.

[1] In the preparation of this text assistance has been received from the translation in *British and Foreign State Papers*, Vol. LXVII (1875–76), p. 118.

ART. 2. Foreigners may freely establish themselves in Spanish territory, may exercise their calling therein, and may practice any profession for the exercise of which the laws do not require certificates of fitness issued by Spanish authorities.

Persons not naturalized cannot hold in Spain any office conferring authority or jurisdiction.

ART. 3. Every Spaniard is under obligation to bear arms in the defense of the country when called upon by law, and to contribute, in proportion to his wealth, toward the expenses of the state, of the province, and of the municipality.

No person shall be required to pay a tax which has not been voted by the Cortes, or by a corporation legally authorized to impose the same.

ART. 4. No Spaniard or foreigner shall be arrested except in the cases and in the manner prescribed by law.

Every person arrested shall be set at liberty or handed over to the judicial authority within twenty-four hours after his arrest.

Every arrest shall be without effect, or shall be converted into imprisonment within seventy-two hours of the delivery of the arrested person to a competent judge.

The action taken in the matter shall be made known to the interested party within the same time.

ART. 5. No Spaniard shall be imprisoned except by virtue of an order of a competent judge.

The writ containing the order [of arrest] shall be approved or annulled, after a hearing of the suspected offender, within seventy-two hours after the arrest.

Every person detained or imprisoned without the legal formalities, or in cases not provided by the constitution and the laws, shall be set at liberty on the petition of himself or of any Spaniard. The law shall provide the form of summary procedure in such cases.

ART. 6. No one shall enter the house of a Spaniard or of

a foreigner resident in Spain, without his consent, except in the cases and in the manner expressly provided by law.

The examination of papers and effects shall always take place in the presence of the interested party or of a member of his family, and in default thereof, in the presence of two witnesses from the same town.

ART. 7.   Correspondence intrusted to the post shall not be detained or opened by the governmental authorities.

ART. 8.   Every order for imprisonment, for the search of domicile, or for the detention of correspondence shall contain a statement of the cause of its issuance.

ART. 9.   No Spaniard shall be compelled to change his domicile or residence except by virtue of the order of a competent authority, and in the cases provided by law.

ART. 10.   The penalty of confiscation of property shall never be imposed, and no one shall be deprived of his property except by the competent authority, and for a proved cause of public utility, always after due compensation.

If this requirement is not fulfilled, the judges shall protect the dispossessed person and, in such case, shall return the property to his possession.

ART. 11.   The Apostolic Roman Catholic religion is the religion of the state. The nation binds itself to maintain this religion and its ministers.

No one shall be molested in Spanish territory on account of his religious opinions, or for the exercise of his particular form of worship, provided he show the respect due to Christian morality.

Ceremonies and public manifestations other than those of the state religion, however, shall not be permitted.

ART. 12.   Everyone shall be free to choose his profession and to learn it as he may think best.

Any Spaniard may found and maintain institutions of instruction or of education, in conformity with the law.

The state shall have the power to issue professional diplo-

mas, and to determine the qualifications of those who desire
to obtain them, and the manner in which such persons shall
prove their fitness therefor.

A special law shall determine the duties of teachers and
the rules to which teaching is to be subjected in the institutions
of public instruction supported by the state, the provinces, or
the municipalities.

ART. 13. Every Spaniard shall have the right:

To give free expression to his ideas and opinions, either
verbally or in writing, through the medium of the press or of
any other similar process, without subjection to previous
censorship.

To hold peaceful meetings.

To become a member of associations for the purpose of
promoting the objects of human life.

To address petitions, either individually or with others, to
the King, to the Cortes, or to the authorities.

The right of petition shall not be exercised by any kind of
armed force.

Those who form a part of an armed force shall not exercise individually the right of petition, except in accordance
with the laws of their organization, in regard to matters relating thereto.

ART. 14. Proper rules shall be provided by law to secure
to Spaniards the mutual observance of the rights recognized in
this title, without detriment to the rights of the nation or to
the essential attributes of public authority.

The law shall also determine the civil and penal liability
incurred by judges, officers, and functionaries of all classes
who attempt to violate the rights enumerated in this title.

ART. 15. All Spaniards shall be eligible to public offices
and employments, according to their merit and capacity.

ART. 16. No Spaniard shall be tried or sentenced except
by the proper judge or court, by virtue of laws passed prior
to the offense, and in the manner prescribed therein.

ART. 17. The guaranties expressed in Arts. 4, 5, 6, and 9, and in the first, second, and third paragraphs of Art. 13 shall not be suspended throughout the kingdom or in any portion thereof, except temporarily and by means of a law, when, in extraordinary circumstances, the security of the state may require it.

When the Cortes is not in session and the case is grave and clearly urgent, the government, upon its own responsibility, may order the suspension of the guaranties mentioned in the previous paragraph, submitting its action to the approval of the Cortes as soon as possible.

But in no case shall other guaranties than those mentioned in the first paragraph of this article be suspended.

Nor shall the military or civil authorities have power to establish any other penalty than that previously prescribed by law.

TITLE II.   THE CORTES

ART. 18. The legislative power shall reside in the Cortes together with the King.

ART. 19. The Cortes shall be composed of two legislative bodies, equal in powers: the Senate and the Congress of Deputies.

TITLE III.   THE SENATE

ART. 20. The Senate shall be composed:

1) Of senators in their own right.

2) Of life senators appointed by the crown.

3) Of senators elected by the corporations of the state and by the larger taxpayers, in the manner to be determined by law.[a]

[a] The election of senators is regulated by the law of February 8, 1877. The 180 elected senators are chosen as follows: (1) One member by the clergy of each of the nine Archbishoprics, 9; (2) One by each of the six royal academies, 6; (3) One by each of the ten universities, 10; (4) Five by the Economic Societies of the Friends of the Country, 5; (5) The remaining 150 senators are chosen by electoral colleges in each province. These

The number of senators in their own right and of life senators shall not exceed one hundred and eighty.

There shall be the same number of elected senators.

ART. 21. The following shall be senators in their own right:

The sons of the King and of the heir presumptive to the throne, upon the attainment of their majority.

Grandees of Spain in their own right, who are not subjects of another power and have a proven yearly income of 60,000 pesetas derived from real property of their own or from rights legally equivalent to real property.

The captains-general of the army and the admiral of the navy.

The patriarch of the Indies and the archbishops.

The presidents of the Council of State, of the Supreme Court, of the Court of Accounts of the Kingdom, and of the Supreme Councils of War and of the Navy, after two years of service.

ART. 22. Only the Spaniards who belong, or shall have belonged, to one of the following classes shall be senators by royal appointment, or through election by the corporations of the state and the larger taxpayers:

1) President of the Senate or of the Congress of Deputies.

2) Deputies who shall have belonged to three different congresses, or who shall have served during eight sessions.

3) Ministers of the crown.

4) Bishops.

5) Grandees of Spain.

6) Lieutenant-generals of the army and vice-admirals of the navy, two years after their appointment.

7) Ambassadors, after two years of active service, and ministers plenipotentiary after four years of service.

colleges are composed of members of the provincial deputations, and of representatives chosen from among the municipal councilors and largest taxpayers of the several towns and municipal districts.

8) Councilors of state, the *fiscal*[a] of that council, ministers, and *fiscals* of the Supreme Court and of the Court of Accounts of the Kingdom, supreme councilors of war and of the navy, and the dean of the Court of Military Orders, after two years of service.

9) Presidents or directors of the Royal Academies, viz.: The Royal Spanish Academy; The Royal Academy of History; The Royal Academy of Fine Arts of San Fernando; The Royal Academy of Exact, Physical, and Natural Sciences; The Royal Academy of Moral and Political Sciences, and The Royal Academy of Medicine.

10) Members of the aforesaid academies who shall in point of seniority come within the first half of the list of members of their respective bodies; first-class inspectors-general of the Corps of Engineers of roads, mines, and forests; and head-professors of the universities, if they have held that rank and performed the duties thereof for four years.

Persons included in the above categories must also have an annual income of 7,500 pesetas, derived from property of their own, or from salaries of employments that can be lost only for cause legally proven, or from a pension, or retirement or dismissal allowance.

11) Persons who for two years shall have possessed an annual income of 20,000 pesetas, or who shall have paid into the public treasury a direct tax of 4,000 pesetas, if, in addition, they possess titles of nobility, or shall have been deputies to the Cortes, provincial deputies, or mayors in capitals of provinces or in towns of more than 20,000 inhabitants.

12) Persons who shall have been senators at any time before the promulgation of this constitution. Those who, in order to become senators, shall have proved their income at any time, may give evidence thereof, in order that it may be computed for them, upon their becoming senators in their own

---

[a] *Fiscal* is an officer corresponding to the American state attorney or attorney-general.

right, by certificate of the register of property, proving that they still own the same property.

The appointment of senators by the King shall be made by special decree, which shall always set forth the foundation upon which, in accordance with the provisions of this article, the appointment is based.

ART. 23. The qualifications necessary for the appointment or election of a senator may be altered by law.

ART. 24. One-half of the elected senators shall be renewed every five years, and all shall be renewed when the King dissolves the elected part of the Senate.

ART. 25. Senators shall not accept employment, promotion (except that strictly governed by seniority), titles, or decorations during the sessions of the Cortes.

However, the government may confer upon them, within the sphere of their respective posts or ranks, such commissions as the public service may require.

The office of minister of the crown is excepted from the provisions of the first paragraph of this article.

ART. 26. To become a senator one must be a Spaniard, have completed the age of thirty-five years, not have been subjected to criminal proceedings, nor have been deprived of the exercise of his political rights, and have the free management of his property.

TITLE IV.   THE CONGRESS OF DEPUTIES

ART. 27. The Congress of Deputies shall be composed of those named by the electoral bodies, in the form determined by law. At least one deputy shall be chosen for every 50,000 inhabitants.[4]

[4] The election of deputies is regulated by a law of August 8, 1907. Male Spaniards of the age of twenty-five, who are in possession of their civil rights, and have resided in the district for two years, enjoy the privilege of voting. The exercise of this privilege is compulsory, the only exceptions to this rule being persons over the age of seventy and certain judicial officers. Deputies are directly elected from districts into which the

ART. 28. Deputies shall be elected and may be re-elected an indefinite number of times in the manner provided by law.

ART. 29. To be elected as a deputy, one must be a Spaniard, a layman, of full age,[5] and in the enjoyment of all civil rights. The law shall determine what classes of functions are incompatible with the office of deputy and with re-election to this office.

ART. 30. Deputies shall be elected for five years.

ART. 31. Deputies upon whom the government or the royal household confers a pension, office, promotion (except promotion governed by seniority), commission with remuneration, honors, or decorations, shall cease to exercise their functions as deputies, without the necessity of any declaration, unless within one fortnight after their appointment they inform the Congress of their refusal of the favor.

The provisions of the preceding paragraph do not relate to deputies who may be appointed ministers of the crown.

TITLE V. THE MEETINGS AND POWERS OF THE CORTES

ART. 32. The Cortes shall meet every year. The King shall have power to convene, to suspend, and to close the sessions of the Cortes, and to dissolve, simultaneously or separately, the elective part of the Senate and the Congress of Deputies; in case of dissolution, the King is obliged to convene and assemble the dissolved body or bodies within three months.

ART. 33. The Cortes must be convened as soon as the crown becomes vacant, or when the King is in any way incapacitated for governing.

country is divided. In districts choosing more than one deputy a system of limited voting prevails; if less than four deputies are to be chosen, each person votes for one less than the number to be elected; if more than four are to be chosen he votes for two less than the whole number; if more than eight are to be chosen he votes for three less than the total number; if more than ten are to be elected he votes for four less than the total number.

[5] Twenty-five years is fixed as full age by the electoral law.

ART. 34. Each of the legislative bodies shall adopt its own rules for its internal direction, and shall determine both the qualifications of its members and the legality of their election.

ART. 35. The Congress of Deputies shall choose its president, vice-presidents, and secretaries.

ART. 36. The King shall appoint, for each session, from among the senators themselves, the president and vice-presidents of the Senate; but the Senate shall elect its secretaries.

ART. 37. The King shall open and close the Cortes, either in person or through the medium of his ministers.

ART. 38. Neither of the legislative bodies shall be assembled without the other, except in the case in which the Senate exercises judicial functions.

ART. 39. The legislative bodies shall not deliberate in joint session, or in the presence of the King.

ART. 40. The sessions of the Senate and of the Congress shall be public, and secret sessions shall be held only when privacy is necessary.

ART. 41. The King and each of the legislative bodies shall have the right to initiate laws.

ART. 42. Laws relating to taxation and to the public credit shall be presented, in the first instance, in the Congress of Deputies.

ART. 43. Resolutions may be passed in either of the legislative bodies by a majority vote; but the presence of one more than half of the total number of members is necessary in order to vote on laws.

ART. 44. If one of the legislative bodies should reject any bill or should the King refuse his sanction thereto, no other bill upon the same subject shall be introduced in that session.

ART. 45. In addition to the legislative power which the Cortes exercises with the King, it shall possess the following powers:

1) To receive from the King, from the immediate suc-

cessor to the throne, and from the regency or regent of the kingdom, the oath to maintain the constitution and the laws.

2) To elect the regent or regency of the kingdom, and to appoint a guardian for the minor King, under the provisions of the constitution.

3) To make effective the responsibility of the ministers, who may be impeached by the Congress and tried by the Senate.

ART. 46. Senators and deputies are inviolable for their opinions and votes in the exercise of their functions.

ART. 47. Judicial proceedings shall not be begun against senators, nor shall they be arrested without the previous determination of the Senate, unless they have been taken in the commission of an offense or when the Senate is not in session; but in every case a report shall be made to that body as soon as possible, in order that it may determine what action shall be taken. Neither shall judicial proceedings be begun against deputies nor shall they be arrested during a session without the permission of the Congress unless they have been taken in the commission of an offense; but in this event and in the event of their being proceeded against or arrested when the Cortes is not in session, a report shall be made as soon as possible to the Congress for its information and action. The Supreme Court shall take cognizance of criminal proceedings against senators and deputies in the cases and in the manner provided by law.

TITLE VI.   THE KING AND HIS MINISTERS

ART. 48. The person of the King is sacred and inviolable.

ART. 49. The ministers are responsible.[6]

No order of the King shall be executed unless countersigned by a minister, who by this act alone becomes responsible for it.

[6] Besides the president of the council, there are at present nine ministers, viz.: the ministers of state; of justice; of war; of marine; of the treasury; of government; of public instruction, fine arts, and agriculture; of industry; and of commerce and public works.

ART. 50.   The power of executing the laws shall be vested
in the King, and his authority shall extend to everything which
conduces to the preservation of public order at home and the
security of the state abroad, in conformity with the constitution
and the laws.

ART. 51.   The King sanctions and promulgates the laws.

ART. 52.   He shall have supreme command of the army
and navy, and direct the land and naval forces.

ART. 53.   He bestows ranks, promotions, and military
rewards, in accordance with the laws.

ART. 54.   The King shall also have power:

1) To issue decrees, regulations, and instructions which
may be conducive to the execution of the laws.

2) To see that justice is fully and promptly administered
throughout the kingdom.

3) To pardon criminals in accordance with the law.

4) To declare war and to make peace, furnishing afterward a report with documents to the Cortes.

5) To conduct diplomatic and commercial relations with
other powers.

6) To have control of the coinage of money, upon which
shall be stamped his head and name.

7) To decree the distribution of the funds appropriated to
each department of the administration, in accordance with the
budgetary law.

8) To confer civil employments, and to grant honors and
distinctions of every class, in accordance with the law.

9) Freely to appoint and to dismiss his ministers.

ART. 55.   The King must be authorized by a special law:

1) To alienate, cede, or exchange any part of Spanish
territory.

2) To incorporate any other territory with that of Spain.

3) To admit foreign troops into the kingdom.

4) To ratify treaties of offensive alliance, which relate
especially to commerce, or which stipulate the payment of

subsidies to any foreign power, and all treaties which may be
binding individually upon Spaniards.

In no case shall secret articles of a treaty annul public ones.

5) To abdicate the crown in favor of the heir presumptive.

ART. 56. The King, before contracting marriage, shall
inform the Cortes, to whose approbation shall be submitted the
marriage contracts and stipulations, which shall be the object
of a law.

The same formalities shall be observed with respect to the
heir presumptive to the throne.

Neither the king nor the heir presumptive shall contract
marriage with any person who is by law excluded from the
succession to the throne.

ART. 57. The revenue of the King and of his family shall
be fixed by the Cortes at the beginning of each reign.

ART. 58. Ministers may be senators or deputies and may
take part in the discussions of both legislative bodies, but shall
vote only in the one to which they belong.

TITLE VII. THE SUCCESSION TO THE THRONE

ART. 59. The legitimate king of Spain is Don Alfonso
XII of Bourbon.[7]

ART. 60. The succession to the throne of Spain shall
follow the regular order of primogeniture and representation,
the elder line always being preferred to the younger ones; in
the same line the nearer degree of kinship to the more remote;
in the same degree of kinship, the male to the female; in the
same sex, the older to the younger person.

ART. 61. If the lines of legitimate descendants of Don
Alfonso XII of Bourbon should be extinguished, his sisters
shall succeed in the established order; then his aunt, the sister
of his mother, and her legitimate descendants, and those of his
uncles, the brothers of Don Fernando VII, if they should not
have been excluded.

[7] Alfonso XIII who became of age in 1902 is the present king.

ART. 62. If all of the above-named lines should be extinguished the Cortes shall make such new choice as may be most suitable to the nation.

ART. 63. Any doubts as to facts or rights which may occur in the order of the succession to the crown shall be settled by a law.

ART. 64. Those who may be incapable of governing, or who may have committed some act for which they deserve to lose their right to the crown, shall be excluded from the succession by a law.

ART. 65. When a woman reigns, the prince consort shall have no share whatever in the government of the kingdom.

TITLE VIII.   THE MINORITY OF THE KING AND THE REGENCY

ART. 66. The King shall be a minor until he has attained the age of 16 years.

ART. 67. When the King is a minor, the father or the mother of the King, or in default thereof, the relative nearest to the succession to the crown, according to the order established in the constitution, shall at once enter upon the duties of the regency, and shall exercise them during the whole minority of the King.

ART. 68. In order that the nearest relative may exercise the regency, he must be a Spaniard, have reached the age of twenty years, and not be excluded from the succession to the crown. The father or mother of the King shall exercise the regency only so long as they do not remarry.

ART. 69. The regent shall take before the Cortes an oath of fidelity to the minor King, and to preserve the constitution and the laws.

If the Cortes is not assembled the regent shall convoke it immediately, and in the meanwhile shall take the above-mentioned oath before the Council of Ministers, promising to repeat it before the Cortes as soon as it has assembled.

ART. 70. If there be no person to whom the regency falls

by right, the Cortes shall appoint a regency which may consist
of one, three, or five persons.

Until this appointment shall have been made, the Council
of Ministers shall provisionally govern the kingdom.

ART. 71.   When the King is incapacitated for the exercise
of authority, and his incapacity shall have been recognized by
the Cortes, his eldest son, provided he be 16 years of age, shall
exercise the regency during the incapacity of the King; if
there be no son, the wife of the King, and in her default, those
summoned to the regency.

ART. 72.   The regent or the regency, in case there is one,
shall exercise the full authority of the King, in whose name the
acts of the government shall be published.

ART. 73.   The guardian of the minor King shall be the
person named in the will of the deceased monarch, provided
that he be a Spaniard by birth.   If no person should be so
named, the father or mother shall be the guardian, so long as
they do not remarry.   If there be no father or mother, the
Cortes shall appoint the guardian, but the duties of regent and
of guardian of the King shall not be united in the same person,
except in that of the father or mother of the King.

TITLE IX.   THE ADMINISTRATION OF JUSTICE

ART. 74.   Justice shall be administered in the name of the
King.

ART. 75.   The same codes shall be in force throughout the
whole monarchy, without prejudice to variations which the law
may determine upon for particular circumstances.

In the codes shall be established but one system of law for
all Spaniards, in ordinary civil and criminal cases.

ART. 76.   The power of applying the laws in civil and
criminal cases shall belong exclusively to the courts, which
shall exercise no other functions than those of judging and of
enforcing their judgments.

ART. 77.   A special law shall determine the cases in which previous authorization shall be required in order to proceed before the ordinary courts against the public authorities and their agents.

ART. 78. The laws shall determine what courts shall be created, the organization of each, its powers, the manner of exercising them, and the qualifications which its members must possess.

ART. 79. Proceedings in criminal matters shall be public, and in the form provided by law.

ART. 80. Magistrates and judges shall be irremovable and shall not be removed, suspended, or transferred, except in the cases and in the manner prescribed by the organic law of the courts.

ART. 81. Judges shall be personally responsible for any violation of the law which they may commit.

TITLE X. THE PROVINCIAL DEPUTATIONS AND THE MUNICIPAL COUNCILS

ART. 82. In each province there shall be a provincial deputation, elected in the manner provided by law and composed of the number of members fixed by law.[8]

ART. 83. In the towns there shall be mayors and municipal councils. The members of the municipal council shall be chosen by the inhabitants upon whom the law confers such right.[8]

ART. 84. The organization and powers of the provincial deputations and of the municipal councils shall be regulated by their respective laws.

Laws for this purpose shall be based on the following principles:

[8] The law of June 28, 1890, provides that all male Spaniards of the age of 25 may vote for members of the provincial deputations and municipal councils. The law of 1890 has been partially superseded by the law of August 8, 1907.

1) Government and direction of the local interests of the province or of the town by their respective deputations or councils.

2) Publication of the estimates, accounts, and official acts of such local bodies.

3) Intervention of the King, and in certain cases, of the Cortes, in order to prevent the provincial deputations and municipal councils from exceeding their powers to the prejudice of general and established interests.

4) Determination of their powers in the matter of taxation in order that the provincial and municipal corporations may never be in conflict with the financial system of the State.

TITLE XI.   TAXATION

ART. 85.   The government shall annually present to the Cortes, for its examination and approval, the general estimates of the expenses of the state for the following year, and the plan of taxation and means of meeting such expenses, as well as the accounts of the collection of taxes and of the expenditure of the public funds.

If the budget cannot be voted before the first day of the next fiscal year, that of the previous year shall remain in force, provided always that the latter had been discussed and voted by the Cortes and sanctioned by the King.

ART. 86.   The government must have authority by law in order to dispose of property of the state and to borrow money on the credit of the nation.

ART. 87.   The public debt shall be under the special protection of the nation.

TITLE XII.   THE MILITARY FORCES

ART. 88.   The Cortes shall annually fix, upon the proposal of the King, the permanent military force on land and sea.

TITLE XIII.   THE GOVERNMENT OF THE COLONIES

ART. 89.   The colonies shall be governed by special laws, but the government is authorized to apply to them, with the modifications which it may think proper, the laws promulgated or which may be promulgated for the peninsula, giving an account thereof to the Cortes.

Cuba and Puerto Rico shall be represented in the Cortes of the kingdom in the manner to be determined by a special law, which may be different for each one of the two provinces.[9]

---

[9] By the treaty of Paris of 1898 Spain renounced sovereignty over Cuba, and ceded to the United States Puerto Rico, Guam, and the Philippine Islands. The Caroline, Marianne (Ladrones), and Palaos Islands were sold to Germany by Spain on February 12, 1899.

SWEDEN

Sweden in the Middle Ages was an aristocratic monarchy with an elective ruler. For over a hundred years after the union of Kalmar in 1397 the three Scandinavian kingdoms of Denmark, Norway, and Sweden were united under one ruler. Sweden was ruled from and in the interests of Denmark. Sweden gained her independence, the powers of the nobles and clergy were reduced, and by a law of 1544 the crown became hereditary. Under Gustavas Vasa and his immediate successors the kingdom was reorganized and for a time became one of the great powers of Europe. The provincial assemblies gave way in the sixteenth century to the national legislature or Riksdag, composed of representatives of the nobles, clergy, cities, and peasantry.

Under Gustavus Adolphus laws were enacted for the systematic organization of the government. The law of 1617 on the organization of the Riksdag, that of 1626 defining the powers of the nobility, and the constitution of 1634 issued by Chancellor Oxenstjerna after Gustavus' death at Lützen fixed with precision the powers of the great departments of the government. The powers of the Riksdag were extended by the additional act of 1660. In 1680 and 1682 the king, with the consent of the Riksdag, assumed almost complete power and the absolute monarchy lasted until 1718.

Charles XII, who had governed Sweden arbitrarily and had ruined the country by foreign wars, aroused strong feeling in favor of a return to popular government. After his death, by the laws of 1719, 1720, and 1723, all power was vested in the Riksdag. Only the name of king remained. The executive conduct of government was vested in a Council in which the King was given a casting vote. During the sessions of the Riksdag all powers of government were exercised by its Secret Committee which was dominated by the nobles. The King became a state decoration rather than a ruler.

The system of legislative dominance continued for over fifty years, during which Sweden gained neither internal peace nor

honor abroad. A conspiracy was organized in 1772 with King
Gustavus III at its head and the Riksdag was forced on August
21 of that year to adopt a constitution which restored the crown
to the position which it had occupied before 1719. By the Act
of Union and Security of 1789 the King's power was still further
augmented, and the special privileges of the nobles were curtailed. These acts so angered the nobility that Gustavus was
assassinated in 1792. His successor, the half-crazy Gustavus
IV, involved Sweden in war with Russia, with the result that
Finland was lost and the independence of Sweden was threatened. Gustavus was deposed and a new king, Charles XIII, was
chosen. A new constitution was adopted on June 6, 1809.

The constitution has been amended at almost every session
of the Riksdag since 1809. The most important alterations have
been (1) that of 1866 substituting a bicameral legislature for the
four estates; (2) the reorganization of the Council of State in
1840 and the creation of the office of the president of the Council
in 1876. By Art. 85 of the constitution the law organizing the
Riksdag, the act of succession, and the law relating to the freedom of the press are fundamental laws and may be amended only
in the manner provided for changing the constitution. A new
Riksdag law was enacted on June 22, 1866, to provide for the
new organization of the two houses of the legislature.

SELECT BIBLIOGRAPHY

UPPSTRÖM, W. *Sveriges Grundlager och konstitutionela stadgar jemte
    kommunallagarne samt Norges Grundlov.* (6th ed., Stockholm [1903].)
    An excellent collection of Swedish constitutional laws.

NAUMANN, CHRISTIAN. *Sveriges statsförfatningsrätt.* (2d ed., Stock-
    holm, 1879–84. 4 vols.) The leading treatise; the editor has not had
    an opportunity to examine this work.

FAHLBECK, PONTUS. *La constitution suédoise et le parlementarisme
    moderne.* (Paris, 1905.) Contains a brief sketch of Swedish con-
    stitutional history and government.

HILDEBRAND, EMIL. *Svenska statsförfattningens historiska utveckling
    från äldsta tid våra dagar.* (Stockholm [1896].)

ASCHEHOUG, T. H. *Das Staatsrecht der vereinigten königreiche Schwe-
    den und Norwegen.* (Freiburg, 1886. Handbuch des oeffentlichen
    Rechts.)

CONSTITUTION OF SWEDEN

(June 6, 1809)

We the estates of the Swedish Kingdom, counts, barons, bishops, nobles, clergy, burghers, and peasants, assembled in general session on our own behalf and in behalf of our brethren at home, publicly declare that, whereas we the deputies of the Swedish people have gained the opportunity of improving the condition of our country through the establishment of a revised constitution in consequence of the recent change of government to which we have given our unanimous consent, we do hereby repeal the fundamental laws which have been more or less in force up to this time, viz.: the constitution of August 21, 1772, the act of union and security of February 21 and April 3, 1789, the Riksdag ordinance of January 24, 1617, and all other such old or new laws, acts, ordinances, enactments, or resolutions as have heretofore gone under the name of fundamental laws; and we do hereby make known the adoption of the following constitution for the Swedish Kingdom and its dependencies, which from henceforth shall be the foremost fundamental law of the land, reserving to this diet the right to adopt, in the manner herein prescribed, the other fundamental laws mentioned in Art. 85 of this constitution:

ARTICLE 1.   Sweden shall be governed by a king and shall be a hereditary monarchy with the order of succession established by the law of succession.[1]

ART. 2.   The King shall always belong to the pure evangelical faith as adopted and explained in the unaltered Augsburg Confession and in the resolution of the Upsala Synod of 1593.

[1] By Art. 85 of the constitution the law of succession is included as one of the fundamental laws. The succession is regulated by law of September 26, 1810, which confirmed the election of Marshal Bernadotte, prince of Ponte Corvo, as crown prince of Sweden. The crown is transmitted in the male line in the order of primogeniture, to the exclusion of females and of their descendants.

Art. 3. The person of the King shall be sacred and inviolable; he shall not be subject to any prosecution for his actions.

Art. 4. The King alone shall govern the kingdom in accordance with the provisions of this constitution; he shall, however, in the cases hereafter specified, ask the opinion and advice of a Council of State; he shall appoint the members of this Council from among capable, experienced, honest persons of good reputation, who are Swedes by birth, and who belong to the pure evangelical faith.

Art. 5. The Council of State shall be composed of eleven members, one of whom the King shall appoint as minister of state and president of the Council. These members shall be present whenever any business is transacted. Neither father and son nor brothers shall be members of the Council of State at the same time.

Art. 6. Eight of the members of the Council of State shall be heads of departments, and each of them shall present reports upon the affairs of his department; viz.:

The minister of foreign affairs for the Department of Foreign Affairs.

The head of the Department of Justice.

The head of the War Department, who shall also be the King's adviser in matters relating to the command of the army.

The head of the Navy Department who shall also be the King's adviser in matters relating to the command of the navy.

The head of the Home Department.

The head of the Department of Agriculture.

The head of the Department of the Treasury.

The head of the Department of Public Worship.

The further distribution of business among the departments shall be regulated by the King, in a special order, publicly issued.

Of the three councilors of state without a department at least two shall have held civil office.

ART. 7. All measures of the government except those mentioned in Arts. 11 and 15 shall be laid before the King in Council, and shall be there decided upon.

ART. 8. The King shall not render a decision upon a measure about which the Council of State should be consulted, unless at least three councilors of state are present in addition to the one who properly presents the measure. Unless they have a legitimate excuse, all members of the Council shall be present for the consideration of measures of special weight and importance touching the general administration of the king-dom; by the order of the day previous notice shall be given of such measures, which are: questions and projects regarding the adoption of new general laws; the repeal or amendment of existing general laws; the establishment of new organizations within the several branches of the government, and other ques-tions of a similar character.

ART. 9. Minutes shall be kept of all measures discussed in the Council of State. Such members as are present shall, under the responsibility for their advice referred to in Arts. 106 and 107, positively express and explain their opinions which shall be entered upon the minutes; however, the King alone shall have the power to decide; in case of the unexpected event that the King's decision is plainly contrary to the consti-tution of the kingdom or to its general laws, it shall be the duty of the members of the Council of State to enter a vigorous protest against such decision. The member who does not sepa-rately enter his opinion in the minutes shall be held responsible as if he had advised the King to make such a decision.

ART. 10. Before matters are presented to the King in Council they shall be prepared by the member presenting them, who shall gather for this purpose necessary information from the proper administrative offices.

ART. 11. Ministerial affairs (i. e., all matters which bear upon the relations of the kingdom with foreign powers) shall be prepared, as the King may think proper, by the minister for foreign affairs, whose duty it shall be to present them to the King in the presence of the minister of state and of one other member of the Council of State, or if the minister of foreign affairs is also minister of state, in the presence of two other members of the Council of State summoned for that purpose. If the minister of state is prevented from being present, the King shall summon another member of the Council of State in his place. If the minister for foreign affairs is absent the matter shall be presented by a member of the Council of State whom the King shall designate for that purpose. After having received and entered upon the minutes the advice of these officers, for which they are responsible, the King shall make his decision in their presence; the minutes of such meetings shall be kept by a person specially designated for this purpose. The King shall inform the Council of State of as much as he may think proper of such decisions, in order that they may also have some knowledge of this department of the government. All diplomatic correspondence with foreign countries or with the ministers of the King in foreign countries without regard to its character shall take place through the minister of foreign affairs.

ART. 12. The King shall have power to conclude treaties and alliances with foreign powers after having, in the manner set forth in the preceding article, consulted the minister of state, the minister of foreign affairs, and one other member of the Council of State summoned for this purpose, or two other members of the Council of State, if the minister of foreign affairs is also minister of state.

ART. 13. If the King wishes to declare war or to conclude peace he shall convene all the members of the Council of State into extraordinary council, shall lay before them the causes and circumstances to be considered, and shall require their opinions concerning the matter; each of them shall separately enter his opinion in the minutes, under the responsibility referred to in

Art. 107. The King may then make and execute such a decision as he considers for the best interests of the country.

Art. 14. The King shall be commander-in-chief of the land and naval forces of the kingdom.

Art. 15. Matters of military command (i. e., those in which the King personally acts in his capacity as commander-in-chief of the land and naval forces) shall be decided by the King, when he is personally exercising the executive power, in the presence of the head of the military department within whose province the matter comes. The head of such department is bound, under his responsibility, to express his opinion upon the measures adopted by the King at the time when such measures are under consideration; should he disapprove of the decision of the King he shall enter his objections and advice upon a minute which the King shall verify by his royal signature. If this officer believes that the measures are of a dangerous character or tendency, or are founded upon resources uncertain or insufficient for their execution, he shall recommend, in addition, that the King summon into a council of war two or more of the higher military officers who may be at hand; the King shall, however, have the right to comply with or to reject the recommendation for a council of war; if he approves it he may take such action as he thinks best with reference to the opinion of the council of war, which shall be entered upon the minutes.

Art. 16. The King shall maintain and further justice and truth, prevent and forbid iniquity and injustice; he shall not deprive anyone nor cause anyone to be deprived of life, honor, personal liberty, or well-being unless he has been legally tried and condemned; he shall not deprive anyone nor permit anyone to be deprived of any real or personal property without trial and judgment in accordance with the provisions of Swedish law; he shall not disturb or cause to be disturbed the peace of any person in his home; he shall not banish any person from one place to another; he shall not constrain nor cause to be constrained the conscience of any person, but shall protect every-one in the free exercise of his religion, provided he does not thereby disturb public order or occasion general offense. The King shall cause everyone to be tried by the court under the jurisdiction of which he properly belongs.

ART. 17. The judicial power of the King shall be vested in not less than twelve nor more than twenty-one men learned in the law, who shall be appointed by the King; they must have the qualifications required by law for the exercise of judicial functions, and shall, as judges, have shown knowledge, experience, and honesty. They shall be called councilors of justice and shall constitute the Supreme Court of the King. Their number shall not exceed twelve unless the King and the Riksdag should decide, in accordance with Art. 87, sec. 1, that the Supreme Court be divided into sections; in this case, the number of councilors of justice within the limits defined above, and the distribution of business between the sections shall be regulated in the same decree.

ART. 18. The Supreme Court shall also receive and decide petitions asking that the King set aside judgments that have gained legal force or that he grant relief from forfeiture resulting from the expiration of a legal term.

ART. 19. In case requests are made to the King by courts or officials regarding the proper interpretation of a law, the Supreme Court shall furnish such interpretation, if the matter is a proper one for the courts.

ART. 20. In time of peace cases appealed to the King from the military courts shall be heard and decided by the Supreme Court. Two military officers of high rank, selected and appointed by the King for this purpose, shall, subject to judicial challenge and responsibility and without special remuneration, be present in the Supreme Court and have a voice in the decision of such cases; but the number of judges shall not exceed eight.

In time of war such cases shall be tried according to the provisions of the articles of war.

ART. 21. The King shall have two votes in the cases heard and decided when it is his pleasure to be present in the Supreme Court. All questions regarding the interpretation of the law shall be laid before the King, and his votes shall be taken and counted, even though he did not take part in the deliberations of the Supreme Court.

ART. 22. Cases of slight importance may be heard and decided in the Supreme Court by five members, and even by four, where all agree. In more important cases at least seven members shall take part in the judgment. No more than eight members shall at the same time take part in the trial of any case, except in certain cases otherwise provided for by Art. 87, sec. 1.

ART. 23. All decisions of the Supreme Court shall be issued in the name of the King and under his signature or under his privy seal.

ART. 24. The King's office of judicial affairs shall prepare judicial business for trial and decision by the Supreme Court.

ART. 25. The King shall have power to grant pardons in criminal cases, to commute death penalties, to restore honors, and to return property forfeited to the crown. However, the Supreme Court shall be consulted with respect to applications of this kind, and the King's action shall be taken in the Council of State. The offender shall then have the right to accept the pardon granted by the King or to suffer the punishment imposed upon him.

ART. 26. When judicial affairs are laid before the Council of State two councilors of justice shall be present in addition to the head of the Department of Justice and two other members of the Council of State; it shall be their duty to enter their opinions in the minutes, as provided in Art. 9.

ART. 27. The King shall appoint as attorney-general an

able, impartial person, well versed in the law, who has had experience as a judge. It shall be the principal duty of the attorney-general as the highest legal officer of the King, personally or through his subordinate officers, to prosecute, in the name of the King, all cases which affect the public safety or the rights of the crown; and also, on behalf of the King, to exercise supervision over the administration of justice, and in this capacity to prosecute offenses committed by judges or other officers.

ART. 28. Sec. 1. The King in the Council of State shall have power to appoint and promote native Swedes to all offices and positions, high or low, within the kingdom, for which the King's commissions are granted; however, the proper authority shall first submit nominations, if such a practice has heretofore been customary. The King may, likewise, after having taken the advice of the proper authorities or upon their nomination, appoint or promote foreigners of distinguished merit, professing the pure evangelical faith, to professorships in the universities excepting however the chairs of theology, to professorships or other positions in other institutions for science, manual training, or fine arts, and as physicians. The King may likewise employ foreigners of unusual ability in the military service, but not as commanders of fortresses. In all appointments the King shall consider only the candidate's merit and ability, and not his extraction. Only persons professing the pure evangelical faith shall be appointed to the office of preacher or to other offices carrying with them the obligation to give instruction in the Christian religion or in theology. To all other offices and positions, excepting membership in the Council of State as provided by Art. 4, persons belonging to another Christian faith or adherents of the Mosaic belief may be appointed; however, no person not belonging to the pure evangelical faith shall take part, as judge or in any other position, in the discussion or decision of questions relating to divine worship, to religious instruction, or to appointments within the

Swedish church. Each chief of a department shall present and conduct all business relative to the appointment, commission, leave of absence, and discharge of all officers and employees in the bureaus and divisions belonging to his department.

Sec. 2. The King shall have power to confer Swedish nationality by means of naturalization, in the manner and upon the conditions to be determined by a special law passed in the manner provided by Art. 87, sec. 1. A naturalized foreigner shall enjoy the same rights and privileges as native-born Swedes except that he may not be appointed to membership in the Council of State.

ART. 29. The King shall appoint the archbishop and bishops, one from a list of three candidates presented to him in the manner provided by the church law.

ART. 30. The King shall, in the manner heretofore practiced, appoint the incumbents of the royal benefices. The so-called consistorial benefices shall retain their right of election.

ART. 31. Residents of cities qualified to vote in the election of the Riksdag shall have the right to propose three competent persons, of whom the King shall choose one as mayor. The same principle shall apply to aldermen and city clerks of Stockholm.

ART. 32. Ministers to foreign powers and the officers of legations shall be appointed by the King in the manner prescribed by Art. 11 for the conduct of diplomatic affairs.

ART. 33. When the King is to appoint to offices for which nominations are made in advance, the members of the Council of State shall express their opinion regarding the aptitude and merit of the candidates; they shall also have the right to make humble representations against the King's appointments to other offices and positions.

ART. 34. The minister of state and the minister for foreign affairs shall have the highest rank in the kingdom, and councilors of state shall rank next. Members of the Council of State shall not at the same time perform the duties of or receive income from any other office; neither shall a councilor of justice hold any other office or perform other duties.

ART. 35. Members of the Council of State, presidents and heads of administrative boards or of institutions established in their place, the attorney-general, the heads of the prisons, of the surveying service, of the state railroads, of the pilot, postal, telegraph, customs, and forestry services; the under secretaries of the departments of the government, the governor, deputy governor, and chief of police of the capital; the governors of provinces, field marshals, generals, and admirals of all grades, adjutants-general, adjutants-in-chief and adjutants of the staff, commanders of fortresses, colonels of regiments, lieutenant-colonels of both cavalry and infantry regiments of guards and of the household guards as well as of other military corps and battalions having a separate organization, the chiefs of artillery, of fortifications, and of the topographical and hydrographic surveys; ministers, envoys, and commercial agents in foreign countries, as well as officers and employees of the King's cabinet for foreign correspondence and of the legations, shall hold their offices during the pleasure of the King, who may remove them whenever he thinks it for the good of the state. He shall, however, make known his action to the Council of State, whose members shall make humble remonstrances if they think that they have reason to do so.

ART. 36. Persons occupying judicial positions, higher as well as lower, and all officers or employees other than those mentioned in the preceding article shall not be removed from office by the King, except after trial and judgment; nor shall they be promoted or transferred to other offices, except upon their own application.

ART. 37. The King shall have power to grant titles of nobility to persons who, by fidelity, courage, virtue, learning, or zeal, have deserved well of the King and of the country. The King may also, as a reward for important and distin-

guished services, confer upon a noble the rank of baron, or
upon a baron the rank of count. The rank of nobility and the
titles of baron and count hereafter granted shall be borne only
by the person ennobled or elevated in rank, and, after his death,
descending lineally, by the eldest male heir of the oldest branch
of his family and after its extinction, by the nearest male heir
of the ancestor belonging to the oldest branch in existence, and
so forth. If noble rank should pass by inheritance to a person
who has already been ennobled or has received a title by previous inheritance, his own rank shall lapse, unless it is of a
higher grade, in which case the lower rank shall go to the
nearest branch of the family; if no such branch is in existence,
the title shall become extinct. If anyone should forfeit his
noble rank, the title shall go to the nearest heir, in accordance
with the rules herein established.

An ordinance regarding the nobility, to be adopted by the
King in concert with the knights and nobles, shall prescribe
the manner in which knights and nobles may assemble to decide
upon matters which they have in common.

ART. 38. All dispatches and orders issued by the King,
except in matters of military command, shall, in order to be
valid, be signed by the King and bear the countersignature of
the person presenting the matter, whose duty it shall be to see
that the action taken is in agreement with the minutes made
concerning it. The heads of departments may issue directly to
proper parties instructions and memoranda regarding the execution of orders already given. Should the person presenting a
matter think that any order of the King is in conflict with this
constitution he shall make a representation to the Council of
State concerning it; if the King should still insist upon issuing
such order, it shall be the minister's right and duty to refuse
his countersignature thereto and as a consequence to withdraw
from his office, which he shall not resume until the Riksdag
has examined and approved his conduct. In the meantime his
salary and other emoluments shall continue.

ART. 39.   Should the King desire to travel beyond Sweden
and Norway he shall make known his intention at a full meeting of the Council of State and ask its opinion, as provided by
Art. 9.   Should the King decide to take such a trip and put his
decision into execution he shall not take part in the government
or exercise the royal power while he is outside the kingdom;
but, during his absence, the government shall be conducted in
the King's name by the heir apparent to the throne, if he has
attained the age fixed by Art. 41.   This prince shall govern as
regent with all the royal power and authority, in accordance
with this constitution; he shall not, however, confer ranks or
titles of nobility, raise persons to the ranks of count or baron,
or confer honorary orders; and all officers of trust appointed
by the regent shall hold only by temporary appointment.

If there should be no heir apparent, or if the nearest heir
to the throne has not reached the age fixed by Art. 41, or if by
illness or by absence from Sweden and Norway he is prevented from assuming the government, the Council of State
shall govern with the same power as a regent.

Art. 91 provides for the measures to be taken in case the
King remains out of the kingdom for more than twelve months.

ART. 40.   Should the King become too ill to perform his
functions the government shall be conducted in accordance
with the preceding article.

ART. 41.   The King shall reach his majority at the age of
eighteen.   The same holds true for the heir apparent to the
throne.   Should the King die before the heir apparent has
reached this age, the Council of State shall, in conformity with
Art. 39, conduct the government in the name of the King, until
the Riksdag convenes and until the regency established by it
has entered upon its duties; the Council of State shall conform
strictly to this constitution.

ART. 42.   If the misfortune should happen that the whole
royal family, to which the succession belongs, becomes extinct
in the male line, the Council of State shall also conduct the

government, in conformity with Art. 39, until the Riksdag
assembles and chooses a new royal house, and until the King-
elect assumes his function.

ART. 43. When the King takes active part in a war, or
when he visits distant parts of the kingdom or the kingdom of
Norway, he shall designate three members of the Council of
State, under a president separately appointed from among the
princes of his house or from among the members of the Council of State, to conduct such matters of government as he may
direct. Matters in which the King himself acts shall be conducted in accordance with Art. 8.

The above provisions regarding the King shall also apply
to the regent when he conducts the government.

ART. 44. No prince of the royal house, whether crown
prince, hereditary prince, or prince, shall marry without the
King's knowledge and consent. Should he do so, he forfeits
all hereditary right to the crown, for himself, his children,
and his descendants.

ART. 45. Neither the crown prince of Sweden, his heir
apparent, nor the princes of the royal house shall hold any
civil office or territorial rights of government; they may,
however, according to ancient custom, bear the titles of duchies
and principalities, without any rights over the territory of
which they bear the name.

ART. 46. The country shall remain divided into provinces
under the customary provincial governments. No governor-
general shall hereafter be appointed within the kingdom.

ART. 47. The courts of appeal of the kingdom and all
other courts shall decide cases in accordance with the laws.
The administrative boards of the kingdom, provincial governments, and all other offices together with superior or inferior
officers of the government shall perform their duties and functions in accordance with the instructions, regulations, and
orders already issued or which may hereafter be issued; they
shall obey all orders and commands of the King and assist one

another in the execution of such orders and in the performance of all functions which the good of the kingdom may require of them, being responsible to the King, in accordance with the law, for any omission and negligence or for illegal actions.

ART. 48.   The King's court shall be under his own direction, and he may give orders regarding it, according to his own pleasure.   He may, at will, appoint or dismiss all officials of his court.

ART. 49.   The Riksdag shall represent the Swedish people. All rights and duties now vested in the estates of the kingdom shall hereafter be vested in the Riksdag.   The Riksdag shall be composed of two houses, whose members shall be chosen in the manner provided by the Riksdag law.[2]   The houses shall have equal power and authority in all matters.   The Riksdag shall by virtue of this constitution, convene in regular session on the 15th of January of each year, or, if this day is a holiday, on the succeeding day; the King shall, however, have the power to call an extraordinary session of the Riksdag, in the intervals between its regular sessions.

[2] By constitutional amendments of 1866 a legislature of two branches was substituted for the representation of the four estates.   The Riksdag law of June 22, 1866, as amended to 1900, regulates the manner of election and the procedure of the two houses, which are placed upon a complete equality. The Riksdag meets annually and may remain in session for four months, but may be dissolved by the King at any time; however, new elections must be ordered immediately if the two houses or either of them is dissolved.   The upper house is composed of one hundred and fifty members who are elected for a term of nine years; they are chosen indirectly by electoral bodies in the rural districts and in the cities not represented in the rural electoral bodies.   Membership in the upper house is confined to persons thirty-five years of age who for three years prior to the election have owned taxable property valued at 80,000 rix-dollars or have paid taxes upon an annual income of at least 4,000 rix-dollars; a member ceasing to possess these qualifications loses his seat.   Members of the upper house receive no salary. The members of the lower house are elected from single districts for a term of three years; of the two hundred and thirty members, one hundred and fifty are chosen by the rural districts and eighty by the cities; in general the elections are indirect, but in the smaller towns and rural communes which are united for the election of a representative, elections may be

The extraordinary session of the Riksdag shall consider only the matters which occasioned its being called or other matters submitted to it by the King, and questions which may be inseparably connected with such matters.

ART. 50. The Riksdag shall meet in the capital of the kingdom, except when invasion of an enemy, pestilence, or some other equally grave obstacle makes it impossible or dangerous to the liberty and security of the Riksdag. In such a case the King, after conferring with the persons elected by the Riksdag as commissioners of the state bank and of the office of the national debt, shall decide upon and announce another place of meeting.

ART. 51. In case the Riksdag is convened by the King, regent, or Council of State the time of meeting fixed shall not be less than seven days nor more than twenty days after the summons is published in the general newspapers.

ART. 52. The presidents and vice-presidents of the houses shall be appointed by the King.

ART. 53. When in regular session, the Riksdag shall appoint the following committees for the preparation of busi-

direct if a majority of the qualified voters so desire. Persons qualified as municipal voters who pay taxes on an annual income of at least 800 rix-dollars, own real estate of a taxable value of at least 1,000 rix-dollars, or who have a leasehold interest for five years or for life of a taxable value of 6,000 rix-dollars, may vote for members of the lower house; according to statistics of 1902 about 34 per cent. of the male population above the age of twenty-one years possessed these qualifications. Qualified voters of twenty-five years of age may be elected from the districts within which they reside. Members of the lower house receive traveling expenses, and a compensation of 1,200 rix-dollars for each regular session; for extraordinary sessions they receive a per diem.

On May 14, 1907, a law was passed introducing universal male suffrage for the election of members of the lower house of the Riksdag, and reducing the property qualification of members of the upper house to 50,000 kroner or to the payment of a tax on an annual income of 3,000 kroner. As a fundamental law this measure must be passed at two successive sessions of the Riksdag, but its passage is assured. This is one of the most important steps yet taken in Sweden toward democratic government, and is comparable with the parliamentary reform of 1866.

ness: a Constitutional Committee to raise and consider questions regarding changes in the fundamental laws and to report thereon to the Riksdag, and also to examine the minutes kept by the Council of State; a Committee of Finance to examine and to report to the Riksdag upon the condition, administration, and needs of the public treasury and of the office of the national debt; an Appropriation Committee to consider questions of appropriations; a Committee on the Bank to superintend the management and condition of the bank and to give directions regarding its administration; and a Committee on Laws, to elaborate projects submitted to it by the houses for the improvement of the civil, criminal, municipal, and ecclesiastical laws.

At the extraordinary sessions of the Riksdag no more committees shall be appointed than are necessary for the preparation of the measures to be considered.

ART. 54.   Should the King ask that special delegates of the Riksdag consult with him upon matters which he thinks should be kept secret, such delegates shall be chosen by the houses; however, they shall have no power to make decisions, but shall merely advise the King with regard to the measures submitted for their consideration.   The delegates shall take an oath of secrecy if required to do so by the King.

ART. 55.   Neither the Riksdag, its houses, nor any of its committees shall deliberate or decide upon any matter in the presence of the King.

ART. 56.   The Riksdag law shall determine the order of proceeding with reference to propositions of the King and with reference to questions raised by members of the houses.

ART. 57.   The ancient right of the Swedish people to tax themselves shall be exercised by the Riksdag alone.   The municipal laws, to be enacted by the King and Riksdag acting together, shall determine the manner in which the separate areas of local government may tax themselves for their own needs.

ART. 58. At each regular session the King shall present to the Riksdag a statement of the financial condition of the country in all of its branches, both income and expenses, assets and debts. Should the country receive any revenue because of treaties with foreign powers, it shall be accounted for in the same manner.

ART. 59. In connection with the statement of the condition and needs of the treasury the King shall present to the Riksdag a proposal relative to the appropriation of funds which the state may need in addition to its ordinary revenues.

ART. 60. The customs and excise taxes, postal charges, stamp taxes, taxes on domestic distillation, and all such other taxes as each Riksdag may vote shall be reckoned as public revenues. No general tax, of whatever name or character, may be increased without the consent of the Riksdag, the duties on imported and exported grain alone excepted; nor shall the King lease the revenues of the state, or establish any monopoly for the benefit of himself and the crown or of individuals and corporations.

ART. 61. All taxes voted by the Riksdag, under the headings mentioned in the preceding article, shall be collected until the end of the year within which the new taxes are to be voted by the Riksdag.

ART. 62. It devolves upon the Riksdag, after examining the needs of the treasury, to vote supplies to meet such needs, and also to prescribe the special purposes for which the separate items of appropriation may be used, and to grant these items under definite budgetary headings.

ART. 63. In addition to this, two separate amounts, of sufficient size, shall be voted and placed subject to payment by the office of the national debt, for use in case of emergency; the one to be available when the King, after having taken the advice of the Council of State at a full meeting, decides that it is absolutely necessary to use it for the defense of the country or for other important and urgent purposes; the other to be

used by the King in case of war, after he has consulted the
Council of State in full session and has convened the Riksdag.
The sealed order of the Riksdag for this latter amount shall
not be opened, nor shall the amount be paid by the commissioners of the office of the national debt, until after the summons of the Riksdag has been published in the general
newspapers.

ART. 64. The regular public funds and revenues, as well
as the supplies voted by the Riksdag as extraordinary advances
or appropriations in the manner above mentioned, shall be at
the disposal of the King for application to the purposes indicated by the Riksdag, in accordance with the budgetary law.

ART. 65. Such funds shall not be applied to other purposes than those specified; the members of the Council of State
shall be responsible if they permit any violation of this rule,
without entering their protests in the minutes of the Council
and calling attention to what the Riksdag has enacted in the
matter.

ART. 66. The office of the national debt shall remain
under the direction, control, and administration of the Riksdag; and, as the Riksdag is responsible for the public debt
which that office administers, it shall, after the condition and
needs of that office have been properly explained, provide by
special appropriation the funds which are found to be necessary
for the payment of the interest and capital of this debt, in
order that the credit of the country may not be impaired.

ART. 67. The delegate of the King in the office of the
national debt shall not attend the meetings of the commissioners of that office except when they desire to consult with
him.

ART. 68. The funds belonging to or appropriated for the
office of the national debt shall not, under any pretext or condition, be withdrawn or applied to other purposes than those
specified by the Riksdag. All orders in conflict with this provision shall be void.

Art. 69. The Riksdag law shall determine how the Riksdag shall proceed in the consideration of the reports of the Committee of Finance with reference to the establishment of the budget, to the whole appropriation necessary to meet the requirements of the budget, to the expenses and revenues of the office of the public debt, or to the principles of its administration. Should the houses reach different conclusions which cannot be brought into agreement, each house shall vote separately upon the matter in dispute; the opinion which receives the majority of the votes of the two houses shall be the decision of the Riksdag.

Art. 70. When the two houses disagree with regard to regulations for the national bank, as to its receipts and expenses, or as to relieving the bank commissioners from their responsibility in cases of supposed misdemeanor, each house shall vote separately as provided in the preceding article.

Art. 71. The same procedure shall also be followed when the houses do not agree upon the principles of an appropriation or upon the manner of its application or payment.

Art. 72. The national bank shall remain under the guaranty of the Riksdag, and shall be administered by commissioners appointed for this purpose, in accordance with a law agreed upon between the King and the Riksdag.

The commissioners shall be seven in number, one of whom the King shall appoint for three years; the King shall also name one deputy commissioner; the other six commissioners and three deputies shall be chosen by the Riksdag for the term and in the manner prescribed by the Riksdag law. The regular member appointed by the King shall preside over the commissioners, but shall perform no other duties in the administration of the bank. Any commissioner whom the Riksdag finds guilty of improper conduct shall lose his position. The commissioner or deputy appointed by the King may be removed at the discretion of the King.

The national bank alone shall have the right to issue bank

notes which may circulate as money in the kingdom. These notes shall be redeemed upon demand, by the bank in gold, at their face value.

ART. 73. No new imposition of taxes, compulsory enrolment of troops, nor levy of money or of goods shall hereafter be ordered, demanded, or executed without the free will and consent of the Riksdag, in the manner provided above.

ART. 74. From the day when, by decision of the King in Council after summoning the Riksdag to convene, the forces of the kingdom are placed upon a war footing, either for the preservation of the neutrality of the kingdom when, in case of war between foreign powers, such neutrality is threatened or violated by any of the belligerent powers or for defense against an imminent or actual attack, until the return to a peace footing, the King shall have power, upon the credit of the state, in the manner and under the conditions prescribed by a special law to be agreed upon between the King and the Riksdag, to make requisitions upon communities or individuals for such supplies and services as may be furnished by the locality, as are indispensably necessary to meet the needs of the army, and which cannot be provided for with sufficient promptness in any other manner.

ART. 75. The annual table of market rates shall be prepared by persons chosen in the manner specially provided by the Riksdag; such table shall be followed until its modification is sought and obtained in the regular manner.

ART. 76. The King shall not, without the consent of the Riksdag, contract loans at home or abroad or burden the kingdom with new debts.

ART. 77. The King shall not, without the consent of the Riksdag, sell, mortgage, grant, or in any other way dispose of royal demesnes and crown lands with the houses and other appurtenances thereto, royal forests, parks, or meadows, the salmon or other fisheries belonging to the crown, or of other crown property. Such property shall be administered in accordance with principles established by the Riksdag; however, persons and communities which, according to present law, are in the possession and enjoyment of such state property shall retain their legal rights therein, and land in the royal forests capable of cultivation may be sold in accordance with laws now in force or hereafter to be enacted.

ART. 78.   No part of the kingdom may be disposed of by sale, mortgage, gift, or in any other similar manner.

ART. 79.   Sec. 1.   No change shall be made in the arms or flag of the kingdom without the consent of the Riksdag.

Sec. 2.   Nor shall any change be made in the standard or weight of the money of the kingdom, either to increase or to decrease it, without the consent of the Riksdag; however, the King's right to coin money shall remain undisturbed.

ART. 80.   The recruiting of the land and naval forces shall remain under the system of equipment duty and military tenure based upon the contracts and agreements to supply troops made with the towns and rural districts; this system shall not be altered in its fundamental principles until the King and the Riksdag agree upon the necessity of some change. No new or increased obligations to furnish recruits shall be imposed except by agreement between the King and the Riksdag.

Should a special law abolish the military tenure system and establish some other principle for the organization of the land and naval forces, no change shall be made in such law except by agreement between the King and the Riksdag.[3]

---

[3] Until recent years the Swedish standing army was based largely upon what were called the *rotering* and *indelning* systems. By *rotering* was meant the obligation of certain proprietors of land to furnish and maintain foot soldiers or seamen, usually in return for exemption from forced enlistment. Under the *indelning* system lands were assigned upon condition that they should furnish and support mounted troops, or provinces agreed to furnish a certain number of such troops in return for a reduction of taxes or of rents due to the state. It has been the policy of the government for some time to abolish these systems; by law of June 14, 1901, universal compulsory military service was introduced, and by 1913 the old standing army will have entirely disappeared.

ART. 81. This constitution and the other fundamental laws shall not be altered or repealed except by resolution of the King and of two regular sessions of the Riksdag.

The decision of the Riksdag upon a proposal made by the King with reference to a fundamental law shall be communicated to him in the manner prescribed by the Riksdag law. If the Riksdag should adopt such a proposal made within its own body, its decision thereon shall be submitted to the King. In the latter case the King, before the adjournment of the Riksdag, shall take the advice of the Council of State in full session and shall, in the hall of state, inform the Riksdag of his consent or of his reasons for not approving its resolution.

ART. 82. Amendments to the fundamental laws adopted by the Riksdag and approved by the King or proposed by the King and adopted by the Riksdag, in the prescribed manner, shall have force as fundamental law.

ART. 83. No interpretation of the fundamental laws to hold good for the future shall be valid unless adopted in the manner provided for amending such laws.

ART. 84. The fundamental laws shall be applied literally in each particular case.

ART. 85. The following shall be considered fundamental laws: this constitution, the Riksdag law, the act of succession, and the law relating to the freedom of the press which shall be adopted by agreement between the King and the Riksdag in accordance with the principles established by this constitution.

ART. 86. By freedom of the press is understood the right of every Swede to publish his writings without any previous interference on the part of public officials; the individual may afterward be prosecuted before a regular court because of the contents of his publication, but shall not be punished unless such publication is plainly in conflict with a law enacted to preserve the public peace, without interfering with public instruction. All proceedings and official minutes of whatever character, except the minutes of the Council of State and those relating to foreign affairs and to matters of military command, shall be published without restriction; the minutes and proceedings of the national bank and of the office of the national debt, concerning matters which should be kept secret, shall not be published.

Art. 87. Sec. 1. The Riksdag shall have power, in concert with the King, to enact civil and criminal laws and criminal laws for the army, and to amend or repeal any laws now in force. Neither the King without the approval of the Riksdag nor the Riksdag without the consent of the King shall have power to enact new laws or to repeal old ones. Proposals may be made in either house, and shall be decided upon by the Riksdag after the committee on laws has reported upon them. If the Riksdag decides to adopt a new law or to amend or repeal an old one, its project shall be submitted to the King, who shall consult the Council of State and the Supreme Court regarding it, and after having reached a decision shall inform the Riksdag of his consent to its proposal or of his reasons for refusing consent. Should the King not be able to make or announce his decision before the adjournment of the Riksdag he may, before the opening of the next session, approve the measure exactly as passed by the Riksdag, and make known his decision. Otherwise the proposal shall be regarded as rejected, and the King shall inform the Riksdag, at its next session, of the reasons which prevented his approving the measure. If the King wishes to propose a bill to the Riksdag, he shall obtain the opinion of the Council of State and of the Supreme Court regarding the matter and shall present his proposal, together with such opinions, to the Riksdag; the Riksdag shall then proceed with the proposal according to the Riksdag law.

Sec. 2. The Riksdag shall also have power, in concert with the King, to enact, amend, or repeal laws relating to the church, but the consent of a general church council shall also be necessary. When a law upon this subject is proposed by the King, the opinions of the Council of State and of the

Supreme Court shall be obtained and submitted to the Riksdag with the proposal, in the manner provided by sec. 1 of this article. If the project in question has not been promulgated as law before the opening of the first session following that in which it was proposed and adopted, it shall be considered rejected and the King shall inform the Riksdag of the reasons which prevented his approving the measure.

ART. 88. With reference to the interpretation of civil, criminal, or church laws the same procedure shall be followed as in the passage of such laws. Interpretations which the King may give through the Supreme Court, during the recess of the Riksdag, in answer to questions regarding the true meaning of a law, may be overruled by the Riksdag at its next session; or if the interpretation related to a church law, it may be overruled by the first general church council meeting after its publication. The interpretations which have thus been overruled shall lose their validity and shall not be observed or relied upon by the courts.

ART. 89. Projects regarding the amendment, interpretation, or repeal of laws and decrees relating to the general economy of the kingdom, new laws of this character, and proposals concerning the principles to be followed in all branches of the public administration, may be introduced in the houses of the Riksdag. In such matters, however, the Riksdag shall merely present an address to the King expressing its wishes and opinions; the King, after consulting the Council of State, shall take such action as he considers most beneficial to the kingdom. If the King wishes to consider with the Riksdag any matters relating to the general administration of the country, the procedure shall be the same as that prescribed in sec. 1 of Art. 87 for the consideration of laws.

ART. 90. Questions relating to the appointment and removal of officers, to decisions, decrees, or judgments of the government or of the courts, to the conduct of individuals or corporations, or to the execution of any law, decree, or undertaking shall in no case or manner be subject to consideration or investigation by the Riksdag, by its houses, or by its committees, except as literally prescribed by the fundamental laws.

ART. 91. When the King, in the case referred to in Art. 39, visiting abroad, shall remain out of the kingdom for more than twelve months, the regent, or the Council of State, if the latter is in charge of the government, shall summon the Riksdag by public proclamation, such summons to be published in the general newspapers within fifteen days after the expiration of the twelve months. The King shall be notified of this action, and if he still remains out of the kingdom, the Riksdag shall take such action as it thinks most proper regarding the government of the country.

ART. 92. The same procedure shall be followed, if illness of the King should prevent his performing the duties of his office for more than twelve months.

ART. 93. If the King should die when the heir apparent is under age, the Council of State shall summon the Riksdag, such summons to be published within fifteen days after the death of the King. The Riksdag shall have power, without regard to anything in the deceased King's will regarding the government, to establish a regency of one, three, or five persons, who shall conduct the government in the King's name, in accordance with this constitution, until the King becomes of age.

ART. 94. Should the unfortunate event occur that the royal family having the right of succession to the throne becomes extinct in the male line, the Council of State shall, within the period after the last King's death fixed by the preceding article, convene the Riksdag, which shall choose a new royal house, always maintaining this constitution.

ART. 95. If unexpectedly the regent or the Council of State should fail to summon the Riksdag immediately, in the cases mentioned in the four preceding articles, it shall be the absolute duty of the courts of appeal of the kingdom publicly to make known such fact, in order that the Riksdag may convene to protect its own rights and the rights of the country. In such a case the Riksdag shall assemble on the twentieth day after the latest date on which the regent or the Council of State should have issued its summons.

ART. 96. The Riksdag shall at each regular session appoint as its attorney a person of known legal ability and of proved honesty; it shall be his duty, in accordance with instructions given him by the Riksdag, to have oversight of the execution of the law by judges and officers, and also to prosecute before the proper courts persons who, because of favoritism or for any other reasons, have acted unlawfully or who have neglected properly to perform their official duties. This officer shall, however, be subject to the same responsibilities and penalties as are provided for public prosecutors by general laws and by the laws of procedure.

ART. 97. This solicitor-general of the Riksdag, who during his term of office shall in every respect have the same rank as the King's attorney-general, shall be chosen in the manner provided by the Riksdag law; another person with the same qualifications shall be chosen at the same time to take the place of the solicitor-general should he die before his successor is elected at the next regular session of the Riksdag, and to perform the duties of solicitor-general in case that officer is prevented from exercising his functions by serious illness or by other cause.

ART. 98. If the solicitor-general resigns from his office or dies during the session of the Riksdag, the Riksdag shall immediately appoint in his place the person who had been chosen as his substitute. Should the substitute resign from his position, be appointed solicitor-general, or die during the session, another qualified person shall be chosen in his place, in the manner provided above. Should a vacancy in either of these positions occur during the recess of the Riksdag, the powers of that body with regard to them shall be exercised by the commissioners of the bank and of the office of the national debt who are elected by the Riksdag.

ART. 99.   The solicitor-general may, whenever he pleases, attend the sessions of the Supreme Court, of the office of judicial affairs, of the courts of appeal, of the administrative boards or of the institutions established in their place, and of all the lower courts, but without the right to take part in their proceedings; he shall also have access to the minutes and records of all courts, administrative boards, and public offices. The King's officers are in general bound to assist the solicitor-general, and all public prosecutors shall aid him in the conduct of cases, if he asks for their assistance.

ART. 100.   The solicitor-general shall present to each regular session of the Riksdag a report of the administration of his office, in which he shall give an account of the administration of justice in the kingdom, call attention to defects in the laws and decrees, and make suggestions for their improvement.

ART. 101.   In case of the unexpected event that the entire Supreme Court or one or more of its members, because of self-interest, partiality, or negligence, shall have rendered such an unjust judgment, in conflict with clear law and with the evidence, that it causes or might have caused loss of life, of personal liberty, of honor, or of property, it shall be the duty of the solicitor-general and shall be within the power of the King's attorney-general to bring charges against the offender before the court provided below and to prosecute him in accordance with the law of the land.

ART. 102.   In this case the court, to be known as the Court of Impeachment, shall be composed of the president of the Svea[4] Court of Appeals, who shall preside, of the presidents of all of the administrative boards of the kingdom, of the

[4] The Svea Court of Appeals is the Court of Appeals having its seat at Stockholm. The term *Riksrätt* which is here rendered as Court of Impeachment may perhaps be more literally translated as Court of the Kingdom.

four senior members of the Council of State, of the highest officer in command of troops stationed at the capital, of the highest naval officer in command of the fleet stationed at the capital, of the two senior members of the Svea Court of Appeals, and of the senior member of each of the administrative boards of the kingdom. When either the attorney-general or the solicitor-general thinks himself justified in accusing the entire Supreme Court or any of its members he shall ask the president of the Svea Court of Appeals, as president of the Court of Impeachment, to issue a summons in legal form to the person or persons to be prosecuted. The president of the Court of Appeals shall then take steps to convene the Court of Impeachment in order that it may issue the summons and further deal with the case according to law. Should he unexpectedly fail to do this or should any of the above-mentioned officers refuse to act in the Court of Impeachment they shall be legally responsible for such intentional neglect of their official duty. If one or more members of the Court of Impeachment have a lawful excuse or if he is properly challenged as incompetent to act, the court shall still be qualified, if it consists of twelve persons. If the president of the Court of Appeals has a lawful excuse or is challenged, the oldest of the remaining presidents shall take his place. After having tried the case and reached a lawful decision, the court shall pronounce its judgment in public session. No one shall have power to change this judgment; the King, however, may grant pardon, which shall not extend to a reinstatement of the sentenced person in the service of the country.

Art. 103. Every third year the Riksdag shall in regular session, in the manner provided by the Riksdag law, appoint a commission whose duty it shall be to decide if all of the members of the Supreme Court deserve to be retained in their important offices, or if any of them ought to be deprived of the exercise of the judicial power, without having clearly committed the errors or crimes referred to in the preceding article.

Should this commission, after voting in the manner prescribed by the Riksdag law, decide that one or more of the members of the Supreme Court are undeserving of the confidence of the Riksdag, the person or persons in question shall be honorably discharged from their offices by the King, to whom the Riksdag shall report its decision. The King shall, however, grant to each such person an annual pension amounting to one-half of his salary.

ART. 104. The Riksdag shall not take under special examination any decision of the Supreme Court, nor shall such a decision be a subject for general consideration before the commission provided above.

ART. 105. The Constitutional Committee of a regular session of the Riksdag shall have power to ask for the minutes kept by the Council of State, except those which relate to foreign affairs or to matters of military command, which may be demanded only in case of matters already generally known and by specific request of the committee.

ART. 106. If the committee discovers, from these minutes, that any member of the Council of State, any person assigned to lay a report before the King, or the officer advising the King in military affairs, has clearly acted in violation of the constitution or of general laws, or has recommended such violation or has omitted to protest against it, or has occasioned or encouraged it by wilful concealment of any information, or that the person presenting a report has failed to refuse his countersignature to the decision of the King, in the cases specified by Art. 38 of this constitution, then the Constitutional Committee shall, through the solicitor-general of the Riksdag, bring charges against such person before the Court of Impeachment, in which, for such cases, the four senior councilors of justice shall take the place of the members of the Council of State; otherwise the procedure shall be as provided by Arts. 101 and 102 for the impeachment of the Supreme Court. When members of the Council of State or the advisers of the

King in military affairs are found to be guilty in the manner
provided above, the Court of Impeachment shall sentence them
in accordance with general law and with a special law to be
enacted by the King and the Riksdag regarding their responsibility.

ART. 107. Should the Constitutional Committee notice
that all of the members of the Council of State or any of them,
in their advice upon public measures, have not had due regard
to the true welfare of the state, or that any person presenting
matters to the King has failed to perform his duties with
impartiality, zeal, ability, and energy, the committee shall lay
the matter before the Riksdag, which, if it thinks the welfare
of the country requires it, may inform the King in writing that
it desires the removal from the Council of State or from office
of the person or persons who have incurred its censure.

Motions of this character may also be made in the houses
of the Riksdag by other committees, but no decision shall be
reached by the Riksdag until after the Constitutional Committee has been heard. In the consideration of such matters
by the Riksdag, decisions of the King with reference to the
rights or affairs of individuals or corporations shall not even
be mentioned, much less shall they be made the subject of any
investigation by the Riksdag.

Everything that the Riksdag, after investigation, shall have
approved or left uncensured shall be regarded as relieved from
responsibility, and no new investigation of the same matter
shall be undertaken by another Riksdag for the purpose of fixing liability; however, in addition to the general supervision
of the administration of public funds exercised by the committee or auditors of the Riksdag, it shall be the duty of the
proper officers to conduct such special audits as pertain to their
official duties.

ART. 108. Every third year the Riksdag in regular session shall, in the manner prescribed by the Riksdag law,
appoint six persons of known intelligence and knowledge, who

with the solicitor-general as president shall watch over the liberty of the press. These commissioners, of whom two in addition to the solicitor-general shall be lawyers, shall have the following duty: In case an author or printer, before publishing, submits a manuscript to them and asks their advice as to whether it would be subject to an action under the law relating to the freedom of the press, the solicitor-general and not less than three of the commissioners, of whom one shall be a lawyer, shall state their opinion in writing. If they decide that the manuscript may be printed, both author and publisher shall be free from all responsibility, but the commissioners shall be responsible.

ART. 109. The regular session of the Riksdag shall not be adjourned, without its own consent, until after a period of four months, unless the King, in accordance with the provisions of the Riksdag law, orders a new election of one or both houses, in which case the Riksdag shall reassemble, within three months after the dissolution, upon the date set by the King, and preserving its character as a regular session, shall not again be adjourned until after four months from the date of its last assembling.

The King may close an extraordinary session of the Riksdag whenever he thinks best, and shall always close it before the time fixed for the meeting of the regular session.

If the unexpected event should happen that the Riksdag, at the close of its session shall not have established the budget nor granted any new general supplies, the former budget and appropriations shall remain in force until the next session. If, however, the total appropriation had been fixed, but the houses disagree as to its distribution, the articles of the last appropriation law shall be increased or decreased in the proportion of such total appropriation to the appropriation voted by the preceding session, and the Riksdag shall intrust the preparation of the budget on these principles to the commissioners of the national bank and of the office of the public debt who are chosen by itself.

ART. 110.   No member of the Riksdag shall be prosecuted or arrested on account of his actions or utterances in that body unless the house to which he belongs has authorized such prosecution or arrest, by special resolution adopted by at least a five-sixths vote.   No member of the Riksdag shall be banished from the place where it meets.   Should any individual or body, civil or military, or any multitude of whatever name, either spontaneously or under direction of others, attempt injury to the Riksdag, its houses, its committees, or to any one of its members, or to disturb the freedom of its discussions and decisions, such actions shall be considered as treason, and the Riksdag may prosecute the offenders in accordance with law.

If a member of the Riksdag, during a session or when going to or from a session, is molested by word or action, the offender being aware of his errand, the offense shall be dealt with according to the general law with reference to assaults upon or insults to the King's officers.   The same law shall apply to assaults upon or insults to the commissioners, auditors, or solicitor-general of the Riksdag, to the secretaries or officers of either house, or of any of their committees, during or in consequence of the performance of their duties.

ART. 111.   If a member of the Riksdag is accused of a serious offense he shall not be arrested until the judge, after investigation, considers such arrest justifiable, provided that he was not caught in the act; however, if he does not obey the summons of the court, he shall be dealt with according to the provisions of the general laws.   No member of the Riksdag shall be deprived of his liberty except in the cases mentioned in this and in the preceding article.

The commissioners of the national bank and of the office of the public debt and the auditors of the Riksdag shall receive no orders relating to their duties except from the Riksdag or in consequence of its instructions, nor shall they be called to account except by the action of the Riksdag.

ART. 112.   No officer shall make an improper use of his authority in the election of members to the Riksdag.   Should he do so he shall be deprived of his office.

ART. 113.   Assessors whose duty it is, on behalf of the Riksdag, to apply the provisions of the appropriation law shall not be held liable because of the performance of their duties.

ART. 114.   The ancient privileges, advantages, rights, and liberties of the estates of the kingdom shall remain in force, except where they are indissolubly connected with the right of representation formerly belonging to the estates and have consequently ceased to exist with the abolition of that right. The rights of the estates shall not be altered or annulled except by agreement between the King and the Riksdag, and with the consent of the nobility if their privileges are in question or of a general church council if the privileges of the clergy are affected.

SWITZERLAND

The Swiss Confederation dates from the league of the three cantons of Uri, Schwyz, and Unterwalden in 1291. Between 1332 and 1353 the five cantons of Luzern, Zürich, Glarus, Zug, and Bern became members of the confederation, which was later increased to thirteen members by the adhesion of Freiburg and Solothurn in 1481, of Basel and Schaffhausen in 1501, and of Appenzell in 1513. No new members were added to the confederation before 1798 although other territories were allied with the cantons, and some lands gained by the confederates were governed as subject territories.

The administration of the Swiss cities became aristocratic and oppressive; the people, influenced by French example and by French intrigue, rose in insurrection; in January, 1798, a French army invaded Swiss territory to aid the revolutionary forces. Under French influence the country was organized into a centralized republic under the title of the Helvetic Republic, with a constitution which was practically a copy of the French constitution of 1795; the constitution of the Helvetic Republic bears the date of April 12, 1798. This constitution was superseded by a constitution of July 2, 1802.

The destruction of the cantons and the centralization of government did not please the majority of the Swiss people. Napoleon, recognizing this fact, called representatives of the Swiss governing bodies to Paris in December, 1802, and on February 19, 1803, the Act of Mediation was promulgated. By this instrument a federal government was re-established, but with greater power than that existing before 1798; the cantonal governments were re-established on the basis of their organization before the creation of the Helvetic Republic, and the subject territories were erected into independent cantons, six in number; the old equality of the cantons was to an extent destroyed by the powers given to the six larger cantons of Bern, Zürich, Vaud, St. Gallen, Aargau, and Grisons, each of which had two votes in the new federal diet, while the other cantons had only one vote.

From 1803 to 1813 Switzerland was treated as a dependency

of France, and Swiss soldiers were enrolled in the French armies. With the fall of Napoleon the Act of Mediation ceased to be in force. Although Switzerland attempted by a declaration in November, 1813, to remain neutral in the struggle between France and the Allies, the allied troops occupied the country in the succeeding month. On the 29th of December, 1813, a conference of fourteen cantons met at Zürich and formally declared the Act of Mediation no longer in force.

Bern and seven of the other old cantons now wished to re-establish the system in existence before 1798, and to reduce to subjection the six new cantons added in 1803. The Allies, however, took the side of the more liberal cantons. An assembly composed of representatives of the nineteen cantons met at Zürich on April 6, 1814, and on August 7, 1815, a constitution or rather a treaty between the cantons was agreed upon. The three cantons of Valais, Neuchâtel, and Geneva were added to the confederation by the Congress of Vienna, entering the union upon an equality with the other cantons.

The constitution of 1815, which restored to the cantons almost all of their former independence, continued in force until 1848. Under the influence of the liberal movement started by the French revolution of 1830, many of the cantonal constitutions were revised so as to give the people a greater share in the government. The liberal cantons were anxious to revise the federal constitution, and a new constitution was drawn up in 1832, but they were not strong enough to accomplish their purpose. Seven of the cantons, unable to obtain the federal guaranty of their new constitutions, united into a league to maintain their liberal institutions. Five conservative cantons united into the league of Sarnen, in November, 1832, which was dissolved after an armed conflict had occurred between Luzern and Schwyz. Religious troubles now contributed to widen still further the breach in the confederation. Beginning in 1834 the Protestant cantons carried on a vigorous movement against the power of the Catholic church over marriage and education, and for the abolition of convents and the expulsion of the Jesuits. In 1845 the seven Catholic cantons entered into a separate league or *Sonderbund*, which was only dissolved after a short war in 1847.

Finally, after about seventeen years of political strife, a new constitution was adopted on September 12, 1848, which forms the basis of the present political organization of Switzerland, and as partially amended in 1866 and completely revised in 1874, remains in force. The confederation now became a federal state, but for a time the movement toward further centralization ceased. In 1872 the Federal Assembly adopted amendments of a centralizing character but they were rejected by the people. The constitution of 1874 increased the power of the federal government, which has been still further augmented by subsequent amendments, of which the most important are those of November 13, 1898 (Arts. 64 and 64 (ii)), extending federal control over the fields of civil and criminal law. Twelve amendments have been adopted since 1874 and are indicated in the proper places in the text printed below.

SELECT BIBLIOGRAPHY

SWITZERLAND. *Sammlung enthaltend die Bundesverfassung und die in Kraft bestehenden Kantonsverfassungen.* (Bern, 1891. Supplements 1–9, 1892–1903.) An official collection in which the federal constitution and amendments are printed in French, German, and Italian.

KAISER, SIMON UND STRICKLER, JOH. *Geschichte und Texte der Bundesverfassungen der schweizerischen Eidgenossenschaft von der helvetischen Staatsumwälzung bis zur Gegenwart.* (Bern, 1901.) A convenient collection of constitutional documents.

SALIS, L. R. VON. *Schweizerisches Bundesrecht.* Staatsrechtliche und verwaltungsrechtliche Praxis des Bundesrates und der Bundesversammlung seit dem 29. Mai 1874. (2d ed., Bern, 1903–04. 5 vols.) A collection of decisions bearing upon the constitution of the Swiss Confederation; there is a French edition by Eugène Borel. For the earlier period consult ULLMER, RUDOLF EDUARD, *Die Staatsrechtliche Praxis der schweizerischen Bundesbehörden aus den Jahren 1848–1863.* (Zürich, 1862–66. 2 vols.) There is also a French edition of the latter collection by Borel.

HILTY, C. *Les constitutions fédérales de la confédération Suisse.* Exposé historique. (Neuchâtel, 1891.) Probably the best constitutional history. The original German edition appeared at the same time.

BLUNTSCHLI, J. C. *Geschichte des schweizerischen Bundesrechtes.* (2d ed., Stuttgart, 1875. 2 vols.) Vol. II is a collection of constitutional documents to 1874.

BLUMER, J. J. *Handbuch des schweizerischen Bundesstaatsrechtes.* (2d ed., herausgegeben von J. Morel. Schaffhausen, 1877–87. 3 vols.) The most important commentary on Swiss constitutional law. A third edition of Vol. I appeared in 1891.

DUBS, JAKOB. *Das oeffentliche Recht der schweizerischen Eidgenossenschaft.* (Zürich, 1877–78. 2 vols.) This work was also published in French (Neuchâtel, 1878). The first volume is devoted to the cantonal governments.

DROZ, NUMA. *Instruction civique.* (Lausanne, 1884.) An excellent elementary treatise. The same author also has an interesting collection of *Études et portraits politiques* (Genève, 1895).

SCHOLLENBERGER, J. *Das Bundesstaatsrecht der Schweiz.* Geschichte und System. (Berlin, 1902.) An excellent general treatise. The same author has also a valuable commentary on the *Bundesverfassung der schweizerischen Eidgenossenschaft* (Berlin, 1905), in which each article of the constitution is separately considered; and *Grundriss des Staats- und Verwaltungsrechts der schweizerischen Kantone* (Zürich, 1898–1900. 3 vols.).

BURCKHARDT, W. *Kommentar der Schweiz. Bundesverfassung vom 29. Mai 1874.* (Bern, 1905.) A commentary upon the federal constitution, similar in character, but more extensive than that of Schollenberger.

ORELLI, ALOIS VON. *Das Staatsrecht der schweizerischen Eidgenossenschaft.* (Freiburg, 1885. Handbuch des oeffentlichen Rechts.)

VINCENT, JOHN MARTIN. *Government in Switzerland.* (New York, 1900.) Of the three principal works in English, no one is satisfactory, but that of Vincent is probably now preferable to Moses or Adams and Cunningham.

MOSES, BERNARD. *The Federal Government of Switzerland.* An essay on the constitution. (Oakland, California, 1889).

ADAMS, FRANCIS OTTIWELL AND CUNNINGHAM, C. D. *The Swiss Confederation.* (London, 1889.)

CURTI, THEODOR. *Le referendum; histoire de la législation populaire en Suisse.* Traduit par Jules Ronjat. (Paris, 1905.) The leading history of the Swiss referendum. The second German edition of this work appeared at Zürich in 1885.

Deploige, Simon. *The Referendum in Switzerland.* Translated into English by C. P. Trevelyan. (London, 1898.) Of value for the operation of the referendum, as is also Stüssi's *Referendum und Initiative in den Schweizerkantonen* (Zürich, 1894).

Klöti, Emil. *Die Proportionalwahl in der Schweiz.* Geschichte, Darstellung und Kritik. (Bern, 1901.)

CONSTITUTION OF THE SWISS CONFEDERATION[1]

(May 29, 1874)

> *In the Name of Almighty God.*

THE SWISS CONFEDERATION, desiring to confirm the alliance of the Confederates, to maintain and to promote the unity, strength, and honor of the Swiss nation, has adopted the following federal constitution:

CHAPTER I. GENERAL PROVISIONS

ARTICLE 1. The peoples of the twenty-two sovereign cantons of Switzerland, united by this present alliance, viz.; Zürich, Bern, Luzern, Uri, Schwyz, Unterwalden (Upper and Lower), Glarus, Zug, Freiburg, Solothurn, Basel (urban and rural), Schaffhausen, Appenzell (the two Rhodes), St. Gallen, Grisons, Aargau, Thurgau, Ticino, Vaud, Valais, Neuchâtel, and Geneva, form in their entirety the Swiss Confederation.

ART. 2. The purpose of the Confederation is, to secure the independence of the country against foreign nations, to maintain peace and order within, to protect the liberty and the rights of the Confederates, and to foster their common welfare.

ART. 3. The cantons are sovereign, so far as their sovereignty is not limited by the federal constitution; and, as such, they exercise all the rights which are not delegated to the federal government.

[1] In the preparation of this text assistance has been received from the translation made by Professor A. B. Hart and issued in *Old South Leaflets,* No. 18, and from that of Professor E. J. James (Philadelphia, 1890).

Art. 4. All Swiss are equal before the law. In Switzerland there are neither political dependents, nor privileges of place, birth, person, or family.

Art. 5. The Confederation guarantees to the cantons their territory, their sovereignty within the limits fixed by Art. 3, their constitutions, the liberty and rights of the people, the constitutional rights of citizens, the rights and powers which the people have conferred upon those in authority.

Art. 6. The cantons are bound to ask of the Confederation the guaranty of their constitutions.

This guaranty shall be accorded, provided:

a) That the constitutions contain nothing contrary to the provisions of the federal constitution.

b) That they assure the exercise of political rights, according to republican forms, representative or democratic.

c) That they have been ratified by the people, and may be amended whenever the majority of all the citizens request it.

Art. 7. All separate alliances and all treaties of a political character between the cantons are forbidden.

On the other hand the cantons shall have the right to make conventions among themselves upon legislative, administrative, or judicial subjects; in all cases they shall bring such conventions to the attention of the federal officials, who are authorized to prevent their execution, if they contain anything contrary to the Confederation, or to the rights of other cantons. Should such not be the case, the contracting cantons are authorized to require the co-operation of the federal officials in carrying out the convention.

Art. 8. The Confederation shall have the sole right of declaring war, of making peace, and of concluding alliances and treaties with foreign powers, particularly treaties relating to tariffs and commerce.

Art. 9. By exception the cantons preserve the right of concluding treaties with foreign powers, respecting the administration of public property, and border and police intercourse;

but such treaties shall contain nothing contrary to the Confederation or to the rights of other cantons.

ART. 10.   Official intercourse between cantons and foreign governments, or their representatives, shall take place through the Federal Council.

Nevertheless, the cantons may correspond directly with the inferior officials and officers of a foreign state, in regard to the subjects enumerated in the preceding article.

ART. 11.   No military capitulations shall be made.[2]

ART. 12.   No members of the departments of the federal government, civil and military officials of the Confederation, or federal representatives or commissioners, shall receive from any foreign government any pension, salary, title, gift, or decoration.

If such persons are already in the possession of pensions, titles, or decorations, they must renounce the enjoyment of their pensions and the bearing of their titles and decorations during their continuance in office.

Nevertheless, inferior officers may be authorized by the Federal Council to receive their pensions.

No decoration or title conferred by a foreign government shall be worn in the federal army.

No officer, non-commissioned officer, or soldier shall accept such distinction.

ART. 13.   The Confederation shall have no right to maintain a standing army.

No canton or half-canton shall, without the permission of the federal government, have a standing force of more than three hundred men; the armed police are not included in this number.

ART. 14.   In case of differences arising between cantons, the states shall abstain from violence and from arming themselves; they shall submit to the decision to be taken upon such differences by the Confederation.

[2] I. e., treaties agreeing to furnish soldiers to other countries.

ART. 15. In case of sudden danger of foreign attack, the authorities of the threatened canton shall request the aid of other members of the Confederation and shall immediately notify the federal government; the subsequent action of the latter shall not thereby be precluded. The cantons summoned are bound to give aid. The expenses shall be borne by the Confederation.

ART. 16. In case of internal disturbance, or if the danger is threatened by another canton, the authorities of the threatened canton shall give immediate notice to the Federal Council, in order that that body may take the measures necessary, within the limits of its power (Art. 102, secs. 3, 10, 11), or may summon the Federal Assembly. In extreme cases the authorities of the canton are authorized, while giving immediate notice to the Federal Council, to ask the aid of other cantons, which are bound to afford such aid.

If the cantonal government is unable to call for aid, the competent federal authority may, and if the safety of Switzerland is endangered, shall, intervene without requisition.

In case of federal intervention, the federal authorities shall take care that the provisions of Art. 5 be observed.

The expenses shall be borne by the canton asking aid or occasioning federal intervention, except when the Federal Assembly otherwise decides on account of special circumstances.

ART. 17. In the cases mentioned in Arts. 15 and 16, every canton is bound to afford undisturbed passage to the troops. The troops shall immediately be placed under federal command.

ART. 18. Every Swiss is bound to perform military service.[3]

Soldiers who lose their lives or suffer permanent injury to their health, in consequence of federal service, are entitled

---

[3] The military organization law of April 12, 1907, imposes the obligation to perform military service upon every male Swiss citizen between the ages of twenty and forty-eight years.

to aid from the Confederation for themselves or their families, in case of need.

Each soldier shall receive without expense his first equipment, clothing, and arms. The arms shall remain in the hands of the soldier, under conditions which shall be prescribed by federal legislation.

The Confederation shall enact uniform provisions as to a tax for exemption from military service.

ART. 19. The federal army shall be composed:

a) Of the cantonal military corps.

b) Of all Swiss who do not belong to such military corps, but who are nevertheless liable to military service.

The Confederation exercises control over the army and the material of war provided by law.

In cases of danger, the Confederation shall also have the exclusive and direct control of men not included in the federal army, and of all other military resources of the cantons.

The cantons shall have authority over the military forces of their territory, so far as this right is not limited by the federal constitution or laws.

ART. 20. The laws on the organization of the army shall be enacted by the Confederation. The enforcement of military laws in the cantons shall be intrusted to the cantonal officials, within limits which shall be fixed by federal legislation, and under the supervision of the Confederation.

Military instruction of every kind shall be under the control of the Confederation. The same applies to the equipment of troops.

The furnishing and maintenance of clothing and equipment shall be within the power of the cantons; but the cantons shall be credited with the expenses therefor, according to a regulation to be established by federal legislation.

ART. 21. So far as military reasons do not prevent, corps of troops shall be formed from soldiers of the same canton.

The composition of these bodies of troops, the maintenance

of their effective strength, the appointment and promotion of
their officers shall belong to the cantons, subject to general
regulations which shall be issued to them by the Confederation.

ART. 22.   Upon the payment of a reasonable compensation, the Confederation shall have the right to use or acquire
drill-grounds and buildings intended for military purposes,
within the cantons, together with the appurtenances thereto.

The method of fixing the compensation shall be settled by
federal legislation.

ART. 23.   The Confederation may construct at its own expense, or may aid by subsidies, public works which concern
Switzerland or a considerable part of the country.

For this purpose it may take private property, on payment
of a reasonable compensation.   Further enactments upon this
matter shall be made by federal legislation.

The Federal Assembly may forbid public works which
endanger the military interests of the Confederation.

ART. 24.   The Confederation shall have the right of super-
intendence over the police of streams and forests.[4]

It may co-operate in the straightening and embankment of
torrents as well as in the afforesting of the districts in which
they rise.   It may prescribe the regulations necessary to assure
the maintenance of these works, and the preservation of existing forests.[5]

ART. 25.   The Confederation shall have power to make

[4] By an amendment of July 11, 1897, the words, "in the upper mountain
regions," were stricken from this clause.

[5] An initiative petition was submitted on June 27, 1906, for the adoption
of a new article, 24 (ii).   A substitute proposal was adopted on September
26, 1907, by the Council of States.   The most important part of this proposed amendment is as follows: "The utilization of hydraulic power is
placed under the supervision of the Confederation.   With reference to the
proper utilization of hydraulic power and with reference to the transmission
and distribution of electric power, federal legislation shall provide the
general regulations necessary to safeguard the public interests.   With the
reservation of such regulation, the cantons shall have power to regulate the
exploitation of hydraulic power."

legislative enactments for the regulation of fishing and hunting, particularly with a view to the preservation of the big game in the mountains, as well as for the protection of birds useful to agriculture and forestry.

[ART. 25 (ii). The killing of animals without benumbing before the drawing of blood is forbidden; this provision applies to every method of slaughter and to every species of animals.[6]]

ART. 26. Legislation upon the construction and operation of railroads is within the province of the Confederation.

ART. 27. The Confederation may establish, besides the existing Polytechnic School, a federal university and other institutions of higher instruction, or may subsidize institutions of such a character.

The cantons shall provide for primary instruction, which shall be sufficient, and shall be placed exclusively under the direction of the secular authority. It shall be compulsory and, in the public schools, free.

The public schools shall be such that they may be frequented by the adherents of all religious confessions, without any offense to their freedom of conscience or of belief.

The Confederation shall take the necessary measures against such cantons as do not fulfil these duties.

[ART. 27 (ii). Subventions shall be granted to the cantons in order to aid them to fulfil their duties in the field of primary instruction.

A law shall regulate the execution of this provision.

The organization, direction, and supervision of the primary schools shall remain within the competence of the cantons, under the reservation of the provisions of Art. 27 of the federal constitution.[7]]

ART. 28. The customs system shall be within the control

[6] This article was introduced by an amendment of August 20, 1893.
[7] Amendment of November 23, 1902.

of the Confederation. The Confederation may levy export and import duties.

, ART. 29. The collection of the federal customs shall be regulated according to the following principles:

1. Duties on imports:

a) Materials necessary for the manufactures and agriculture of the country shall be taxed as low as possible.

b) The same rule shall apply to the necessaries of life.

c) Luxuries shall be subject to the highest duties.

Unless there are imperative reasons to the contrary, these principles shall be observed also in the conclusion of treaties of commerce with foreign powers.

2. The duties on exports shall be as low as possible.

3. The customs legislation shall include suitable provisions for the continuance of commercial intercourse on the frontier.

The above provisions shall not prevent the Confederation from making temporary exceptional provisions, under extraordinary circumstances.

ART. 30. The proceeds of the customs shall belong to the Confederation.

The indemnities which have hitherto been paid to the cantons in lieu of the customs, road and bridge tolls, market fees, and other like dues, are abolished.

By exception, and on account of their international Alpine roads, the Cantons of Uri, Grisons, Ticino, and Valais shall receive an annual indemnity which, considering all the circumstances, is fixed as follows: Uri, 80,000 francs; Grisons, 200,-000 francs; Ticino, 200,000 francs; Valais, 50,000 francs.

The Cantons of Uri and Ticino shall receive in addition, for clearing the snow from the Saint Gotthard road, an annual indemnity of 40,000 francs, so long as that road shall not be replaced by a railroad.

ART. 31. The freedom of trade and of industry is guaranteed throughout the whole extent of the Confederation.

The following subjects are excepted:

. *a*) The salt and gunpowder monopoly, the federal customs, import duties on wines and other spirituous liquors, and other taxes on consumption expressly permitted by the Confederation, according to Art. 32.

b) [The manufacture and sale of distilled liquors, in conformity with Art. 32 (ii).[8]]

c) [Drinking-places, and the retail trade in spirituous liquors; in order that the cantons may by legislation subject the business of keeping drinking-places, and the retail trade in spirituous liquors, to such restrictions as may be required for the public welfare.[9]]

d) Measures of sanitary police against epidemics and cattle diseases.

e) Regulations in regard to the exercise of trades and manufactures, in regard to taxes imposed thereon, and in regard to the police of roads. Such regulations shall not contain anything contrary to the principle of freedom of trade and manufacture.

ART. 32. The cantons are authorized to collect the import duties on wines and other spirituous liquors, provided in Art. 31 *a*), under the following restrictions:

a) The collection of these import duties shall in no wise impede transportation; commerce shall be obstructed as little as possible and shall not be burdened with any other dues.

b) If the articles imported for consumption are re-exported from the canton, the duties paid on importation shall be refunded, without further charges.

[8] Amendment of October 25, 1885. On February 22, 1907, the Federal Council presented to the Federal Assembly an initiative petition proposing a verbal alteration of Art. 31 of the constitution and the addition of a new article, 32 (iii). The essential part of this proposed amendment is as follows: "The manufacture, importation, transportation, sale, or keeping for the purpose of sale, of the distilled liquor known under the name of absinthe is forbidden throughout the whole extent of the Confederation." This prohibition is to come into operation two years after the adoption of the amendment.

[9] Amendment of October 25, 1885.

c) Products of Swiss origin shall be taxed at a lower rate than those of foreign countries.

d) The existing import duties on wines and other spirituous liquors of Swiss origin shall not be increased by the cantons which already levy them. Such duties shall not be imposed upon these articles by cantons which do not at present levy them.

e) The laws and ordinances of the cantons on the collection of import duties shall, before their going into effect, be submitted to the federal government for approval, in order that it may, if necessary, enforce the preceding provisions.

All the import duties now levied by the cantons, as well as the similar duties levied by the communes, shall be abolished without compensation, at the end of the year 1890.[19]

[ART. 32 (ii). The Confederation is authorized to make regulations, by law, for the manufacture and sale of distilled liquors. In this legislation those products which are intended for exportation, or which have been subjected to a process rendering them unfit for use as a beverage, shall be subject to no tax. Distillation of wine, of fruits of any kind or of their by-products, of gentian root, juniper berries, and of other similar substances, shall not be subject to federal legislation as to manufacture or tax.

After the cessation of the import duties on spirituous liquors, provided for in Art. 32 of this constitution, the trade in undistilled alcoholic liquors shall not be subjected by the cantons to any special taxes or to any other restrictions than those necessary for the protection of the consumer against adulterated or noxious beverages. Nevertheless, the powers of the cantons, defined in Art. 31, are retained over the keeping of drinking-places, and the sale at retail of quantities less than two liters.

---

[19] The cantonal duties on spirituous liquors ceased in 1887, by virtue of a federal law, passed in conformity with Art. 32 (ii) and Art. 6, temporary provisions.

The net proceeds resulting from taxation on the sale of alcohol shall belong to the cantons in which the tax is levied.

The net proceeds to the Confederation from the manufacture of alcohol, and from the corresponding increase of the duty on imported alcohol, shall be divided among all the cantons, in proportion to their actual population as established by the most recent federal census. Out of the receipts therefrom the cantons must expend not less than one-tenth in combating drunkenness in its causes and effects.[11]]

ART. 33. The cantons may require proofs of competency from those who desire to practice the liberal professions.

Provision shall be made by federal legislation by which such persons may obtain certificates of competency which shall be valid throughout the Confederation.

ART. 34. The Confederation shall have power to enact uniform laws as to the labor of children in factories, and as to the length of the working day fixed for adults therein, and as to the protection of laborers engaged in unsanitary and dangerous manufactures.

The business of emigration agents and of insurance companies not instituted by the state shall be subject to federal supervision and legislation.

[ART. 34 (ii). The Confederation shall by law establish accident and invalid insurance, having regard for existing invalid funds.

It may declare the participation in this insurance obligatory for all, or for certain classes of the population.[12]]

ART. 35. The opening of gaming houses is forbidden. Those which now exist shall be closed on December 31, 1877.

The concessions which may have been granted or renewed since the beginning of the year 1871 are declared invalid.

[11] Art. 32 (ii) was added by amendment of October 25, 1885. See also Art. 31 and Art. 6, Temporary Provisions.

[12] Art. 34 (ii) was added by amendment of October 26, 1890.

The Confederation may also take necessary measures concerning lotteries.

ART. 36. The posts and telegraphs in all Switzerland shall be controlled by the Confederation.

The proceeds of the posts and telegraphs shall belong to the federal treasury.

The rates shall, for all parts of Switzerland, be fixed according to the same principle and as fairly as possible.

Inviolable secrecy of letters and telegrams is guaranteed.

ART. 37. The Confederation shall exercise general oversight over those roads and bridges in the maintenance of which it is interested.

The sums due to the cantons mentioned in Art. 30, on account of their international Alpine roads, shall be retained by the federal government if such roads are not kept by them in suitable condition.

ART. 38. The Confederation shall exercise all the exclusive rights pertaining to coinage.

It shall have the sole right of coining money.

It shall establish the monetary system, and may enact provisions, if necessary, for the rate of exchange of foreign coins.

ART. 39. The right to issue bank notes and other similar paper money shall belong exclusively to the Confederation.

The Confederation may exercise the exclusive right to issue bank notes by means of a national bank with a special administration, or reserving the right of repurchase, may grant the exercise of this privilege to a central joint stock bank, which should be administered with government co-operation and supervision.

It shall be the chief duty of the bank having the monopoly of note issues to regulate the circulation of currency in the country and to facilitate monetary transactions.

At least two-thirds of the net earnings of the bank, over and above a reasonable interest, or a reasonable dividend upon its capital-shares and the necessary additions to its reserve fund, shall fall to the cantons.

The bank and its branches shall be subject to no taxation in the cantons.

The Confederation shall not declare bank notes or other similar money to be legal tender, except when necessary in time of war.

Federal legislation shall determine the location of the bank, its rules and organization, and the further execution of this article.[18]

ART. 40. The Confederation shall fix the standard of weights and measures.

The cantons, under the supervision of the Confederation, shall enforce the laws relating thereto.

ART. 41. The manufacture and sale of gunpowder throughout Switzerland shall belong exclusively to the Confederation.

Powders used for blasting and not suitable for shooting are not included in the monopoly.

ART. 42. The expenditures of the Confederation shall be met as follows:

a) From the income from federal property.

b) From the proceeds of the federal customs levied at the Swiss frontier.

c) From the proceeds of the post and telegraph.

d) From the proceeds of the powder monopoly.

e) From half of the gross receipts from the tax on military exemptions levied by the cantons.

f) From the contributions of the cantons, which shall be determined by federal legislation, with special reference to their wealth and taxable resources.

ART. 43. Every citizen of a canton is a Swiss citizen.

As such he may participate, in the place where he is domi-

[18] The original Art. 39 forbade the creation of a monopoly for the issue of bank notes. The present article is an amendment of October 18, 1891.

ciled, in all federal elections and popular votes, after having duly proven his qualification as a voter.

No person shall exercise political rights in more than one canton.

The Swiss who acquires a residence outside of his native canton shall enjoy, in the place of his domicile, all the rights of a citizen of the canton, and also all the rights of a citizen of the commune. Participation in municipal and corporate property, and the right to vote in purely municipal affairs, are excepted from such rights, unless the canton by legislation has otherwise provided.

In cantonal and communal affairs he shall gain the right to vote after a residence of three months.

Cantonal laws relating to the right of Swiss citizens to settle outside the cantons in which they were born and to vote on communal questions shall be submitted for the approval of the Federal Council.

ART. 44. No canton shall expel from its territory one of its own citizens, or deprive him of his rights, whether acquired by birth or by settlement.

Federal legislation shall fix the conditions upon which foreigners may be naturalized, as well as those upon which a Swiss may surrender his citizenship in order to obtain naturalization in a foreign country.

ART. 45. Every Swiss citizen shall have the right to settle anywhere in Swiss territory, on condition of submitting a certificate of origin, or a similar document.

By exception, settlement may be refused to or withdrawn from those who, in consequence of a conviction of crime, are not in the enjoyment of civil rights.

In addition, settlement may be withdrawn from those who have been repeatedly punished for serious offenses, and also from those who permanently come upon the charge of public charity, and to whom their commune or canton of origin, as the case may be, refuses sufficient assistance after they have been officially asked to grant it.

In the cantons where the poor are relieved in their place of residence the permission to settle, if it relates to citizens of the canton, may be coupled with the condition that they shall be able to work, and that they shall not, in their former domicile in the canton of origin, have permanently become a charge on public charity.

Every expulsion on account of poverty must be approved by the government of the canton of domicile, and previously announced to the government of the canton of origin.

A canton in which a Swiss establishes his domicile may not require security, nor impose any special burden upon him because of such establishment. Nor may communes impose upon Swiss citizens domiciled in their territory other taxes than those imposed upon their own inhabitants.

A federal law shall establish the maximum fee to be paid to the Chancery Office for a permit to settle.

'ART. 46. Persons settled in Switzerland shall, as a rule, be subject to the jurisdiction and legislation of their domicile, with respect to all matters in the field of civil law.

The Confederation shall by law make the provisions necessary for the application of this principle and for the prevention of the double taxation of a citizen.

ART. 47. A federal law shall establish the distinction between settlement and temporary residence, and shall at the' same time make the regulations to which Swiss temporary residents shall be subject as to their political and civil rights.

ART. 48. A federal law shall provide the necessary regulations concerning the expenses of illness and burial of poor inhabitants of one canton who have fallen ill or died in another canton.

ART. 49. Freedom of conscience and of belief is inviolable.

No person shall be compelled to become a member of a

religious society, to attend religious instruction, or to perform any religious act, nor shall he incur penalties of any kind because of his religious opinions.

The person who exercises the authority of parent or guardian shall have the right, conformably to the principles above enumerated, to control the religious education of children up to the age of sixteen years.

The exercise of civil or political rights shall not be abridged by any provisions or conditions of an ecclesiastical or religious character.

No person shall, on account of his religious opinion, be freed from the performance of any civil duty.

No person shall be bound to pay taxes the proceeds of which are specifically appropriated to the actual expenses of the worship of a religious body to which he does not belong. The further execution of this principle is reserved for federal legislation.

ART. 50. The free exercise of religious worship is guaranteed, within the limits compatible with public order and good morals.

The cantons and the Confederation may take measures necessary for the maintenance of public order and of the peace between members of different religious organizations, and also against encroachments of ecclesiastical authorities upon the rights of citizens and of the state.

Disputes within the fields of either public or private law, which arise out of the formation or the division of religious organizations, may be brought by appeal before the competent federal authorities.

No bishopric shall be created upon Swiss territory without the consent of the Confederation.

ART. 51. Neither the order of Jesuits nor any affiliated society shall be admitted into any part of Switzerland; all activities of their members in church or school are forbidden.

This prohibition may also be extended, by means of a

federal decree, to other religious orders whose activities are dangerous to the state, or disturb the peace between religious denominations.

ART. 52. The foundation of new convents or religious orders, or the re-establishment of those which have been suppressed, is forbidden.

ART. 53. The civil status and the keeping of records thereof shall be subject to the civil authority. The Confederation shall by law enact further provisions upon this subject.

The control of places of burial shall be subject to the civil authority, which shall take care that every deceased person may be decently interred.

ART. 54. The right of marriage is placed under the protection of the Confederation.

No limitation upon marriage shall be based upon religious grounds, nor upon the poverty of either of the contracting parties, nor upon their conduct, nor on any other consideration of good order.

A marriage contracted in a canton or in a foreign country, conformably to the law which is there in force, shall be recognized as valid throughout the Confederation.

By marriage the wife acquires the domicile and citizenship of her husband.

Children born before marriage are made legitimate by the subsequent marriage of their parents.

No tax shall be imposed upon marriage or upon either party thereto.

ART. 55. The freedom of the press is guaranteed.

Nevertheless the cantons, by law, may enact measures necessary for the supression of abuses. Such laws shall be submitted for the approval of the Federal Council.[14]

The Confederation may also enact penalties for the suppression of press offenses directed against it or its authorities.[14]

[14] By amendment of November 13, 1898, these paragraphs will cease to be in force as soon as a federal criminal code is adopted.

ART. 56. Citizens shall have the right to form associations, provided that there be in the purpose of such associations, or in the means which they employ, nothing illegal or dangerous to the state. The cantons by law may take the measures necessary to prevent the abuse of this right.

ART. 57. The right of petition is guaranteed.

ART. 58. No person shall be deprived of his constitutional judge. Therefore no extraordinary tribunal shall be established.

Ecclesiastical jurisdiction is abolished.

ART. 59. Suits for personal claims against a solvent debtor having a domicile in Switzerland, must be brought before the judge of his domicile; consequently, his property outside the canton in which he is domiciled may not be attached in suits for personal claims.

Nevertheless, with reference to foreigners, the provisions of international treaties shall not thereby be affected.

Imprisonment for debt is abolished.

ART. 60. All the cantons are bound to treat the citizens of the other confederated states like those of their own state in legislation and in all judicial proceedings.

ART. 61. Valid judgments in civil cases rendered in any canton may be executed anywhere in Switzerland.

ART. 62. The exit duty on property[15] is abolished in the interior of Switzerland, as well as the right of first purchase[16] by citizens of one canton against those of another canton.

ART. 63. The exit duty on property is abolished as respects foreign countries, provided reciprocity is observed.

ART. 64. The Confederation shall have power to make laws:

[15] *Abzugsrecht:* A tax upon property going out of the canton with the owner or to heirs. Inheritance taxes which may affect property leaving the canton are not forbidden.

[16] *Zugrecht:* The right of relatives, neighbors, or people of the commune to purchase property in preference to any other person.

Upon civil capacity.

[The Confederation shall also have the power to legislate concerning all other matters within the field of the civil law.[17]]

Upon all legal questions relating to commerce and to transactions affecting personal property (the law of obligations, including commercial law and the law of commercial paper).

Upon copyright in literature and art.

Upon the protection of inventions applicable to industry, including designs and models.[18]

Upon the collection of debts and upon bankruptcy.

The organization of the courts, judicial procedure, and the administration of justice shall remain, as heretofore, subject to cantonal control.[19]

[ART. 64 (ii). The Confederation shall have power to legislate upon all matters of criminal law.

The organization of the courts, judicial procedure, and the administration of justice shall remain, as heretofore, subject to cantonal control.

The Confederation may grant subventions to the cantons for the erection of penal and reformatory institutions, and for reforms to be undertaken in the execution of criminal punishments. The Confederation may also co-operate in measures for the protection of foundlings.[20]]

ART. 65. No death penalty shall be pronounced for a political offense.[21]

Corporal punishment is abolished.

---

[17] As amended November 13, 1898. After several years of legislative work a Swiss civil code was adopted on December 10, 1907. This code becomes effective on January 1, 1912.

[18] As amended March 19, 1905. An amendment of July 10, 1887, first extended the federal power over industrial designs and models.

[19] As amended November 13, 1898.

[20] Amendment of November 13, 1898.

[21] The original Art. 65 forbade the death penalty for any offenses; it was changed by amendment of May 18, 1879.

Art. 66. Federal legislation shall determine the conditions upon which a Swiss citizen may be deprived of his political rights.

Art. 67. The Confederation shall provide by law for the extradition of accused persons from one canton to another; however, extradition shall not be made obligatory for political offenses and offenses of the press.

Art. 68. Measures shall be taken by federal law for the granting of citizenship to persons without country (*Heimathlosen*), and for the prevention of new cases of such a character.

Art. 69. Legislation concerning measures of sanitary police against epidemic and cattle diseases, causing a common danger, is included in the powers of the Confederation.

[Art. 69 (ii). The Confederation shall have the power to enact laws:

a) Concerning traffic in food products.

b) Concerning traffic in other articles of use and consumption, in so far as they may be dangerous to life or health.

The cantons shall execute such laws under the supervision and with the financial support of the Confederation.

The regulation of imports at the national frontier shall be under the control of the Confederation.[22]]

Art. 70. The Confederation may expel from its territory foreigners who endanger the internal or external safety of Switzerland.

CHAPTER II. FEDERAL AUTHORITIES

I. FEDERAL ASSEMBLY

Art. 71. With the reservation of the rights of the people and of the cantons (Arts. 89 and 121), the supreme authority of the Confederation shall be exercised by the Federal Assembly, which shall consist of two sections or councils, to wit:

A. The National Council;

B. The Council of States.

[22] Amendment of July 11, 1897.

A. NATIONAL COUNCIL

ART. 72. The National Council shall consist of representatives of the Swiss people, chosen in the ratio of one member for each 20,000 persons of the total population. Fractions of upward of 10,000 persons shall be reckoned as 20,000.

Every canton, and in the divided cantons every half-canton shall choose at least one representative.

ART. 73. The elections for the National Council shall be direct. They shall be held in federal electoral districts, which in no case shall be formed out of parts of different cantons.

ART. 74. Every Swiss who has completed twenty years of age, and who in addition is not excluded from the rights of a voter by the legislation of the canton in which he resides, shall have the right to vote in elections and popular votes.

Nevertheless, the Confederation may by law establish uniform regulations for the exercise of such right.

ART. 75. Every lay Swiss citizen who has the right to vote is eligible for membership in the National Council.

ART. 76. The National Council shall be chosen for three years and shall be entirely renewed at each general election.

ART. 77. Representatives to the Council of States, members of the Federal Council, and officers appointed by that council, shall not at the same time be members of the National Council.

ART. 78. The National Council shall choose from among its own members a president and a vice-president for each regular or extraordinary session.

A member who has held the office of president during a regular session shall not be eligible either as president or as vice-president at the next regular session.

The same member may not be vice-president during two consecutive regular sessions.

When the votes are equally divided the president shall have a casting vote; in elections he shall vote in the same manner as other members.

ART. 79. The members of the National Council shall receive a compensation from the federal treasury.

ART. 80. The Council of States shall consist of forty-four representatives of the cantons. Each canton shall appoint two representatives; in the divided cantons, each half-canton shall choose one.

ART. 81. The members of the National Council and those of the Federal Council may not be representatives in the Council of States.

ART. 82. The Council of States shall choose from among its own members a president and a vice-president for each regular or extraordinary session.

Neither the president nor the vice-president may be chosen from among the representatives of the canton from which the president had been chosen for the regular session immediately preceding.

Representatives of the same canton shall not occupy the position of vice-president during two consecutive regular sessions.

When the votes are equally divided the president shall have a casting vote; in elections he shall vote in the same manner as the other members.

ART. 83. Representatives in the Council of States shall receive a compensation from the cantons.

ART. 84. The National Council and the Council of States shall consider all the subjects which the present constitution places within the competence of the Confederation and which are not assigned to any other federal authority.

ART. 85. The subjects within the competence of the two councils are particularly the following:

1. Laws on the organization and election of federal authorities.

2. Laws and ordinances upon subjects which by the constitution are placed within the federal competence.

3. The salary and compensation of members of the federal governing bodies and of the federal chancellery; the creation of federal offices, and the determination of salaries therefor.

4. The election of the Federal Council, of the Federal Court, and of the chancellor, and also of the commander-in-chief of the federal army.

The Confederation may by law assign to the Federal Assembly other powers of election or of confirmation.

5. Alliances and treaties with foreign powers and also the approval of treaties made by the cantons among themselves or with foreign powers; however, the treaties made by the cantons shall be brought before the Federal Assembly only in case the Federal Council or another canton protests.

6. Measures for external safety and also for the maintenance of the independence and neutrality of Switzerland; the declaration of war and the conclusion of peace.

7. The guaranty of the constitutions and territory of the cantons; intervention in consequence of such guaranty; measures for the internal safety of Switzerland, for the maintenance of peace and order; amnesty and pardon.

8. Measures for enforcing the provisions of the constitution, for carrying out the guaranty of the cantonal constitutions, and for fulfilling federal obligations.

9. The power of controlling the federal army.

10. The determination of the annual budget, the audit of public accounts, and federal ordinances authorizing loans.

11. The supervision of federal administration and of federal courts.

12. Protests against the decisions of the Federal Council upon administrative conflicts (Art. 113).

13. Conflicts of jurisdiction between federal authorities.

14. The amendment of the federal constitution.

ART. 86. The two councils shall assemble annually in

regular session upon a day to be fixed by the standing orders.

They may be convened in extraordinary session by the Federal Council upon the request either of one-fourth of the members of the National Council, or of five cantons.

ART. 87. Neither council may transact business without the presence of a majority of the total number of its members.

ART. 88. In the National Council and in the Council of States decisions shall be reached by a majority of those voting.

ART. 89. Federal laws, decrees, and resolutions shall be passed only by the agreement of the two councils.

Federal laws shall be submitted for acceptance or rejection by the people, if the demand is made by 30,000 voters or by eight cantons. The same principle applies to federal resolutions which have a general application, and which are not of an urgent nature.

ART. 90. The Confederation shall by law establish the forms and intervals to be observed in popular votes.

ART. 91. Members of both councils shall vote without instructions.

ART. 92. Each council shall deliberate separately. But in the case of the elections specified in Art. 85, clause 4, of pardons, or of deciding a conflict of jurisdiction (Art. 85, clause 13), the two councils shall meet in joint session, under the direction of the president of the National Council, and a decision shall be reached by the majority of the members of both councils present and voting.

ART. 93. Measures may originate in either council, and may be introduced by any of their members.

The cantons may by correspondence exercise the same right.[23]

[23] On March 6, 1906, the Federal Council presented to the Federal Assembly a project for the revision of the constitution extending popular initiative to federal legislation. This project was debated in the National Council in December, 1906, and was referred back to the Federal Council for a further report; it will probably be adopted in substance if not in the exact form as

ART. 94. As a rule, the sittings of the councils shall be public.

II. FEDERAL COUNCIL

ART. 95. The supreme directive and executive authority of the Confederation shall be exercised by a Federal Council, composed of seven members.

ART. 96. The members of the Federal Council shall be chosen for three years, by the National Council and Council of States in joint session, from among all the Swiss citizens eligible to the National Council. But not more than one member of the Federal Council shall be chosen from the same canton.

proposed. The project of the Federal Council adds two articles to the constitution, between Arts. 93 and 94, and reads as follows:

Art. 93 (ii). Fifty thousand Swiss voters or eight cantons shall have the right to demand the passage, modification, or repeal of a federal law, as well as the modification or repeal of a federal decree of general application.

Such an initiative petition shall have effect only when the Federal Assembly declares that it violates neither the federal constitution nor obligations resting upon the confederation by virtue of treaties.

The petition for the passage of a federal law, or for the modification of a federal law or of a federal decree of general application, may take the form of a general suggestion or of a completed project.

If the initiative petition is presented in the form of a general suggestion and if the Federal Assembly is in agreement therewith, that body shall draw up a law or a decree in the sense indicated by the petition, and then paragraph 2 of Art. 89 shall have application. Should the two councils not approve of the initiative petition the question whether such petition shall have effect shall be submitted to the decision of the people. Should the majority of voters pronounce in favor of the petition the Federal Assembly shall draw up a law or decree in the sense indicated by the petition, and then paragraph 2 of Art. 89 shall have application.

If the initiative petition is presented in the form of a completed project or if it demands the repeal of a law or of a federal decree of general application, and if the Federal Assembly is in agreement therewith, the initiative petition acquires the force of law, with the reservation of paragraph 2 of Art. 89. If the two councils are not in agreement with the initiative petition it shall without further formality be submitted to the people for acceptance or rejection.

If the popular vote is to be had upon an initiative petition opposed by the Federal Assembly, that body may propose to the people the rejection of the proposal of the petition, or may at the same time submit a counter-project together with the initiative proposal.

Art. 93 (iii). A federal law shall further determine the procedure to be followed in initiative petitions regarding federal laws.

Paragraph 1 of Art. 89 is altered as follows:

The agreement of the two councils is necessary for the passage of federal laws and decrees. However, Art. 93 (iii) is excepted from this provision.

The Federal Council shall be chosen anew after each election of the National Council.

Vacancies which occur during the course of the three years shall be filled at the first ensuing session of the Federal Assembly, for the remainder of the term of office.

ART. 97. The members of the Federal Council shall not, during their term of office, occupy any other office, either in the service of the Confederation or in a canton, nor engage in any other pursuit, nor practice a profession.

ART. 98. The Federal Council shall be presided over by the President of the Confederation. There shall also be a vice-president.

The President of the Confederation and the vice-president of the Federal Council shall be chosen for one year by the Federal Assembly, from among the members of the Council.

The retiring President shall not be chosen as President or vice-president for the ensuing year.

The same member shall not hold the office of vice-president during two consecutive years.

ART. 99. The President of the Confederation and the other members of the Federal Council shall receive an annual salary from the federal treasury.

ART. 100. A quorum of the Federal Council shall consist of four members.

ART. 101. The members of the Federal Council shall have the right to speak, but not to vote, in both houses of the Federal Assembly, and also the right to make motions on the subject under consideration.

ART. 102. The powers and the duties of the Federal Council, within the limits of this constitution, are particularly the following:

1. It shall conduct federal affairs, conformably to the laws and resolutions of the Confederation.

2. It shall take care that the constitution, federal laws, and ordinances, and also the provisions of federal concordats, be

observed; upon its own initiative or upon complaint it shall take measures necessary to cause these instruments to be observed, unless the matter is one which should be brought before the Federal Court, in accordance with Art. 113.

3. It shall enforce the guaranty of the cantonal constitutions.

4. It shall introduce bills or resolutions into the Federal Assembly, and shall give its opinion upon the proposals submitted to it by the councils or by the cantons.

5. It shall execute the laws and resolutions of the Confederation and the judgments of the Federal Court, and also the compromises or decisions in arbitration upon disputes between cantons.

6. It shall make such appointments as are not intrusted to the Federal Assembly, Federal Court, or to other authority.

7. It shall examine the treaties made by cantons with each other, or with foreign powers, and shall approve them, if proper (Art. 85, clause 5).

8. It shall watch over the external interests of the Confederation, particularly the maintenance of its international relations, and shall, in general, be intrusted with foreign relations.

9. It shall watch over the external safety of Switzerland, over the maintenance of its independence and of its neutrality.

10. It shall watch over the internal safety of the Confederation, over the maintenance of peace and order.

11. In cases of urgency, and when the Federal Assembly is not in session, the Federal Council shall have power to raise the necessary troops and to employ them, with the reservation that it shall immediately summon the councils if the number of troops should exceed two thousand men, or if they should remain under arms for more than three weeks.

12. It shall have charge of the military establishment of the Confederation, and of all other branches of administration committed to the Confederation.

13. It shall examine such laws and ordinances of the cantons as must be submitted for its approval; it shall exercise supervision over such departments of the cantonal administration as are placed under its control.

14. It shall administer the finances of the Confederation, introduce the budget, and submit accounts of receipts and expenses.

15. It shall supervise the conduct of all the officers and employees of the federal administration.

16. It shall submit to the Federal Assembly at each regular session an account of its administration, presenting a report upon the internal conditions and foreign relations of the Confederation, and shall recommend to the attention of the Federal Assembly such measures as it thinks desirable for the promotion of the common welfare.

It shall also make special reports when the Federal Assembly or either council requires it.

ART. 103. The business of the Federal Council shall be distributed by departments among its members. This distribution shall have the purpose only of facilitating the examination and dispatch of business; decisions shall emanate from the Federal Council as a body.

ART. 104. The Federal Council and its departments shall have power to call in experts on special subjects.

III. FEDERAL CHANCELLERY

ART. 105. A Federal Chancellery, at the head of which is placed the chancellor of the Confederation, shall perform the duties of secretary for the Federal Assembly and the Federal Council.

The chancellor shall be chosen by the Federal Assembly for the term of three years, at the same time as the Federal Council.

The Chancellery shall be under the special supervision of the Federal Council.

A federal law shall provide for the organization of the Chancellery.

IV. FEDERAL COURT

ART. 106. There shall be a Federal Court for the administration of justice in federal matters.

There shall, furthermore, be a jury for criminal cases (Art. 112).

ART. 107. The members and alternates of the Federal Court shall be chosen by the Federal Assembly, which shall take care that all three national languages are represented therein.

A law shall determine the organization of the Federal Court and of its sections, the number of judges and alternates, their term of office, and their salary.

ART. 108. Any Swiss citizen eligible to the National Council may be chosen to the Federal Court.

The members of the Federal Assembly and of the Federal Council, and officers appointed by these bodies, shall not at the same time be members of the Federal Court.

The members of the Federal Court shall not, during their term of office, occupy any other office, either in the service of the Confederation or in a canton, nor engage in any other pursuit, nor practice a profession.

ART. 109. The Federal Court shall organize its own secretariat and appoint the officials thereof.

ART. 110. The Federal Court shall have jurisdiction in civil suits:

1. Between the Confederation and the cantons.

2. Between the Confederation on the one hand and corporations or individuals on the other, when such corporations or individuals are plaintiffs, and when the amount involved exceeds a certain sum, which shall be determined by federal legislation.

3. Between cantons.

4. Between cantons on the one hand and corporations or individuals on the other, when one of the parties demands it, and the amount involved exceeds a certain sum, which shall be determined by federal legislation.

It shall also have jurisdiction in suits concerning the status of persons not subjects of any government (*Heimathlosigkeit*), and the conflicts which arise between communes of different cantons respecting the right of local citizenship.

ART. 111. The Federal Court is bound to give judgment in other cases when both parties agree to abide by its decision, and when the amount involved exceeds a certain sum, which shall be determined by federal legislation.

ART. 112. The Federal Court, assisted by a jury to decide upon questions of fact, shall have criminal jurisdiction over:

1. Cases of high treason against the Confederation, of rebellion or violence against federal authorities.

2. Crimes and misdemeanors against the law of nations.

3. Political crimes and misdemeanors which are the cause or the result of disturbances which occasion armed federal intervention.

4. Charges against officers appointed by a federal authority, when such federal authority applies to the Federal Court.

ART. 113. The Federal Court shall also have jurisdiction:

1. Over conflicts of jurisdiction between federal authorities on the one hand and cantonal authorities on the other.

2. In disputes between cantons, when such disputes are upon questions of public law.

3. Of complaints of violation of the constitutional rights of citizens, and complaints of individuals because of the violation of concordats or treaties.

Conflicts of administrative jurisdiction are reserved, and are to be settled in a manner prescribed by federal legislation.

In all the above-mentioned cases the Federal Court shall apply the laws passed by the Federal Assembly and the decrees of the Assembly which have a general bearing. It shall in like manner conform to treaties which shall have been ratified by the Federal Assembly.

ART. 114. Besides the cases mentioned in Arts. 110, 112, and 113, the Confederation may by law place other matters within the jurisdiction of the Federal Court; in particular, it may give to that court powers intended to insure the uniform application of the laws provided for in Art. 64.

V.   MISCELLANEOUS PROVISIONS

ART. 115. All that relates to the location of the authorities of the Confederation shall be subject to federal legislation.

ART. 116. The three principal languages spoken in Switzerland, German, French, and Italian, shall be national languages of the Confederation.

ART. 117. The officers of the Confederation shall be responsible for their conduct in office. A federal law shall enforce this responsibility.

CHAPTER III.   AMENDMENT OF THE FEDERAL CONSTITUTION *

ART. 118. The federal constitution may at any time be amended, in whole or in part.

ART. 119. Total revision shall take place in the manner provided for passing federal laws.

ART. 120. When either council of the Federal Assembly resolves in favor of a total revision of the constitution and the other council does not consent thereto, or when fifty thousand Swiss voters demand a total revision, the question whether the federal constitution ought to be revised shall be in either case submitted to a vote of the Swiss people, voting yes or no.

If in either case the majority of those voting pronounce in the affirmative, there shall be a new election of both councils for the purpose of undertaking the revision.

* Chap. iii was revised on July 5, 1891, Arts. 118–23 being substituted for the original Arts. 118–21; the important change is in Art. 121, which extends popular initiative to partial revision of the constitution.

ART. 121. Partial revision may take place either by popular initiative or in the manner provided for the passage of federal laws.

The popular initiative shall consist of a petition of fifty thousand Swiss voters for the adoption of a new article or for the abrogation or amendment of specified articles of the constitution.

When several different subjects are proposed by popular initiative for revision or for adoption into the federal constitution, each one of them must be demanded by a separate initiative petition.

The initiative petition may be presented in general terms or as a completed proposal of amendment.

If the initiative petition is presented in general terms and the federal legislative bodies are in agreement with it, they shall draw up a project of partial revision in accordance with the sense of the petitioners, and shall submit it to the people and the cantons for acceptance or rejection. If, on the contrary, the Federal Assembly is not in agreement with the petition, the question of partial revision shall be submitted to a vote of the people, and if a majority of those voting pronounce in the affirmative, the Federal Assembly shall proceed with the revision in conformity with the popular decision.

If the petition is presented in the form of a completed project of amendment and the Federal Assembly is in agreement therewith, the project shall be submitted to the people and the cantons for acceptance or rejection. If the Federal Assembly is not in agreement with the project, it may prepare a project of its own, or recommend the rejection of the proposed amendment, and it may submit its own counter-project or its recommendation for rejection at the same time that the initiative petition is submitted to the vote of the people and cantons.

ART. 122. The details of procedure in cases of popular

initiative and popular votes on amendments to the constitution shall be determined by federal law.

ART. 123. The amended federal constitution or the revised portion of it shall be in force when it has been adopted by a majority of Swiss citizens voting thereon and by a majority of the cantons.

In making up the majority of cantons the vote of a half-canton shall be counted as half a vote.

The result of the popular vote in each canton shall be considered as the vote of the canton.

, TEMPORARY PROVISIONS

ARTICLE 1. The proceeds of the posts and customs shall be divided upon the present basis, until such time as the Confederation shall take upon itself the military expenses up to this time borne by the cantons.

Federal legislation shall provide, besides, that the loss which may be occasioned to the finances of certain cantons from the changes introduced by Arts. 20, 30, 36, clause 2, and 42 (e), shall fall upon such cantons only gradually and shall not attain its full effect till after a transition period of some years.

Those cantons which, at the going into effect of Art. 20 of the constitution, have not fulfilled the military obligations which are imposed upon them by the former constitution, or by federal laws, shall be bound to fulfil such obligations at their own expense.

ART. 2. The provisions of the federal laws and of the cantonal concordats, constitutions, or laws, which are in conflict with this constitution, shall cease to have effect upon the adoption of the constitution or upon the publication of the laws for which it provides.

ART. 3. The new provisions in regard to the organization and jurisdiction of the Federal Court shall not take effect until after the publication of federal laws relating thereto.

Art. 4. A period of five years shall be allowed to the cantons for the establishment of free instruction in primary public education (Art. 27).

Art. 5. Persons practicing a liberal profession who, before the publication of the federal law provided for in Art. 33, shall have obtained a certificate of competence from a canton or from a joint authority representing several cantons, may practice their profession throughout the Confederation.

[Art. 6. If a federal law for carrying out Art. 32 (ii) be passed before the end of 1890, the import duties levied on spirituous liquors by the cantons according to Art. 32 shall cease upon the going into effect of such law.

If, in such case, the shares of any canton or commune, out of the sums to be divided, are not sufficient to equal the average annual net proceeds of the taxes they had levied on spirituous liquors during the years 1880 to 1884 inclusive, the cantons and communes affected shall, till the end of 1890, receive the amount of the deficiency out of the amount which is to be divided among the other cantons according to population; and the remainder only shall be divided among such other cantons and communes, according to population.

The Confederation shall further provide by law that for such cantons or communes as may suffer financial loss through the effect of this amendment, such loss shall not come upon them immediately in its full extent, but gradually up to the year 1895. The indemnities thereby made necessary shall be previously taken out of the net proceeds designated in Art. 32 (ii), paragraph 4.[25]]

[25] Amendment of October 25, 1885.

UNITED STATES

Before 1776 the British colonies of North America, which later became the United States, had obtained an important share in their own government. Rhode Island and Connecticut under their charters were practically independent. The other colonies were governed by a governor and council,[1] appointed by the English crown, and an assembly chosen by the people. These colonies had what we call representative government in the present British colonial system, but through the increasing powers of the assemblies after 1700 they were rapidly approaching the system of responsible government. The development of self-government was suspended by the reactionary British policy after 1763 and on July 4, 1776, the colonies took the decisive step of declaring themselves independent.

Some union of the colonies was necessary for the conduct of the war with Great Britain, and united action was obtained by means of congresses to which the several colonies sent delegates. The Articles of Confederation, adopted in 1781, for the first time embodied in a written instrument an agreement of union between the previously independent states. The Articles of Confederation were unsatisfactory in that they did not give sufficient power to the central government, and efforts to amend them failed because of the requirement that all states agree upon an amendment.

In pursuance of a recommendation of a convention of five states which met at Annapolis, September 11, 1786, delegates of twelve states met in convention at Philadelphia in May, 1787. This convention drafted a constitution which was finally ratified by all of the thirteen states. Government under this constitution was organized in April, 1789. Since its adoption the constitution has received fifteen amendments; the text of the amendments is given after that of the original constitution.

[1] The council was both a legislative and an executive body, except in Pennsylvania where it was denied legislative power; in Pennsylvania and Maryland appointments were made by proprietors rather than by the crown; in Massachusetts the members of the council were elected by the General Court of the colony.

SELECT BIBLIOGRAPHY

ASHLEY, ROSCOE LEWIS. *The American Federal State: A Textbook in Civics for High Schools and Academies.* (New York, 1902.) Among the elementary treatises on the American government those of Ashley, Hart, and Hinsdale are thought to be the most satisfactory.

HART, ALBERT BUSHNELL. *Actual Government as Applied under American Conditions.* (3d ed., New York, 1908.)

HINSDALE, B. A. *The American Government, National and State.* (4th ed., New York [1905].)

BRYCE, JAMES. *The American Commonwealth.* (3d ed., New York, 1893–95. 2 vols.) Perhaps the most important single work dealing with the American government. An abridged edition in one volume contains the more essential matter, but the unabridged edition is preferable.

WILLOUGHBY, W. W. (*Editor*). "The American States Series." (New York, 1904–08.) A valuable series in eight volumes, in which the agencies of the American government, federal, state, and local, are discussed in detail.

COOLEY, THOMAS M. *The General Principles of Constitutional Law in the United States of America.* (3d ed., Boston, 1898.) The best brief discussion of the technical principles of constitutional law.

MCCLAIN, EMLIN. *Constitutional Law in the United States.* (New York, 1905.) A recent work in the "American Citizen Series," intended mainly for popular use.

STORY, JOSEPH. *Commentaries on the Constitution of the United States.* (5th ed., Boston, 1891.) A classic treatise.

MCCLAIN, EMLIN. *A Selection of Cases on Constitutional Law.* (Boston, 1900.) The best one-volume collection of constitutional cases.

GOODNOW, FRANK J. *The Principles of the Administrative Law of the United States.* (New York, 1905.) A standard work, dealing with a subject heretofore much neglected in the United States.

LANDON, JUDSON S. *The Constitutional History and Government of the United States.* (2d revised ed., Boston, 1905.) The best brief history of the constitutional development of the United States.

STIMSON, FREDERIC JESUP. *The Law of the Federal and State Constitutions of the United States.* (Boston, 1908.) This work is principally made up of a digest of the constitutions in force in the forty-six states of the United States, and is indispensable for the study of state constitutional law.

THE CONSTITUTION OF THE UNITED STATES

(September 17, 1787[1])

We the people of the United States, in order to form a more perfect union, establish justice, insure domestic tranquillity, provide for the common defence, promote the general welfare, and secure the blessings of liberty to ourselves and our posterity, do ordain and establish this Constitution for the United States of America.

ARTICLE I

SECTION I. All legislative powers herein granted shall be vested in a Congress of the United States, which shall consist of a Senate and a House of Representatives.

SEC. 2. The House of Representatives shall be composed of members chosen every second year by the people of the several States, and the electors in each State shall have the qualifications requisite for electors of the most numerous branch of the State Legislature.

No person shall be a Representative who shall not have attained to the age of twenty-five years, and been seven years a citizen of the United States, and who shall not, when elected, be an inhabitant of that State in which he shall be chosen.

Representatives and direct taxes shall be apportioned among the several States which may be included within this Union, according to their respective numbers, which shall be determined by adding to the whole number of free persons, including those bound to service for a term of years, and excluding Indians not taxed, three fifths of all other persons.[2]   The

---

[1] This is the date upon which the constitution was agreed upon by the constitutional convention; according to the terms of the constitution it became effective on June 21, 1788, after ratification by nine states. The date set by Congress for proceedings to begin under the constitution was March 4, 1789, but the government was actually not organized until April of that year.

[2] Amended by the second section of the fourteenth amendment, p. 310.

actual enumeration shall be made within three years after the first meeting of the Congress of the United States, and within every subsequent term of ten years, in such manner as they shall by law direct. The number of Representatives shall not exceed one for every thirty thousand, but each State shall have at least one representative; and until such enumeration shall be made, the State of New Hampshire shall be entitled to choose three, Massachusetts eight, Rhode Island and Providence Plantations one, Connecticut five, New York six, New Jersey four, Pennsylvania eight, Delaware one, Maryland six, Virginia ten, North Carolina five, South Carolina five, and Georgia three.[3]

When vacancies happen in the representation from any State, the Executive authority thereof shall issue writs of election to fill such vacancies.

The House of Representatives shall choose their Speaker and other officers; and shall have the sole power of impeachment.

SEC. 3. The Senate of the United States shall be composed of two Senators from each State, chosen by the Legislature thereof, for six years; and each Senator shall have one vote.

Immediately after they shall be assembled in consequence of the first election, they shall be divided as equally as may be into three classes. The seats of the Senators of the first class shall be vacated at the expiration of the second year, of the second class at the expiration of the fourth year, and of the third class at the expiration of the sixth year, so that one third may be chosen every second year; and if vacancies happen by resignation, or otherwise, during the recess of the Legislature of any State, the Executive thereof may make temporary

---

[3] According to the apportionment act of January 16, 1901, there are now three hundred and ninety-one members of the House of Representatives, there being approximately one member to 193,000 people.

appointments until the next meeting of the Legislature, which shall then fill such vacancies.

No person shall be a Senator who shall not have attained to the age of thirty years, and been nine years a citizen of the United States, and who shall not, when elected, be an inhabitant of that State for which he shall be chosen.

The Vice-President of the United States shall be President of the Senate, but shall have no vote, unless they be equally divided.

The Senate shall choose their other officers, and also a President pro tempore, in the absence of the Vice-President, or when he shall exercise the office of President of the United States.

The Senate shall have the sole power to try all impeachments. When sitting for that purpose, they shall be on oath or affirmation. When the President of the United States is tried, the Chief Justice shall preside; and no person shall be convicted without the concurrence of two thirds of the members present.

Judgment in cases of impeachment shall not extend further than to removal from office, and disqualification to hold and enjoy any office of honor, trust or profit under the United States: but the party convicted shall nevertheless be liable and subject to indictment, trial, judgment and punishment, according to law.

Sec. 4. The times, places and manner of holding elections for Senators and Representatives, shall be prescribed in each state by the Legislature thereof; but the Congress may at any time by law make or alter such regulations, except as to the places of choosing Senators.

The Congress shall assemble at least once in every year, and such meeting shall be on the first Monday in December, unless they shall by law appoint a different day.

Sec. 5. Each House shall be the judge of the elections, returns and qualifications of its own members, and a majority of each shall constitute a quorum to do business; but a smaller number may adjourn from day to day, and may be authorized to compel the attendance of absent members, in such manner, and under such penalties as each House may provide.

Each House may determine the rules of its proceedings, punish its members for disorderly behavior, and, with the concurrence of two thirds, expel a member.

Each House shall keep a journal of its proceedings, and from time to time publish the same, excepting such parts as may in their judgment require secrecy; and the yeas and nays of the members of either House on any question shall, at the desire of one fifth of those present, be entered on the journal.

Neither House, during the session of Congress, shall, without the consent of the other, adjourn for more than three days, nor to any other place than that in which the two Houses shall be sitting.

SEC. 6. The Senators and Representatives shall receive a compensation for their services, to be ascertained by law, and paid out of the Treasury of the United States. They shall in all cases, except treason, felony and breach of peace, be privileged·from arrest during their attendance at the session of their respective Houses, and in going to and returning from the same; and for any speech or debate in either House, they shall not be questioned in any other place.

No Senator or Representative shall, during the time for which he was elected, be appointed to any civil office under the authority of the United States, which shall have been created, or the emoluments whereof shall have been increased during such time; and no person holding any office under the United States, shall be a member of either House during his continuance in office.

SEC. 7. All bills for raising revenue shall originate in the House of Representatives; but the Senate may propose or concur with amendments as on other bills.

Every bill which shall have passed the House of Representatives and the Senate, shall, before it become a law, be presented to the President of the United States; if he approve he shall sign it, but if not he shall return it, with his objections to that House in which it shall have originated, who shall enter the objections at large on their journal, and proceed to reconsider it. If after such reconsideration two thirds of that House shall agree to pass the bill, it shall be sent, together with the objections, to the other House, by which it shall likewise be reconsidered, and, if approved by two thirds of that House, it shall become a law. But in all such cases the votes of both Houses shall be determined by yeas and nays, and the names of the persons voting for and against the bill shall be entered on the journal of each House respectively. If any bill shall not be returned by the President within ten days (Sundays excepted) after it shall have been presented to him, the same shall be a law, in like manner as if he had signed it, unless the Congress by their adjournment prevent its return, in which case it shall not be a law.

Every order, resolution, or vote to which the concurrence of the Senate and House of Representatives may be necessary (except on a question of adjournment) shall be presented to the President of the United States; and before the same shall take effect, shall be approved by him, or being disapproved by him, shall be repassed by two thirds of the Senate and House of Representatives, according to the rules and limitations prescribed in the case of a bill.

SEC. 8. The Congress shall have power to lay and collect taxes, duties, imposts and excises, to pay the debts and provide for the common defence and general welfare of the United States; but all duties, imposts and excises shall be uniform throughout the United States;

To borrow money on the credit of the United States;

To regulate commerce with foreign nations, and among the several States, and with the Indian tribes;

To establish an uniform rule of naturalization, and uniform

laws on the subject of bankruptcies throughout the United States;

To coin money, regulate the value thereof, and of foreign coin, and fix the standard of weights and measures;

To provide for the punishment of counterfeiting the securities and current coin of the United States;

To establish post-offices and post-roads;

To promote the progress of science and useful arts, by securing for limited times to authors and inventors the exclusive right to their respective writings and discoveries;

To constitute tribunals inferior to the Supreme Court;

To define and punish piracies and felonies committed on the high seas, and offences against the law of nations;

To declare war, grant letters of marque and reprisal, and make rules concerning captures on land and water;

To raise and support armies, but no appropriation of money to that use shall be for a longer term than two years;

To provide and maintain a navy;

To make rules for the government and regulation of the land and naval forces;

To provide for calling forth the militia to execute the laws of the Union, suppress insurrections and repel invasions;

To provide for organizing, arming, and disciplining, the militia, and for governing such part of them as may be employed in the service of the United States, reserving to the States respectively, the appointment of the officers, and the authority of training the militia according to the discipline prescribed by Congress;

To exercise exclusive legislation in all cases whatsoever, over such district (not exceeding ten miles square) as may, by cession of particular States, and the acceptance of Congress, become the seat of the government of the United States, and to exercise like authority over all places purchased by the consent of the Legislature of the State in which the same shall be, for the erection of forts, magazines, arsenals, dock-yards, and other needful buildings;—and

To make all laws which shall be necessary and proper for carrying into execution the foregoing powers, and all other powers vested by this Constitution in the government of the United States, or in any department or officer thereof.

SEC. 9.   The migration or importation of such persons as any of the States now existing shall think proper to admit, shall not be prohibited by the Congress prior to the year one thousand eight hundred and eight, but a tax or duty may be imposed on such importation, not exceeding ten dollars for each person.

The privilege of the writ of habeas corpus shall not be suspended, unless when in cases of rebellion or invasion the public safety may require it.

No bill of attainder or ex post facto law shall be passed.

No capitation, or other direct tax shall be laid, unless in proportion to the census or enumeration herein before directed to be taken.

No tax or duty shall be laid on articles exported from any State.

No preference shall be given by any regulation of commerce or revenue to the ports of one State over those of another: nor shall vessels bound to, or from, one State, be obliged to enter, clear, or pay duties in another.

No money shall be drawn from the treasury, but in consequence of appropriations made by law; and a regular statement and account of the receipts and expenditures of all public money shall be published from time to time.

No title of nobility shall be granted by the United States: and no person holding any office of profit or trust under them shall, without the consent of the Congress, accept of any present, emolument, office, or title, of any kind whatever, from any king, prince, or foreign state.

SEC. 10.   No State shall enter into any treaty, alliance,

or confederation; grant letters of marque and reprisal; coin money; emit bills of credit; make anything but gold and silver coin a tender in payment of debts; pass any bill of attainder, ex post facto law, or law impairing the obligation of contracts, or grant any title of nobility.

No State shall, without the consent of the Congress, lay any imposts or duties on imports or exports, except what may be absolutely necessary for executing its inspection laws; and the net produce of all duties and imposts, laid by any State on imports or exports, shall be for the use of the treasury of the United States; and all such laws shall be subject to the revision and control of the Congress.

No State shall, without the consent of Congress, lay any duty of tonnage, keep troops, or ships of war in time of peace, enter into any agreement or compact with another State, or with a foreign power, or engage in war, unless actually invaded, or in such imminent danger as will not admit of delay.

ARTICLE II

SECTION I. The executive power shall be vested in a President of the United States of America. He shall hold his office during the term of four years, and, together with the Vice-President, chosen for the same term, be elected as follows:

Each State shall appoint, in such manner as the Legislature thereof may direct, a number of Electors equal to the whole number of Senators and Representatives to which the State may be entitled in the Congress: but no Senator or Representative, or person holding an office of trust or profit under the United States, shall be appointed an Elector.

The Electors shall meet in their respective States, and vote by ballot for two persons, of whom one at least shall not be an inhabitant of the same State with themselves. And they shall make a list of all the persons voted for, and of the number of

votes for each; which list they shall sign and certify, and transmit sealed to the seat of the government of the United States,
directed to the President of the Senate. The President of the
Senate shall, in the presence of the Senate and House of
Representatives, open all the certificates, and the votes shall
then be counted. The person having the greatest number of
votes shall be the President, if such number be a majority of
the whole number of Electors appointed; and if there be more
than one who have such majority, and have an equal number
of votes, then the House of Representatives shall immediately
choose by ballot one of them for President; and if no person
have a majority, then from the five highest on the list the
said House shall in like manner choose the President. But in
choosing the President, the votes shall be taken by States, the
representation from each State having one vote; a quorum for
this purpose shall consist of a member or members from two
thirds of the States, and a majority of all the States shall be
necessary to a choice. In every case, after the choice of the
President, the person having the greatest number of votes of
the Electors shall be the Vice-President. But if there should
remain two or more who have equal votes, the Senate shall
choose from them by ballot the Vice-President.[4]

The Congress may determine the time of choosing the
Electors, and the day on which they shall give their votes;
which day shall be the same throughout the United States.

No person except a natural-born citizen, or a citizen of the
United States at the time of the adoption of this Constitution,
shall be eligible to the office of President; neither shall any
person be eligible to that office who shall not have attained to
the age of thirty-five years, and been fourteen years a resident
within the United States.

In case of the removal of the President from office, or of
his death, resignation, or inability to discharge the powers and
duties of the said office, the same shall devolve on the Vice-

[4] This clause has been superseded by the twelfth amendment, p. 309.

President, and the Congress may by law provide for the case of removal, death, resignation, or inability, both of the President and Vice-President, declaring what officer shall then act as President, and such officer shall act accordingly, until the disability be removed, or a President shall be elected.

The President shall, at stated times, receive for his services a compensation, which shall neither be increased nor diminished during the period for which he shall have been elected, and he shall not receive within that period any other emolument from the United States, or any of them.

Before he enter on the execution of his office, he shall take the following oath or affirmation:—"I do solemnly swear (or affirm) that I will faithfully execute the office of President of the United States, and will to the best of my ability, preserve, protect and defend the Constitution of the United States."

Sec. 2. The President shall be commander-in-chief of the army and navy of the United States, and of the militia of the several States, when called into the actual service of the United States; he may require the opinion, in writing, of the principal officer in each of the executive departments, upon any subject relating to the duties of their respective offices, and he shall have power to grant reprieves and pardons for offences against the United States, except in cases of impeachment.

He shall have power, by and with the advice and consent of the Senate, to make treaties, provided two thirds of the Senators present concur; and he shall nominate, and by and with the advice and consent of the Senate, shall appoint ambassadors, other public ministers and consuls, judges of the Supreme Court, and all other officers of the United States, whose appointments are not herein otherwise provided for, and which shall be established by law; but the Congress may by law vest the appointment of such inferior officers, as they think proper, in the President alone, in the courts of law, or in the heads of departments.

The President shall have power to fill up all vacancies that may happen during the recess of the Senate, by granting commissions which shall expire at the end of their next session.

SEC. 3. He shall from time to time give to the Congress information of the state of the Union, and recommend to their consideration such measures as he shall judge necessary and expedient; he may, on extraordinary occasions, convene both Houses, or either of them, and in case of disagreement between them, with respect to the time of adjournment, he may adjourn them to such time as he shall think proper; he shall receive ambassadors and other public ministers; he shall take care that the laws be faithfully executed, and shall commission all the officers of the United States.

SEC. 4. The President, Vice-President and all civil officers of the United States, shall be removed from office on impeachment for, and conviction of, treason, bribery, or other high crimes and misdemeanors.

ARTICLE III

SECTION 1. The judicial power of the United States shall be vested in one Supreme Court, and in such inferior courts as the Congress may from time to time ordain and establish. The judges, both of the Supreme and inferior courts, shall hold their offices during good behavior, and shall, at stated times, receive for their services a compensation, which shall not be diminished during their continuance in office.

SEC. 2. The judicial power shall extend to all cases, in law and equity, arising under this Constitution, the laws of the United States, and treaties made, or which shall be made, under their authority; to all cases affecting ambassadors, other public ministers and consuls; to all cases of admiralty and maritime jurisdiction; to controversies to which the United States shall be a party; to controversies between two or more States, between a State and citizens of another State, between citizens of different States, between citizens of the same State claiming lands under grants of different States, and between a State, or the citizens thereof, and foreign states, citizens or subjects.

In all cases affecting ambassadors, other public ministers and consuls, and those in which a State shall be party, the Supreme Court shall have original jurisdiction. In all the other cases before mentioned, the Supreme Court shall have appellate jurisdiction, both as to law and fact, with such exceptions, and under such regulations, as the Congress shall make.

The trial of all crimes, except in cases of impeachment, shall be by jury; and such trial shall be held in the state where the said crimes shall have been committed; but when not committed within any State, the trial shall be at such place or places as the Congress may by law have directed.

SEC. 3. Treason against the United States, shall consist only in levying war against them, or in adhering to their enemies, giving them aid and comfort. No person shall be convicted of treason unless on the testimony of two witnesses to the same overt act, or on confession in open court.

The Congress shall have power to declare the punishment of treason, but no attainder of treason shall work corruption of blood, or forfeiture except during the life of the person attainted.

ARTICLE IV

SECTION 1. Full faith and credit shall be given in each State to the public acts, records, and judicial proceedings of every other State. And the Congress may by general laws prescribe the manner in which such acts, records and proceedings shall be proved, and the effect thereof.

SEC. 2. The citizens of each State shall be entitled to all privileges and immunities of citizens in the several States.

A person charged in any State with treason, felony, or other crime, who shall flee from justice, and be found in another State, shall on demand of the executive authority of the

State from which he fled, be delivered up to be removed to the
State having jurisdiction of the crime.

No person held to service or labor in one State, under the
laws thereof, escaping into another, shall, in consequence of
any law or regulation therein, be discharged from such service
or labor, but shall be delivered up on claim of the party to
whom such service or labor may be due.

SEC. 3. New States may be admitted by the Congress
into this Union; but no new State shall be formed or erected
within the jurisdiction of any other State; nor any State be
formed by the junction of two or more States, or parts of
States, without the consent of the Legislatures of the States
concerned as well as of the Congress.

The Congress shall have power to dispose of and make all
needful rules and regulations respecting the territory or other
property belonging to the United States; and nothing in this
Constitution shall be so construed as to prejudice any claims
of the United States, or of any particular State.

SEC. 4. The United States shall guarantee to every State
in this Union a republican form of government, and shall
protect each of them against invasion; and on application of
the Legislature, or of the Executive (when the Legislature
cannot be convened) against domestic violence.

ARTICLE V

The Congress, whenever two thirds of both houses shall
deem it necessary, shall propose amendments to this Constitution, or, on the application of the Legislatures of two thirds
of the several States, shall call a convention for proposing
amendments, which, in either case, shall be valid to all intents
and purposes, as part of this Constitution, when ratified by
the Legislatures of three fourths of the several States, or by
conventions in three fourths thereof, as the one or the other
mode of ratification may be proposed by the Congress; pro-

vided that no amendment which may be made prior to the year one thousand eight hundred and eight shall in any manner affect the first and fourth clauses in the ninth section of the first article; and that no State, without its consent, shall be deprived of its equal suffrage in the Senate.

ARTICLE VI

All debts contracted and engagements entered into, before the adoption of this Constitution, shall be as valid against the United States under this Constitution, as under the Confederation.

This Constitution, and the laws of the United States which shall be made in pursuance thereof; and all treaties made, or which shall be made, under the authority of the United States, shall be the supreme law of the land; and the judges in every State shall be bound thereby, anything in the constitution or laws of any State to the contrary notwithstanding.

The Senators and Representatives before mentioned, and the members of the several State Legislatures, and all executive and judicial officers, both of the United States and of the several States, shall be bound by oath or affirmation, to support this Constitution; but no religious test shall ever be required as a qualification to any office or public trust under the United States.

ARTICLE VII

The ratification of the conventions of nine States, shall be sufficient for the establishment of this Constitution between the States so ratifying the same.

ARTICLES IN ADDITION TO, AND AMENDMENT OF, THE CONSTITUTION OF THE UNITED STATES OF AMERICA

ARTICLE I

Congress shall make no law respecting an establishment of religion, or prohibiting the free exercise thereof; or abridging the freedom of speech, or of the press, or the right of the people peaceably to assemble, and to petition the government for a redress of grievances.[5]

ARTICLE II

A well regulated militia being necessary to the security of a free state, the right of the people to keep and bear arms shall not be infringed.

ARTICLE III

No soldier shall, in time of peace be quartered in any house, without the consent of the owner, nor in time of war, but in a manner to be prescribed by law.

ARTICLE IV

The right of the people to be secure in their persons, houses, papers, and effects, against unreasonable searches and seizures, shall not be violated, and no warrants shall issue but upon probable cause, supported by oath or affirmation, and particularly describing the place to be searched, and the persons or things to be seized.

ARTICLE V

No person shall be held to answer for a capital, or otherwise infamous crime, unless on a presentment or indictment of a grand jury, except in cases arising in the land or naval forces, or in the militia, when in actual service in time of war or public danger; nor shall any person be subject for the same offence to be twice put in jeopardy of life or limb; nor shall be compelled in any criminal case to be a witness against himself, nor be deprived of life, liberty, or property, without due process of law; nor shall private property be taken for public use without just compensation.

[5] The first ten amendments were proposed by the first Congress, on September 25, 1789, and were ratified by three-fourths of the states during the two succeeding years.

ARTICLE VI

In all criminal prosecutions, the accused shall enjoy the right to a speedy and public trial, by an impartial jury of the State and district wherein the crime shall have been committed, which district shall have been previously ascertained by law, and to be informed of the nature and cause of the accusation; to be confronted with the witnesses against him; to have compulsory process for obtaining witnesses in his favor, and to have the assistance of counsel for his defence.

ARTICLE VII

In suits at common law, where the value in controversy shall exceed twenty dollars, the right of trial by jury shall be preserved, and no fact tried by a jury shall be otherwise re-examined in any court of the United States, than according to the rules of the common law.

ARTICLE VIII

Excessive bail shall not be required, nor excessive fines imposed, nor cruel and unusual punishments inflicted.

ARTICLE IX

The enumeration in the Constitution, of certain rights, shall not be construed to deny or disparage others retained by the people.

ARTICLE X

The powers not delegated to the United States by the Constitution, nor prohibited by it to the States, are reserved to the States respectively, or to the people.

ARTICLE XI

The judicial power of the United States shall not be construed to extend to any suit in law or equity, commenced or prosecuted against one of the United States by citizens of another State, or by citizens or subjects of any foreign state.[6]

ARTICLE XII

The Electors shall meet in their respective States, and vote by ballot for President and Vice-President, one of whom, at least, shall not be an inhabitant of the same State with themselves; they shall name in their ballots the person voted for as President, and in distinct ballots the person voted for as Vice-President; and they shall make distinct lists of all persons voted for as President, and of all persons voted for as Vice-President, and of the number of votes for each, which lists they shall sign and certify, and transmit sealed to the seat of the government of the United States, directed to the President of the Senate;—the President of the Senate shall, in the presence of the Senate and House of Representatives, open all the certificates, and the votes shall then be counted;—the person having the greatest number of votes for President, shall be the President, if such number be a majority of the whole number of Electors appointed; and if no person have such majority, then from the persons having the highest numbers not exceeding three on the list of those voted for as President, the House of Representatives shall choose immediately, by ballot, the President. But in choosing the President, the votes shall be taken by States, the representation from each State having one vote; a quorum for this purpose shall consist of a member or members from two thirds of the States, and a majority of all the States shall be necessary to a choice. And if the House of Representatives shall not choose a President whenever the right of choice shall devolve upon them, before the fourth day of March next following, then the Vice-President shall act as President, as in the case of the death or other constitutional disability of the President. The person having the greatest

[6] The eleventh amendment was proposed to the states on March 12, 1794, and was declared adopted on January 8, 1798.

number of votes as Vice-President, shall be the Vice-President,
if such number be a majority of the whole number of Electors
appointed, and if no person have a majority, then from the
two highest numbers on the list, the Senate shall choose the
Vice-President; a quorum for the purpose shall consist of two
thirds of the whole number of Senators, and a majority of the
whole number shall be necessary to a choice. But no person
constitutionally ineligible to the office of President shall be
eligible to that of Vice-President of the United States.[7]

ARTICLE XIII

SECTION 1. Neither slavery nor involuntary servitude,
except as a punishment for crime whereof the party shall have
been duly convicted, shall exist within the United States, or
any place subject to their jurisdiction.

SEC. 2. Congress shall have power to enforce this article
by appropriate legislation.[8]

ARTICLE XIV

SECTION 1. All persons born or naturalized in the United
States, and subject to the jurisdiction thereof, are citizens of
the United States and of the State wherein they reside. No
State shall make or enforce any law which shall abridge the
privileges or immunities of citizens of the United States; nor
shall any State deprive any person of life, liberty, or property,
without due process of law; nor deny to any person within its
jurisdiction the equal protection of the laws.

SEC. 2. Representatives shall be apportioned among the
several States according to their respective numbers, counting
the whole number of persons in each State, excluding Indians

[7] The twelfth amendment was proposed to the states on December 12,
1803, and was declared adopted, September 25, 1804.

[8] The thirteenth amendment was proposed on February 1, 1865, and was
declared adopted on December 18, 1865.

not taxed. But when the right to vote at any election for the choice of Electors for President and Vice-President of the United States, Representatives in Congress, the executive and judicial officers of a State, or the members of the Legislature thereof, is denied to any of the male inhabitants of such State, being twenty-one years of age, and citizens of the United States, or in any way abridged, except for participation in rebellion or other crime, the basis of representation therein shall be reduced in the proportion which the number of such male citizens shall bear to the whole number of male citizens twenty-one years of age in such State.

SEC. 3. No person shall be a Senator or Representative in Congress, or Elector of President and Vice-President, or hold any office, civil or military, under the United States, or under any State, who, having previously taken an oath, as a member of Congress, or as an officer of the United States, or as a member of any State Legislature, or as an executive or judicial officer of any State, to support the Constitution of the United States, shall have engaged in insurrection or rebellion against the same, or given aid or comfort to the enemies thereof. But Congress may, by a vote of two thirds of each House, remove such disability.

SEC. 4. The validity of the public debt of the United States, authorized by law, including debts incurred for payment of pensions and bounties for services in suppressing insurrection or rebellion, shall not be questioned. But neither the United States nor any State shall assume or pay any debt or obligation incurred in aid of insurrection or rebellion against the United States, or any claim for the loss or emancipation of any slave; but all such debts, obligations and claims shall be held illegal and void.

SEC. 5. The Congress shall have power to enforce, by appropriate legislation, the provisions of this article.[9]

[9] The fourteenth amendment was proposed to the states on June 16, 1866, and was declared adopted on July 21, 1868.

ARTICLE XV

Section 1. The right of citizens of the United States to vote shall not be denied or abridged by the United States or by any State on account of race, color, or previous condition of servitude.

Sec. 2. The Congress shall have power to enforce this article by appropriate legislation.[10]

[10] The fifteenth amendment was proposed on February 27, 1869, and was declared adopted on March 30, 1870.

INDEX

INDEX

315

members not to receive instructions, I, 82; term of members, I, 82; no voting by proxy in, I, 82; dissolution, I, 82, 83.

—Imperial Court: jurisdiction, I, 84, 85; organization, I, 85.

—Laws: may not be declared invalid by courts, I, 86; promulgation of, I, 89; decrees for the enforcement of, I, 89.

—Ministers: entitled to be present in Reichsrat, I, 83; may be required to furnish information to Reichsrat, I, 83; responsibility and impeachment of, I, 81, 88.

—Provinces: legislative power of diets, I, 79, 80; government of, I, 80, *note.*

—Reichsrat: organization and membership, I, 74–77; sessions, I, 77; powers, I, 78, 79; proposal and passage of laws, I, 80, 81; immunity of members, I, 82; adjournment, I, 83; publicity of sessions, I, 83; order of business, I, 83; nomination of members of Imperial Court by, I, 85.

Austria-Hungary, *see also* Austria. Hungary.

—Affairs common to Austria and Hungary, I, 114, 115; expense of such affairs, I, 115, 116, 122.

—Affairs regulated upon uniform principles in Austria and Hungary, I, 115; method of reaching agreement regarding such matters, I, 121.

—Bosnia and Herzegovina: joint administration, I, 122, 123.

—Commercial affairs, I, 115.

—Customs legislation, I, 115, 123.

—Delegations: composition of Austrian Delegation, I, 116–18; composition of Hungarian Delegation, I, 117, *note;* sessions and organization, I, 118; powers, I, 118; passage of laws by, I, 118, 120, 121; joint sessions of Delegations, I, 118, 120, 121; quorum, I, 119; separate sessions, I, 119; voting by delegates, I, 119; immunities of delegates, I, 119; dissolution, I, 119; public sessions, I, 120, 121; communications between Delegations, I, 120; procedure, I, 121.

—Emperor: power to fix proportion of expense of affairs administered in common, I, 115; control of joint

army by, I, 116; approval of laws by, I, 118.

—Finances, I, 115, 116, 122, 123.

—Foreign affairs, I, 114.

—Joint ministry, I, 116; may present projects of laws to Delegations, I, 118; impeachment of, I, 118, 119; participation by, in deliberations of Delegation, I, 120; must furnish information to Delegations when requested, I, 120.

—Military and naval affairs, I, 115.

—Monetary system, I, 115, 123.

—Public debt, I, 116.

—Railways, I, 115, 122.

Bail: Brazil, I, 173; Chile, I, 258; Denmark, I, 278; Mexico, II, 43; Portugal, II, 176; United States, II, 308.

Bank, national: Argentine Nation, I, 15; Norway, II, 143; Sweden, II, 234, 237, 250.

Banking: Australia, I, 46; Austria, I, 78; Canada, I, 206; Germany, I, 327; Mexico, II, 59.

Banks of issue: Argentine Nation, I, 29; Austria, I, 78; Brazil, I, 151, 158; Switzerland, II, 268.

Bankruptcy: Argentine Nation, I, 16, 29; Australia, I, 44, 45, 46; Canada, I, 192, 206; Hungary, I, 104, 110; Norway, II, 131, 142; Switzerland, II, 275; United States, II, 298.

Belgium—

—Court of Cassation: trial of impeached ministers by, I, 140, 147; jurisdiction of, I, 140, 141, 142; appointment of judges, I, 141, 147.

—Colors and coat of arms, I, 145.

—Court of Accounts, I, 144.

—Courts: jurisdiction of, I, 130, 140; sessions to be public, I, 141; appointment, salary, and tenure of judges, I, 141, 147; courts of appeal, I, 142; military and commercial courts, I, 142.

—House of Representatives: exclusive power to originate money bills and bills relating to the army contingent, I, 130; election, I, 132, 133; apportionment of representatives, I, 134; qualifications of representatives, I, 134; term, I, 134; dissolution, I, 134; compensation of members, I, 134;

gary, I, 94; Mexico, II, 59; Netherlands, II, 84; United States, II, 298.

Catholic church: Argentine Nation, I, 3, 16, 17, 20, 23, 24; Chile, I, 229, 247; Italy, II, 5, 6, 8, 16–21; Portugal, II, 147, 155, 163, 164; Spain, II, 201. *See also* Church, Papacy, Religion, Religious orders.

Census: Argentine Nation, I, 10, 11; Australia, I, 46, 66; Austria, I, 79; Brazil, I, 156; Canada, I, 187, 205; United States, II, 294.

Charities: Canada, I, 207; Denmark, I, 279; Netherlands, II, 118; Portugal, II, 178.

Chile—
—Congress: composition, I, 232; immunities of members, I, 232; powers, I, 235–37, 247, 248; sessions, I, 240, 246; power of Executive Committee to call extraordinary sessions of, I, 242; election of President by, I, 243; exclusive power to levy taxes, I, 259; actions taken in presence of an armed force void, I, 261.

—Council of State: impeachment of members, I, 237, 253; share in executive powers, I, 246, 247; composition, I, 251; powers, I, 252, 253.

—Courts: impeachment of judges, I, 237; control by President over judicial administration, I, 245; appointment of judges, I, 246, 252; judicial power exercised by, I, 253; tenure of judges, I, 253; responsibility of judges, I, 253, 254; qualifications of judges, I, 254; organization of courts, I, 254.

—Executive Committee: action with reference to members of Congress accused of crime, I, 232; impeachment of members, I, 237; composition, I, 241; powers, I, 241, 242; its share in the appointment of officers by the President, I, 246; its consent to command of army by President, I, 247.

—Form of government, I, 229.
—House of Deputies: apportionment and election of members, I, 232, 233; term, I, 233; qualifications of deputies, I, 233; persons ineligible as deputies, I, 233; offices compatible with that of deputy, I, 234, 249; powers, I, 237, 238; quorum, I, 240; sessions when Senate is not in session, I, 241;

impeachment of ministers by, I, 249, 250.

—Laws: procedure in the enactment of, I, 238–40, 253.

—Local government: organization of, I, 254–57.

—Minister of State: may at the same time be a member of the House of Deputies, I, 234, 249; impeachment, I, 237, 249–51; appointment and removal, I, 246; qualifications, I, 248; responsibility of, I, 248; relations with Congress, I, 248, 249.

—Municipal government, I, 255–57.
—President: decision by Congress with reference to resignation or disability of, I, 235; duties of Congress with reference to election of, I, 235, 236; power to initiate legislation, I, 238, 252; veto power, I, 239, 253; qualifications of, I, 242; term, I, 242, 244; election, I, 242–44, 245; succession in case of President's disability, I, 244; may not leave Chilean territory without consent of Congress, I, 244; oath of office, I, 245; powers, I, 245–48; responsibility of ministers of state for acts of, I, 248; impeachment, I, 248; Council of State as an advisory body, I, 252, 253; establishment of municipalities by, I, 255; action taken in presence of an armed body void, I, 260; powers vested in, during a state of siege, I, 261.

—Senate: composition, I, 234; term and election of senators, I, 234, 235; qualifications of senators, I, 235; powers, I, 238; quorum, I, 240; sessions when House of Deputies is not in session, I, 240; its share in the appointment of officers by the President, I, 246; its consent to command of army by President, I, 247; trial of impeached ministers by, I, 250.

Church, established: Argentine Nation, I, 3; Chile, I, 229; Denmark, I, 267, 278; Italy, II, 5; Norway, II, 123; Portugal, II, 147; Spain, II, 201; Sweden, II, 219, 220, 226, 227, 242. *See also* Catholic church, Religion.

Citizenship: Argentine Nation, I, 16, 29; Austria, I, 71, 79; Belgium, I, 127, 146; Brazil, I, 171, 172; Chile, I, 229, 230; Germany, I, 326, 327; Japan, II, 26; Mexico, II, 46–49, 60; Netherlands, II, 81; Norway, II, 140;

Breinigsville, PA USA
24 January 2010
231257BV00002B/28/A

9 781432 683191